Contemporary Cinema and the Philosophy
of Iris Murdoch

For Jean Bolton and Richard Menzies

In loving memory of Kat Lindner

Contemporary Cinema and the Philosophy of Iris Murdoch

Lucy Bolton

Edinburgh University Press is one of the leading university presses in
the UK. We publish academic books and journals in our selected subject
areas across the humanities and social sciences, combining cutting-edge
scholarship with high editorial and production values to produce academic
works of lasting importance. For more information visit our website:
edinburghuniversitypress.com

© Lucy Bolton, 2019, 2021

Edinburgh University Press Ltd
The Tun – Holyrood Road
12 (2f) Jackson's Entry
Edinburgh EH8 8PJ

First published in hardback by Edinburgh University Press 2019

Typeset in 11/13 Ehrhardt MT by
IDSUK (DataConnection) Ltd

A CIP record for this book is available from the British Library

ISBN 978 1 4744 1639 9 (hardback)
ISBN 9781474481359 (paperback)
ISBN 978 1 4744 1640 5 (webready PDF)
ISBN 978 1 4744 1641 2 (epub)

The right of Lucy Bolton to be identified as author of this work has been
asserted in accordance with the Copyright, Designs and Patents Act 1988
and the Copyright and Related Rights Regulations 2003 (SI No. 2498).

Contents

List of Figures	vi
Acknowledgements	vii
List of Abbreviations	ix
Frontispiece: Iris Murdoch pays loving attention to art	x
1 Introduction	1
2 Film as Art, and Cinema as a Hall of Reflection	21
3 Film as a Moral Fable	51
4 Film and the Existential Hero(ine)	75
5 Film, Love and Goodness	104
6 Film, Comedy and Tragedy	130
7 Film and Women's Stories	167
8 Metaphysics as a Guide to Movies	203
Bibliography	223
Filmography	229
Index	231

Figures

1.1	The face of Lee Miller, in *The Blood of a Poet/Le sang d'un poète*	15
1.2	Iris Murdoch's thoughts on Rin Tin Tin on the reverse of a postcard	16
2.1	Anna's complex emotions on display, in *Birth*	32
2.2	Jackie Kennedy sees the crowds lining the streets, in *Jackie*	36
2.3	Footage of Diane Polley from *Stories We Tell*	42
2.4	The alien looks at her own 'human' face, in *Under the Skin*	48
3.1	Lisa looks at the driver and says 'green', in *Margaret*	55
3.2	Jasmine breaks down after Dwight's call, in *Blue Jasmine*	65
3.3	Becky knows there's nothing she can do, in *Compliance*	70
4.1	Maria Enders realises Val has left, in *Clouds of Sils Maria*	88
4.2	Dr Cemal looks us straight in the eye, in *Once Upon a Time in Anatolia*	93
4.3	Eliza and Romeo have a frank conversation, in *Graduation*	100
5.1	Susanne helps Nejat recall his father's love, in *The Edge of Heaven*	119
5.2	Juliette and Léa learn to live together, in *I've Loved You So Long/Il y a longtemps que je t'aime*	123
5.3	Eva perseveres with realism and love, in *We Need to Talk about Kevin*	126
6.1	Khrushchev and Malenkov argue over who invited the bishops, in *The Death of Stalin*	139
6.2	Michèle offers a cognac, in *Elle*	150
6.3	Lee Chandler dreams of his children, in *Manchester by the Sea*	160
7.1	The rancher lovingly looks at Elizabeth, in *Certain Women*	182
7.2	The girl who rang, in *The Unknown Girl/La fille inconnue*	189
7.3	Dr Jenny Davin's steady attention yields results, in *The Unknown Girl/La fille inconnue*	194
7.4	Marieme realises she cannot go to high school, in *Girlhood*	198
8.1	Iris Murdoch refers to film in an annotation on a page of her copy of Gilbert Ryle's *The Life of the Mind*	211
8.2	Mary Magdalene as a spiritual leader, in *Mary Magdalene*	214
8.3	Eve encourages Adam to dance, in *Only Lovers Left Alive*	221

Acknowledgements

Thank you to Gillian Leslie from EUP for her enthusiasm for this book right from my first mention of it, and to her colleagues Richard Strachan, Emma Rees and Rebecca Mackenzie for their help over the last couple of years. Thank you to all the readers of this book along the way, including the anonymous reviewers and those who have given me invaluable feedback on specific chapters and the whole thing: Jean Bolton, Miles Leeson, Richard Menzies, Anat Pick, Hollie Price, Lindsey Smith, Catherine Wheatley and Emma Wilson. Many thanks to colleagues at Queen Mary University of London for facilitating the sabbatical I needed to write the book: David Adger, Janet Harbord, Sue Harris and Shirley Jordan.

Thanks to those who have invited me to speak about Iris Murdoch and film over the past three or four years and who have given me the opportunity to receive so many comments and helpful suggestions on this as work in progress. In particular, Robert Sinnerbrink for the Cinematic Ethics event at Macquarie University (2015); Miles Leeson at the University of Chichester (2017); Lisa Downing and Kate Ince at the University of Birmingham (2014); David Sorfa at the University of Edinburgh (2015). And very special thanks to Fiona Smith at the National Portrait Gallery, and Aga Baranowska and David Edgar at the British Film Institute, who have so generously allowed me to pedal my film philosophical work to the public.

My most sincere thanks go to my friends and colleagues at *Film-Philosophy*, who have always supported my work, given me encouragement and friendship, and infinite, good humoured, intellectual companionship. Thanks to William Brown, Catherine Constable, John Ó Maoilearca (especially for stories about Iris Murdoch), David Martin-Jones, Richard Rushton, Robert Sinnerbrink, David Sorfa and Catherine Wheatley in particular.

Thank you to my friends and colleagues at Queen Mary University of London, especially in the Centre for Film and Ethics. Particular thanks to my undergraduate and postgraduate film philosophy students over the past ten years, and to my PhD students Simon Dickson and Alice Pember, whose film philosophical discussions have enriched my work no end.

I am grateful beyond measure to my Murdochian fellow travellers Miles Leeson, Pamela Osborne, Anne Rowe and Frances White. Thank you for welcoming me to your community of scholarship, sharing your knowledge so generously, and inviting me to be part of the *Iris Murdoch Review*. You have supported me far beyond my expectations and I am truly in your debt.

For connections, ideas and suggestions that have added to this project in many ways, thanks to Laura Adams, Lucy Fawcett, Lucas Hare, Ian Killick, Carly McLaughlin, Lucy H. Oulton, Anat Pick and Sercan Şenozan.

Special love and thanks to my goddaughters Jess Wilson, Charlotte Hathaway and Asha Stobbart, and to my support system: Laura Adams, Tanya Aplin, Bela Kapur, Julie Lobalzo Wright, Natalie Marcus and Ludo, Caraline Menzies, Lindsey Smith, Megan Smith and The Wilsons. That support system includes Laverne, Babs and the team at The Currant, Wanstead – thanks to you all.

I thank my intellectual spirit animals, Lisa Downing, Anat Pick, Libby Saxton, Lindsey Smith and Catherine Wheatley, with gratitude and humility. And all my love, forever, to Jean Bolton and Richard Menzies. I could not have written this book without you.

Part of my analysis of *Blue Jasmine* in Chapter 3 was published in my essay, 'Attention to the details of film and form: *Blue Jasmine* as Murdochian Moral Vision' (2017a). Part of the work on *Margaret* in Chapter 3 appeared in my article, 'Murdoch and *Margaret*: Learning a Moral Life' (2017b). Some of my analysis of *Only Lovers Left Alive* features in my review of the film in the *Times Higher Educational Supplement*, 20 February 2014.

Finally, I want to thank Fatih Akin for granting me permission to use the image of Lotte from *The Edge of Heaven* on the cover. Her smiling face in this scene means a great deal to me and substantially contributes to the meaning of this book.

Abbreviations

These are abbreviations for works written by Iris Murdoch. Where possible, essay references are given to the reprints of Murdoch's philosophical works in the collection, *Existentialists and Mystics* (*E&M*; Conradi 1997).

A&E	'Art and Eros' [1980], *E&M* 464–95
AD	'Against Dryness' [1961], *E&M* 287–95
E&M	'Existentialists and Mystics' [1970], *E&M* 221–34
EB	'Existentialist Bite' [1957], *E&M* 151–3
EPM	'The Existential Political Myth' [1952], *E&M* 130–45
F&S	'The Fire and the Sun: Why Plato Banished the Artists' [1977], *E&M* 386–463
HT	'A House of Theory' [1958], *E&M* 171–86
IP	'The Idea of Perfection' [1964], *E&M* 299–336
KV	'Knowing the Void' [1956], *E&M* 157–60
L&P	'Literature and Philosophy' [1977], *E&M* 3–30
M&E	'Metaphysics and Ethics' [1957], *E&M* 59–75
MGM	*Metaphysics as a Guide to Morals* [1992] (2003), London: Vintage
OGG	'On "God" and "Good"' [1969], *E&M* 337–62
OTC	'On the Cinema' (1956), British *Vogue*, 112, August, pp. 98–9
S&G	'The Sublime and the Good' [1959], *E&M* 205–20
SBR	'The Sublime and the Beautiful Revisited' [1959], *E&M* 261–86
SGC	'The Sovereignty of Good over Other Concepts' [1967], *E&M* 363–85
SRR	*Sartre: Romantic Rationalist* [1953] (1989), London: Penguin
T&L	'Thinking and Language' [1951], *E&M* 33–42
VCM	'Vision and Choice in Morality' [1956], *E&M* 76–98

Iris Murdoch pays loving attention to art, by Sophie Bassouls. Ashmolean Museum, Oxford, 25 January 1977. Copyright Sophie Bassouls.

CHAPTER I

Introduction: Thinking about Cinema and Iris Murdoch

> Where virtue is concerned we often apprehend more than we clearly understand and *grow by looking*. ('The Idea of Perfection' (IP): 324)

> The 'world' of *The Concept of Mind* is the world in which people play cricket, cook cakes, make simple decisions, remember their childhood and go to the circus, not the world in which they commit sins, fall in love, say prayers or join the Communist Party. (*Sartre: Romantic Rationalist* (SRR): 78–9)

Iris Murdoch was a philosopher concerned with morality and goodness, art and experience. She believed that moral philosophy is something we all undertake in our everyday lives, and that paying attention to art is a way of developing our moral visions and becoming better people. Cinema is an art form that shows people grappling with moral choices and living ethical relationships, and undoubtedly experiencing cinema can be morally challenging and affecting for the filmgoer. In this book, I bring Murdoch's thinking into dialogue with cinema in a sustained way for the first time, and explore how experiencing film can be an exercise in moral training, and how the philosophical challenges of contemporary cinema can be illuminated by Murdoch's philosophical writings. Among other things, this book asks, can cinema make me a better person?

Iris Murdoch wrote very little about the cinema. She is well known as a writer of twenty-six novels, and her biography has been written from the perspective of several significant individuals in her life and depicted on-screen in the film *Iris* (Richard Eyre, 2001). What is lesser known is that she was also an influential philosopher who worked in the fields of moral and political philosophy. Her writings about the role and function of art in our lives, and her visual and practical philosophical examples, suggest possibilities for thinking about film through a Murdochian lens. Connections between film and philosophy are well established in academia, and indeed the consideration of film as a philosophical medium has taken place since the first days of seeing images of our world projected on a wall or a screen. Questions of how the contents of a film relate to the world around us, and how film is uniquely able to show us ourselves as social beings, reconfigured, reshaped and in sharp focus, have been the subject of enquiry for philosophical filmmakers from Jean Epstein, Maya Deren and Sergei Eisenstein to Ingmar Bergman, Jane Campion and Kelly Reichardt. The images and operations of cinema have formed the basis of the writings of film critics such as André Bazin and the enquiries of philosophers such as Stanley Cavell, and the mysteries of the cinema have fascinated writers such as Virginia Woolf and indeed Murdoch, who expressed interest in and respect for cinema as I shall explore. The academic discipline of film studies has analysed cinema in various ways, including cultural conditions of production, theoretical approaches about authorship and genre, critical perspectives such as realism and post-modernism, and psychoanalysis, which dominated film theory in the 1970s and 1980s. Recognising the philosophical content of individual films, and indeed proposing that a film can be philosophy in action, has formed a valuable contribution to the understanding of how cinema works as a provocative, contemplative, productive experience. Drawing on the film studies tradition of close analysis of image, movement and sound, the nuances of a film's, a scene's or even a moment's philosophical content can be made abundantly clear.

This approach can reveal the way in which a film is posing a question, or offering a perspective, or arguing a position: in this film world, this happens. Another aspect of the film philosophy relationship is where the work of a particular philosopher is brought into dialogue with a film or selection of films, as I am doing here. The question then arises as to the nature of the relationship: are the films being used to illustrate the philosopher, or is the philosopher being explained through the films in some way? Or perhaps it is being suggested that the films can be better understood by knowing the philosophy of a particular thinker. Does any of this matter? Well, only inasmuch as there may be a perceived superiority of the work of the philosopher over the work of the film in some way, and this is not what is intended by the film philosophy approach and certainly not by this book. This work is a meeting of equals: the concepts and thought of Iris Murdoch, and the content of the selected films. How this relationship works will be developed across the pages of this book, but the equivalence of the two elements is fundamental.

In this introduction, I will give some background to Iris Murdoch's philosophical work and career before explaining her significance as a philosopher and outlining the remit of her work. I will begin to explain her thinking about morality, goodness and art, thereby setting up the chapters that follow to stage an encounter between Murdoch's philosophy and a range of international contemporary films. This will further the discipline of film studies, and the sub-discipline of film philosophy, by bringing Murdoch's thinking into relation with cinema in a sustained and detailed analysis, and introduce a British philosopher into the discipline who bridges the divisions between analytic and continental philosophical traditions.

MURDOCH'S PHILOSOPHICAL CONTEXT

As Justin Broackes argues, 'Iris Murdoch was a professional philosopher before she was a professional novelist and her work was brave, brilliant, and independent' (Broackes 2012: preface). Murdoch had studied 'Mods and Greats' (ancient history, Greek, Latin and philosophy) at Somerville College, Oxford between 1938 and 1942. At this time, she was studying with 'the golden generation' of women philosophers at Oxford: Philippa Foot, Mary Midgley, Elizabeth Anscombe, and, a little later, Mary Warnock. Murdoch then worked as a civil servant, for His Majesty's Treasury in London, and then as an administrative officer with the United Nations Rehabilitation and Relief Association (UNRRA) between 1944 and 1946, travelling to Belgium and Austria. She met Sartre in Brussels in 1945 when he gave a lecture there, and her notes are carefully recorded in a notebook held in the Iris Murdoch Archive at Kingston University.[1] In 1947, Murdoch took up a studentship at Newnham College, Cambridge, where she met Wittgenstein and, although he was leaving Cambridge, she was able to work in close proximity with those he had influenced (Broackes 2012: 4). She was elected to a fellowship at St Anne's College, Oxford, in 1948, where she stayed until 1963. She published her first book, *Sartre: Romantic Rationalist* in 1953. This was the first book to be published on Sartre in the English language, and, according to Mary Warnock, 'remains one of the most penetrating studies of the early Sartre' (1996: 155). Murdoch published her first novel, *Under the Net*, in 1954. She was building a body of philosophical work which included the Sartre book, papers given to and published by the Aristotelian Society, and radio talks and lectures on existentialism, theology and politics. During this time of her philosophical career, in the 1950s, she was challenging the philosophy of her elders, such as Gilbert Ryle (author of *The Concept of Mind* (1960) referred to in the epigraph to this chapter), and her peers such as R. M. Hare, Stuart Hampshire and A. J. Ayer (with their emphasis on language and behaviour). In her 1951 paper 'Thinking and Language' (T&L), Murdoch investigates how Wittgenstein and Ryle fail to account for any kind of 'inner experience' (T&L: 38). She gave a talk on 'Metaphysics and Ethics' (M&E) for BBC Radio (Third Programme,

1955; M&E). In her 1956 paper given to the Aristotelian Society, 'Vision and Choice in Morality' (VCM), Murdoch demonstrates the inadequacy of Hare's moral philosophy to account for everyday human behaviour and individuality, and ends the piece by looking to 'contemporary continental philosophers' where such an 'imaginative exploration of the moral life' is being practised (VCM: 97).

Murdoch had clearly been excited by Sartre but she came to find his brand of existentialism to be a solipsistic void, for which 'the supreme virtue is reflective self-awareness' (SRR: 105). This will be examined in detail in Chapter 4. The work of Simone Weil was far more influential upon her. Justin Broackes writes how reviewing *The Notebooks of Simone Weil* for *The Spectator* in November 1956 'made a huge impact on Murdoch':

> Her review was penetrating – it was a real achievement to weave together for the review a presentation of ideas so clear, expressive, and fundamental out of the six hundred pages of Weil's wandering and brilliant text. And the material that Murdoch found there was, I think, both fruitful and not at all easily domesticated in the house of Oxford philosophy. (Broackes 2012: 19)

In an earlier talk given on BBC Third Programme in 1951, Murdoch expresses clearly how much of an impression Weil has made on her:

> What she writes is striking. She expresses herself vividly, sometimes violently; and her work has that unmistakable fresh tang. She is that rare thing, an original thinker. One gets too the impression of an exceptional degree of seriousness. We are not surprised to learn that she impressed people she met as a truly spiritual person. (Murdoch 2017: 10)[2]

The qualities that Murdoch admires in Weil are revealing of the values and passions of Murdoch herself. The rarefied linguistic philosophy of the Oxford tradition, and the self-centred romanticism of Sartre, were devoid of imagination, spirit and fellow feeling. Weil's qualities stood apart as consisting of selflessness and commitment missing from these others. But Murdoch did not follow Weil's philosophical commitments wholesale. Not one for such asceticism or self-restraint, Murdoch did not embrace the austerity that so characterises Weil's lived philosophy. The influence of Weil's concept of 'attention' on Murdoch was profoundly significant; as Broackes argues, 'prior and perhaps even greater in some ways than the influence of Plato' (Broackes 2017: 17). The Platonic influence on Murdoch can be seen in her consideration, and prioritisation, of 'the good': there is such a thing as a transcendent good, and we are all aiming for it. As Peter Conradi explains, 'Iris Murdoch poses two questions that link her intimately to Plato: what is goodness or what is a good man like? And what is the place of love and desire within the quest for goodness?' (Conradi 1994: 330). In Weil, writes Broackes, Murdoch found 'a form of Platonism expressed with a heady religious tone' (2012: 20), and this helped her to formulate language, concepts and imagery to express her moral thinking. Murdoch's philosophical writings, however, were overtaken by her prolific writing of fiction. Usefully, Broackes identifies three elements that led Murdoch away from being a professional philosopher at Oxford in the late 1950s: enjoying writing successful novels; the increasing impact of Hare's moral philosophy and the lack of impact of her own work; and thirdly 'the difficulty of domesticating within the existing philosophical world the new ideas she was developing from Weil' (2012: 20). Murdoch's following as an academic philosopher was not really taken up until John McDowell in the 1970s, by which time Murdoch had become known much more as a novelist who used to do some philosophy.[3]

There was a resurgence of popular interest in Murdoch at the turn of the century, which began with the publication of her husband John Bayley's memoirs in three volumes, detailing their struggles with Murdoch's Alzheimer's disease. The wave of interest continued with the film *Iris*, which saw both actresses who portrayed her, Kate Winslet and Judi Dench, nominated for Oscars, and saw Jim Broadbent win for his performance as Bayley. Peter Conradi's authorised biography, *Iris Murdoch: A Life*, was published in 2001, and his study of her work originally published in 1986, *The Saint and the Artist*, was republished that same year. Academic interest in Murdoch's work and life was bolstered by the acquisition of her archive in an Arts and Humanities Research Council (AHRC) funded project led by Dr Anne Rowe at the University of Kingston in 2004. Out of Rowe's work evolved the Centre for Iris Murdoch Studies, the *Iris Murdoch Review* and a biennial international conference. Upon Anne Rowe's retirement, the Centre for Iris Murdoch Studies moved to the University of Chichester in 2016 under the directorship of Miles Leeson, and is going from strength to strength as The Iris Murdoch Research Centre. BBC Radio 4 had a Murdoch season in August 2015, during which they broadcast dramatisations of two of her novels, *The Sea, the Sea* (1978) and *A Severed Head* (1961). There is, in popular culture at least, less focus on her work as a philosopher than there is as a novelist and public figure. However, the burgeoning field of Murdoch studies is remedying her exclusion and placing her in the forefront of their literary and philosophical work, including life writing, biography, and moral and political philosophy. There has certainly been an upsurge in interest in her philosophy in Oxford, evidenced by several conferences in the past few years, and also the development of the Women (In Parenthesis) project on the work of Elizabeth Anscombe, Philippa Foot, Murdoch and Mary Midgley, based at the University of Durham.[4]

Murdoch never closed the door on philosophy, and more works followed across her career, ranging from essays and a collection of articles to her lengthy final philosophical book. The works are: *Sartre: Romantic Rationalist*, first published in 1953; the compilation of three essays in *The Sovereignty of Good*, first published in 1970; 'The Fire and the Sun: Why Plato Banished the Artists' (1977); *Acastos: Two Platonic Dialogues* (1986), where Murdoch engages in arguments about the nature of religion and of art; and *Metaphysics as a Guide to Morals* (MGM), first published in 1992, the work that some might call her magnum opus, but others might call a baggy monster.[5] There is also the collection of essays, interviews and reviews compiled by Peter Conradi in 1997, *Existentialists and Mystics* (which includes essays such as 'Vision and Choice' and 'The Existentialist Hero'). All of these works will feature across the chapters of this book, in relation to different films and concepts. The essays in *Existentialists and Mystics* will be cited as they arise, rather than set out in full here, but references will be made to at least fifteen essays, talks and articles, published between 1950 and 1980. This demonstrates the length of time that Murdoch was writing non-fiction, but there was also a long period of her career where the focus was clearly on writing novels. Her philosophical concerns were consistent across her career, however, and developed and evolved, and these are what I will consider in relation to film in this book.

PHILOSOPHICAL CONCERNS

Murdoch was concerned with the moral life and moral vision of everyday experience, in contrast with the behaviourist analytics and the existentialists who were the leading philosophical voices at the time. Murdoch's perspective is referred to by many as moral realism, as Broackes explains, 'allowing the world to contain such things as the courage of an individual person or the meanness of some petty act' (Broackes 2012: 1). Broackes describes this approach as broadly Wittgensteinian, which Murdoch also combined with moral psychology and the idea of moral training, influenced by Plato. In other words, for Murdoch, rather than abstract or artificial choices, moral philosophy is concerned with the question of how I can become a better person. She wrote in 1967 that,

> Moral philosophy is the examination of the most important of all human activities, and I think that two things are required of it. The examination should be realistic. Human nature, as opposed to the natures of other hypothetical spiritual beings, has certain discoverable attributes, and these should be suitably considered in any discussion of morality. Secondly, since an ethical system cannot but commend an ideal, it should commend

a worthy ideal. Ethics should not be merely an analysis of ordinary mediocre conduct, it should be a hypothesis about good conduct and about how this can be achieved. How can we make ourselves better? is a question moral philosophers should attempt to answer. ('The Sovereignty of Good over Other Concepts' (SGC): 363–4)

This passage contains the heart of Murdoch's moral philosophy: thinking about real people and how we work, how we make moral choices, how we might make better ones, and what 'better' might be. In *Sartre: Romantic Rationalist*, she engages with Sartre the novelist, the human, the cultural figure and the philosopher; and also with his existentialist philosophy. Murdoch finds 'the general impression of Sartre's work is certainly that of a powerful but abstract model of a hopeless dilemma, coloured by a surreptitious romanticism which embraces the hopelessness' (SRR: 111). In 'Vision and Choice in Morality' in 1956, she distances herself from the prevailing moral philosophical thinking at Oxford, considering that their 'picture is simple, behaviouristic, anti-metaphysical, and leaves no place for commerce with "the transcendent"' (VCM: 80).

These are the two major departure points for Murdoch's philosophy: she moves away from her peers and establishes new modes of thinking and a new attitude to morality in everyday life and in art. In this way, Murdoch is positioned between the British tradition and the continental tradition, drawing on both but finding a new perspective. As mentioned above, she was very influenced by Simone Weil, and her concept of attention; especially in relation to the idea of 'the Good' as a transcendent reality and the idea that progress in morality is a matter of meditation, not just action. Bringing this thinking to the debates in film philosophy will enable the divide between the two traditions to be seen in a fresh light and perhaps not as polarising as can sometimes be the case. Murdoch offers an alternative framework, mindset and vocabulary for thinking about film as moral philosophy, and the role of film in our individual moral thinking and training.

Murdoch is particularly concerned with the idea of moral perception, and this is where many of her visual metaphors come into play. This is enlarged upon in Chapter 3, but for now let me clarify that this is about the perceptions of individuals. Broackes describes Murdoch's model of morality as being about the 'perception of particulars', and how this was 'radically distinctive' (2012: 11). This was not morality as instinct or passion, or intellectual intuition, or linguistic puzzle-solving, and was not about judgement or issuing prescriptions. Murdoch argues that different moral choices are made on the basis of different conceptual schemes. She writes, 'I can only choose within the world I can *see*' (IP: 329): a person's conceptual apparatus focuses their range of options, which determines their moral world. It is through attention, in the Weilian sense, that we are able to 'un-self', or become less focused on ourselves, in order to determine a more 'just and loving gaze directed upon an individual reality' (IP: 327). This invites an encounter with the gazes of cinema, both on- and off-screen, of character, camera and filmgoer, to see how moral thinking about film might be enlivened by these notions of attention and inner vision. It is here that I propose Murdoch's contention in the epigraph, that we might apprehend more than we understand and might grow by looking, becomes pertinent to the experience of cinema. Indeed, it seems from some glimpses of her writings that she was aware of cinema's potential in this regard, despite the fact that she did not develop these ideas beyond one essay.

MURDOCH AND THE CINEMA

To celebrate British *Vogue*'s centenary year in 2016, the magazine's website published 100 archive pieces from the magazine, described as 'some of our favourite pieces'. As she is introduced, 'Booker-prize winning author Iris Murdoch' had written a short piece for the August 1956 issue of British *Vogue* on the particular art of the cinema.[6] This essay is remarkable for several reasons. Firstly, when it was written: in 1956, the year that Murdoch gave the paper 'Vision and Choice in Morality' to the Aristotelian Society. In VCM she talks about the limitations of language to conduct moral philosophy, and calls upon philosophers to be like poets, to extend the limits of language and enable it 'to illuminate regions of reality which were formerly dark' (VCM: 90). She also refers to the type of fantasy that 'a private film show *à la* Walter Mitty' might be (VCM: 85).[7] Although, in that paper, she does not suggest cinema is a way to conduct moral philosophy, the *Vogue* article shows that cinema was on her mind, and that it could be an art form she would consider capable of the requisite humanity and insight: an illuminating, external, truth-seeking light, not a purely imaginary deceptive fantasy. Secondly, the cinematic references that Murdoch draws upon to illustrate her thinking are canonical, before the film critics' canon had been invented! This shows that Murdoch was seeing international films such as *Seven Samurai* (Akira Kurosawa, 1954), as well as British fare such as *Brief Encounter* (David Lean, 1945), and major American works such as *The Magnificent Ambersons* (Orson Welles, 1942), and that she was recognising their significance and understanding their complexities. Thirdly, she recognises the specific abilities and potential of the cinema as distinct from the other arts, of which she more frequently writes in her philosophy. The essay is no more than 1,000 words, and I am going to examine it in detail here, so as to open out a range of possible encounters between the cinema and Murdoch's thinking about cinema as art in 1956.

'ON THE CINEMA'

Murdoch begins by setting out her stall in relation to film:

> I was told at school that the cinema resembles the Cave in the *Republic* of Plato: a dark hole into which one retires in order to escape from reality and be entertained by shadows. Perhaps for that reason, and feeling too that shadows have their place, I used to expect films to resemble dreams, and was disappointed. ('On the Cinema' (OTC): 98)

Already, a philosophical link with the chained prisoners and deluded shadow play of Plato's cave is established. Several books and articles have emerged in the last twenty or thirty years that overtly make this connection, but Murdoch was contemplating this link as a school child.[8] The implications of this similarity are clear: that the cinema is a place of delusions, escape and entertainment. Entertainment is true. But 'escape from reality' is something that this book disputes, and indeed Murdoch does not maintain that early outlook. The idea that 'shadows have their place' is an insight into the realm of art and imagination in which Murdoch is interested, and yet she finds that they do not resemble dreams. Does this mean in fact that they resemble reality?

> I make the assumption that the art of the cinema is visual, and that its task is to delight and enlarge the imagination by the creation of visual images. How should a film achieve this? I speak, of course, as an outsider with strong prejudices and no expertise. (Ibid.: 98)

Here Murdoch states a clear understanding of cinema as more than a storytelling medium, and also as a field which has a measure of expertise.[9] Film should 'enlarge the imagination by the creation of visual images': this sounds like a tall order, but one that perceives cinema as having lasting value beyond mere entertainment, and indeed beyond the cinema theatre. In order to understand how film does do this, Murdoch interrogates the medium further.

> The film is, for better or worse, the medium which can most exactly reproduce the moment-to-moment vagaries of the human consciousness. It is in fact the most natural image for the consciousness, which Locke, for want of this example, likened to a magic-lantern show. The film presents an animated visual picture, observed from a certain point of view and experienced in a non-reversible order. From a painting we can stand back, with a novel we can pause and ponder, but a film is as near to us as our own self-awareness, and comes over us with the inevitability of time itself. One result of this is that the film can be the most

> profoundly boring and demoralizing of all art forms. What can compare with the feeling of blunted dreariness with which one leaves a bad film, especially if one has been unwise enough to visit it in the afternoon? (Ibid.: 98)

Here Murdoch aligns the art form with human consciousness by engaging with the element of time: film can show time moment by moment, making it 'the most natural image' for consciousness. Again forging a link with the endeavour of philosophers to capture this visual element of human thinking, she reminds us of Locke's use of the example of the magic lantern, or camera obscura, which he likened to the human mind.[10] Murdoch then captures the formal essence of the art: 'an animated visual picture, observed from a certain point of view and experienced in a non-reversible order'. This phrasing encompasses the cinematic specificity of movement, vision, direction and experience, as well as the inevitability of time passing as we watch a film. Just as Virginia Woolf had teased out the differences between experiencing a film and reading a novel in her essay on cinema thirty years earlier, Murdoch here differentiates the film from the distance we can impose on a painting, and the controlled consumption we have of a novel (Woolf 2009: 172–6). We experience film on a plane akin to our own self-awareness, or how we experience the world we look at, and its passage through time – even if it is the film's time, rather than the real time in which we live it – is out of the control of our hands and minds. Murdoch then cuts to the fact that, seeing as our experience of the world can be dull, so can the experience of a film, and indeed it can demoralise. This is undoubtedly true: and it is interesting that Murdoch chooses not purely to celebrate cinema in this essay but to pursue her analysis of its likeness to human experience of the world. In the delightfully evocative vignette one can imagine a demoralised Murdoch leaving a disappointing matinee, having been taken on an unhappy experience: but an experience nonetheless. She goes on to refine her thinking about film in relation to narrative:

> A good story will always benefit a film, though a weak one will not necessarily ruin it. *The Magnificent Ambersons* is admirable in spite of its story, but what makes *Seven Samurai* mythological in the memory is that in addition to its other merits it is a great archetypal tale. (OTC: 98)

This is strikingly insightful in that Murdoch here acknowledges the formal and visual attractions of the Welles film aside from its tale of a family's fortunes. She goes so far as to say that the story fails to hamper the film, clearly indicating that the attractions of the film are seen on the screen, not in the story. Then to describe *Seven Samurai* as 'mythological in the memory' conveys the power of the film's images to stay with the viewer, and to resonate with the stories of the ages which film has the power to evoke. But clearly Murdoch sees film as being about more than evocative storytelling.

> Now what can the movie camera do which nothing else can do, and what should it therefore busy itself doing? It can present to us human drama and feeling in the form of momentary awareness. A film should not attempt objectivity; it should not be 'as if we were there ourselves' (why are most travel films so depressing?). It should resemble, not a vague detached awareness of things going forward, but a tense heightened awareness, such as we have in dreams or moments of emotional vision. After all, this is a form of *Art*. Therefore, objects in films ought never to look *normal*, since objects do not do this in ordinary life in our moments of most acute observation. A film should show us a strange and startling world, disintegrated and distorted, and full of dramatically significant objects. Compare the surrealist painter, who attempts by curious juxtapositions to revive our jaded awareness of our surroundings. (Ibid.: 98)

The language of this passage shows Murdoch fully engaged with the experience of cinema. She describes the emotional impact through talking about 'human drama and feeling', but also understands how these are conveyed 'in the form of momentary awareness': the form of the content is unique, and it moves from moment to moment. In another comment redolent of Woolf, Murdoch's consideration of moments recalls Woolf's discussion of the value of a moment in her novel *Mrs Dalloway* (1925), as emphasised in the novel *The Hours* (1998) written by Michael Cunningham and conveyed so exquisitely in the 2003 film adaptation (Bolton 2014). In *The World Viewed* (1979) Stanley Cavell discusses the significance of a moment in a film, and of returning to that moment again and again (Klevan 2011: 53–5). Murdoch prefigures this line of scholarship, drawing attention to this temporal, formal and experiential element of film. With her comment about objectivity she identifies the bland voiceover of the travelogue as the type of film she finds depressing. This comment reveals that she is not interested in film's ability simply to record and relay images from other places in the world. Murdoch is keen to see film show life as only it can: 'a tense heightened awareness, such as we have in dreams or moments of emotional vision'. Here Murdoch links explicitly the images we can see on-screen with the images we see in our own minds and imaginations, thereby signalling the kinship between the content of both. She then states, unequivocally, 'after all, this is a form of Art' (capital A!). This is a vital insight into Murdoch's thought, as so much of her work is concerned with the power and meaning of art, and here we can see that cinema might be included in those conversations. There is then an unexpected foray into the idea that objects should not 'look normal', which she clarifies by saying that objects do not look normal in everyday life when we study them 'in moments of acute observation'. This links with her thinking about attention to art, which will be considered at length in this book, and also the notion that acute observation distorts and changes perceptions. So the sharp focus of the camera can and should alter the appearance of its object just as our directed attention changes what it focuses on. The description of the film world Murdoch desires sounds like the surrealist films she admires: strange and startling, disintegrated and distorted, full of dramatically significant objects. This reveals that Murdoch sees cinema as a realm of immense creativity and invention, which is formally equipped to use focus on objects as a way of changing their significance. She then makes the comparison to surrealism explicit, invoking the surrealist painter who uses 'curious juxtapositions' (sounds like 'montage') 'to revive our jaded awareness of our surroundings'. This is a way of thinking about the filmmaker in terms similar to those of Cavell nearly twenty years later: our reality as reshaped and given back to us in ways that challenge our understanding of our surroundings (Cavell 1979: 199). This is Murdoch speaking about form and aesthetics in 1956 in ways that resonate with the film and philosophy debates of the 1990s and 2000s. Murdoch then again reveals her preference for the sharp focus on objects.

> I am tempted to say that the cinema is an art of indoors. Few outdoor shots linger in my memory except as reminders of other landscapes; and perhaps the most totally depressing, as well as one of the most common types of cinema-going experience is to be presented with a sunny field of waving corn to the accompaniment of mediocre music. (OTC: 98)

While this may bring to *our* minds many epic outdoor sequences we love, and specific scenes from *Ratcatcher* (Lynne Ramsay, 1999), *Gladiator* (Ridley Scott, 2000) or *Days of Heaven* (Terrence Malick, 1978), Murdoch is not talking here about exterior arable images per se. Bear in mind that when she is writing, she may not have seen films made in CinemaScope, which was invented in Hollywood in the early 1950s. Landscapes would probably not have appeared to her in their full cinematic beauty using panoramas, CinemaScope or VistaVision. She recalls her dislike of the simple recording of other landscapes from the comment about travel films, but the real problem for her here is lack of meaning. 'Sunny field of waving corn' suggests cliché and banality, accompanied by 'mediocre music', which again fails to forge a new path or drive home an original insight. This is a bland image of reality mechanically reproduced and conveyed, not focused or reshaped in the way that film can do. It is now that Murdoch begins to make clear what she does see as cinema's prime ability.

> There is, however, one natural object with which the cinema is supremely concerned, and that is the human body, and more especially that 'most interesting surface', the human face. Here we can find tragedy and comedy made minutely concrete in the movement of a muscle, and human character on display at the point where spirit and matter are most intensely fused. If cinema could do nothing but present faces it would have enough material to be a major art. (Ibid.: 98)

Cinema's forte is in the realm of focusing on the human, and the face in particular. Murdoch's description of finding 'tragedy and comedy made minutely concrete' conveys the human embodiment of emotions and themes, and indeed archetypes, to use Murdoch's term about *Seven Samurai*. This sentence conveys the idea that cinema can show the archetypal genres of the ages, tragedy and comedy, and through its ability to focus in extreme close-up can convey the human experience of these phenomena. The facial close-up is one of the most intense and affective shots in cinema, and can yield great plaudits for the performers of such moments. The labile emotions on Connie Sumner's face in *Unfaithful* (Adrian Lyne, 2002), as she travels back on the train from her lover to her husband, was a feature of Diane Lane's Oscar-nominated performance in 2003, as was the agony wreaked across Fantine's face in Anne Hathaway's performance in *Les Misérables* (Tom Hooper, 2012), for which she won an Academy Award. Murdoch's description of the face as 'where spirit and matter are most intensely fused' inspires me to write in detail about faces in this book, and indeed explains the cover image of Lotte (Patrycia Ziolkowska) from *The Edge of Heaven/Auf der anderen Seite* (Fatih Akin 2007), which will be discussed further in Chapter 5. The fusing of spirit and matter is a description that conveys how the image on-screen can convey interiority, or inner life, as Murdoch would more likely say. This in turn enables the face to be a means of affective and cognitive connection with the viewer, conveying far more than the story or even the reaction of a character, but rather their internal battles, responses and experiences. Murdoch recognised this and its potential, while declaring that presenting faces in the way it does means film has 'enough material to be a major art'. Murdoch's understanding of art, and the role it plays in moral philosophical thinking, will be explained and explored in Chapter 2, as it forms a major part of her philosophical writings. In this short essay for *Vogue*, however, Murdoch makes it clear that she takes cinema seriously.

> It follows from all this that I admire Cocteau and Orson Welles: that frankly dream-like quality of the former, the everyday grotesque quality of the latter. The conversations in the dark house in *The Magnificent Ambersons*, for instance, overwhelmingly create an image of despair which is at the same time a delight to remember, a piece of intensified

consciousness transformed into the material of art. These scenes also illustrate a careful combining of vision and sound. (I do not go so far as to lament the disappearance of the silent film; but how often the addition of sound merely makes for facile story-telling, and how rarely it is treated seriously as an aspect of the image.) (Ibid.: 98)

Murdoch returns to *The Magnificent Ambersons* to clarify her thoughts on the film. The form, the darkness, the oppressiveness, 'create an image of despair': a visual depiction of an emotional state, or, in Murdoch's words, 'a piece of intensified consciousness transformed into the material of art'. And indeed this is not just visual, as Murdoch notes the efficacious combination of vision and sound, when used to create such an evocation. Again, this observation on the misuse, or waste, of sound and the need for its serious consideration demonstrates Murdoch's nuanced, thoughtful and medium-specific attention to film. But she does not take it all entirely seriously as she does recognise the humour in delightful slapstick: 'Such a grotesque intensity of presentation need not, of course, be alarming; it can also be funny, as we see from the films of Chaplin, and from *The Italian Straw Hat*, which is perhaps the funniest film ever made' (Ibid.: 99). The fact that Murdoch liked Chaplin films, and the sight of a horse eating a straw hat, shows that she is not ignoring cinema's function as entertainment, and indeed takes pleasure in it. In some of her correspondence she reveals great enjoyment of films (and some irritation, which I set out below). In fact, perhaps cinema brings out some of the romantic in her:

> It follows, too, that I like emotion minutely expressed. What a commentary on the dramas of love would be possible here! Yet films too rarely deal with love. The love scene in which tensions, ambiguities, calculations and hopes appear in minute signs – this is not often to be found. Examples that occur to me are the touching scene in the café in *Brief Encounter*, where the doctor begs the girl to see him again, and the scene in the conservatory in *Le jour se lève*. I don't think there are many others. (Ibid.: 99)

It is unusual to hear these scenes discussed without the names of Laura (Celia Johnson) and Alec (Trevor Howard), or Francois (Jean Gabin) and Clara (Arletty) being mentioned, but Murdoch here is talking about the emotions that these scenes evoked rather than recalling the details of the characters or actors. It is of course the case that 'tensions, ambiguities, calculations and hopes appear in minute signs' in *Brief Encounter*, where the passionate adulterous love that Alec and Laura feel for each other is concealed under English etiquette as well as by the necessity of their situation. Murdoch clearly enjoyed the suppressed emotion in these scenes, and sees the potential for many more. She is not thinking of the fairly staple cinematic scenes of romantic declaration, but rather the more deeply affecting scenes of conflicting emotion and repressed passions. She sees the lack of such scenes as a matter of regret, as does she see images of beauty:

> Add to this the screen tendency to prefer vacuous regular faces to irregular and interesting ones. For a serious treatment of the face we turn to Japan, where perhaps the cinema is aided by a dramatic tradition which interested itself in facial expression. Even in the surely not impossibly difficult task of presenting the magic of feminine beauty the cinema has not often succeeded, and for all their undeniable charms I would exchange the whole pack of Italian gamines for the memory of Lee Miller in *Le Sang d'un Poète*. (Ibid.: 99)

Murdoch clearly sees the conventional faces of the movies as uninteresting, and lacking in emotional depth. The Japanese faces to which she refers, and perhaps she is again thinking of *Seven Samurai* here, would have seemed exaggeratedly theatrical to most, but Murdoch yearns for evident emotion. Similarly, she sees convention and predictability in the depiction of female beauty, thinking, it would seem, of Italian actresses of the era, such as Alida Valli, Marina Berti and Adriana Benetti. Her preference is for the striking androgyny of Lee Miller, standing in as the Venus de Milo in Cocteau's *Blood of a Poet* (1932) (Figure 1.1). Miller also contributed an essay on the cinema for the same issue of *Vogue*, which begs the question as to whether this prompted Murdoch's praise for Miller in the film.

Figure 1.1 The face of Lee Miller, in *The Blood of a Poet/Le sang d'un poète*, directed by Jean Cocteau, 1932.

There are interesting connections here with the biography of Lee Miller, who was acquainted with both Charlie Chaplin, whose films Murdoch has expressed a liking for, and Raymond Queneau, whom Murdoch regarded as a mentor.[11] In a letter to David Morgan from 1964, Murdoch again mentions the Cocteau film as being 'one of the two or three films in the world that I love – at least I love certain images from it. The face of Lee Miller is really beautiful, not like most film stars.'[12] Clearly this image of beauty stayed with Murdoch long after seeing the film. She does then go on to say to Morgan that, 'It's years now though since I stopped going to films. Do they mean much to you?' Sadly, then, it seems that Murdoch's examination of cinema in the *Vogue* essay did not lead to a lifelong engagement with films. There are, however, some other mentions of films in Murdoch's correspondence which are of note.

MURDOCH THE CORRESPONDENT

The Iris Murdoch Archive held at Kingston University holds many letter runs between Murdoch and her multiple correspondents, including Brigid Brophy, Philippa Foot and Raymond Queneau. I do not assert that the following is comprehensive coverage by any means; it is simply intended to show some evidence of the role that cinema played in Murdoch's thinking about life and art. A photograph of canine film star Rin Tin Tin on a postcard to Brigid Brophy (undated), says on the reverse, 'Dear old pal! How nice films were then – primal innocence' (Figure 1.2).[13]

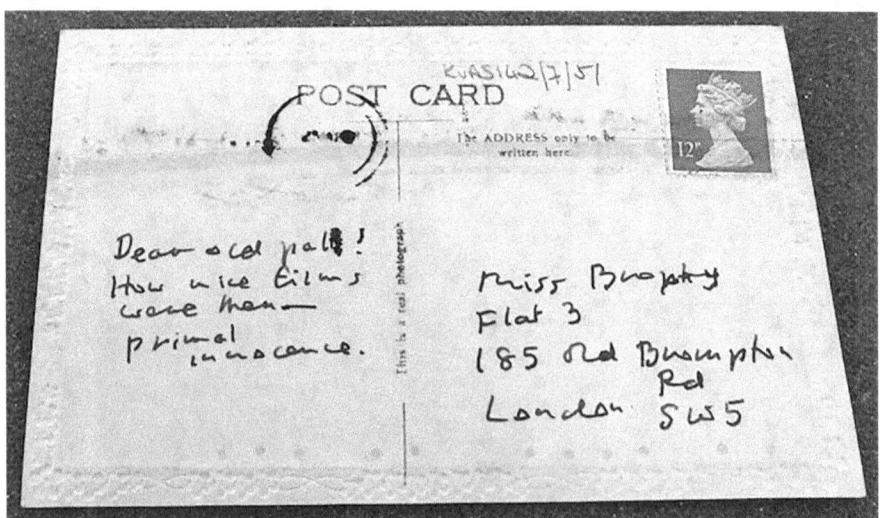

Figure 1.2 Iris Murdoch's thoughts on Rin Tin Tin on the reverse of a postcard written by Murdoch to Brigid Brophy. From the Iris Murdoch Collections in Kingston University Archives. Copyright Kingston University. Photograph is author's own.

In a letter to Raymond Queneau, dated 28 October 1946, Murdoch writes, 'I was glad to hear you are venturing into the cinema. In France anyway, a most honourable region of art, judging by the excellent French films we've been seeing over here lately.'[14] In an undated letter to Philippa Foot, Murdoch writes 'By the way, see if you can the excellent German film "The Murderers Are Amongst Us" [sic]. It suddenly occurred to me that I'd never met Germany. A whole universe to discover.'[15] Writing to Brophy, it is clear that Murdoch was looking forward to seeing the film made by the Beatles: 'Someone has given me the Beatles latest record, and tells me the Beatles film is super, the show stolen by Ringo. That is all that I hoped.'[16] And in another letter to Brophy, she writes 'Sorry I missed the Tallulah film, it sounds marvellous!'[17] These comments show an enthusiasm for some films and that, at this stage in her life, they were still part of her cultural experiences.

However, Murdoch expresses a very negative view of cinema in a letter to Brigid Brophy (no date). Murdoch is clearly in a bad mood, due to a postal strike, and the fact that

> My military brother-in-law is here, hewing down trees and laying pavements, and doing other things suitable to a huge taciturn man who cannot communicate with the human race by the usual channels, and he seems to control all the forms of transport. Though actually J and I escaped briefly this morning.

She then pronounces that 'Films hold my attention but too much. That is one reason why I detest them. I just undergo them, and as they are usually rotten . . .'[18]

These items of correspondence show some ambivalence towards cinema, but I am inclined to set the comment about 'detesting' film in the context of that bad-tempered letter, which finds the prolific correspondent frustrated by a postal strike, inducing 'postal despair', and aggravated by the presence of her brother-in-law. The majority of the opinions expressed elsewhere are positive, even praiseworthy and idealistic, suggesting that perhaps Murdoch had higher hopes of cinema than her subsequent viewing enabled her to sustain.

A couple of other comments are of note before proceeding. Once, in interview in 1985, Murdoch was asked why she is so interested in images associated with water, and she concedes that there is water in all her books. She then says, in relation to the drowning of one of her characters in her novel *The Philosopher's Pupil*,

> one image printed on my mind is from a film that I saw a hundred years ago, *Les Enfants du Paradis*, where there is a murder in a swimming bath (though the character in the film is not drowned but shot I think). (Dooley 2003: 127)

(In fact, the character Lacenaire kills the Count in the Turkish baths, but it is not clear how.) Another passing reference reveals that Murdoch also watched Leni Riefenstahl's films of the 1936 Berlin Olympic Games, and the swimming movies featuring Esther Williams. In her review of the book, *Haunts of the Black Masseur: The Swimmer as Hero*, she discusses the inspirational role that water and swimming can play for a novelist, and she refers to Esther Williams and the fact that she 'scorned to wear a bikini' (Murdoch 1993).

These scattered references to stars and scenes in cinema show that Murdoch knew of popular American film and European cinema. This brief survey of some of the mentions in Murdoch's non-fiction writing, including personal correspondence, simply aims to reveal that she saw film, was interested in it, and was genuinely struck by some lasting images and moments. It is the work of this book to develop the conceptual and philosophical connections between Murdoch's work and the cinema, as an experience of art but also within the artworks themselves.

MURDOCH AND CONTEMPORARY FILMS

This book will examine Murdoch's thinking in relation to contemporary films from a range of countries and genres, including art cinema and more mainstream works. All the films have been released in the last ten years, since 2008. The reason why contemporary cinema is the focus is because part of this project is to demonstrate the relevance of Murdoch's philosophy to film experiences now, and to our critical thinking and contemporary society. Through the connections forged, and methodology conducted, I aim to show the rigour and relevance of Murdoch's philosophical thinking, as well as to celebrate her originality and to demonstrate how her unique voice can contribute to the field of film philosophy.

Just because Murdoch uses the terminology of transcendence, metaphysics and morals does not mean that her thinking is outmoded. On the contrary, this book will show how contemporary cinema is increasingly occupied with the questions that occupied Murdoch, such as how to become a better person, how to act justly and how to learn from experience. The selected films demonstrate political, social, moral and artistic concerns that merit analysis in light of an open-minded approach to moral vision, and to learning by watching, that Murdoch called for and promoted. For Murdoch, paying attention to art is a way of learning about morality and goodness, and she spoke about these ideas in language that uses a great deal of visual metaphors, such as attention, sight, vision and pictures (Blum 2014: 307–23). These concepts can be fruitfully and excitingly applied to film in ways that not only further our understanding of the moral value of cinema as an art form, but also in relation to the moral messages and operations of individual films. This book will examine the idea that film itself can be part of our individual moral training as Murdoch envisages art can be. This is not just a question of relationships to and within the text, but also as part of the experience of the film that we take with us into the world, and of, in Murdoch's words, growing by looking.

The book's approach is to examine concepts that are related between the films and Murdoch's philosophy in the next seven chapters, thereby picking out the main themes in Murdoch and some fundamental themes in contemporary cinema. Through the selection of films that make philosophical contributions to the debates raised by Murdoch, the book will forge an original pathway in the field of film philosophy, bringing a new philosopher into focus, highlighting a set of questions about goodness that have been overlooked by contemporary work on film and ethics, and offering a fresh set of film readings to the discipline. I propose that the films themselves are the type of philosophical work that Murdoch believes good art can be. Murdoch talks about art as painting, sculpture and novels, including her own novels. Indeed, many of the interviews with Murdoch – both on YouTube and in print – are at least partly concerned with the question of the difference between novels and philosophy, and how philosophical her novels are. Some Murdoch scholars may say that you cannot appreciate Murdoch's philosophy without including the novels; that what is referred to as 'her' philosophy is contained as much in the novels as it is in her overtly philosophical texts. My project refocuses Murdoch's philosophy onto films that I consider to be examples of her philosophical thinking in action. My fundamental questions are, can films be the type of art that Murdoch considers constitutes philosophy, and, if so, how does this work? Where is the philosophy found? And, ultimately, how does this help us more fully understand what the films are doing?

NOTES

1. Kingston University, London, holds archives of Murdoch's correspondence, books, photographs and other materials (<https://www.kingston.ac.uk/faculties/faculty-of-arts-and-social-sciences/research/iris-murdoch-archive/> (last accessed 17 December 2018)). Murdoch's Sartre notebook is listed in this way: Murdoch, I. *Notes on a lecture given by Jean Paul Sartre*: Brussels Oct 24 1945 ; [Notes on works by Sartre: Equisse d'une théorie des émotions; L'imaginaire; L'être et le néant]. The Archive reference is IML 682.
2. Iris Murdoch: 'Waiting on God': A Radio Talk on Simone Weil (1951), with a Prefatory Note by Justin Broackes. The text of the talk is set out in Broackes (2017: 8, 10–16). The talk was discovered in typed form by Justin Broackes, who has produced this printed version, with a prefatory note and commentary article, for the *Iris Murdoch Review*.
3. See Justin Broackes's comprehensive account of Murdoch's philosophical trajectory in his introduction (2012: 21–92).

4. Why Iris Murdoch Matters, 13–14 November 2015; The Philosophy of Iris Murdoch, 16 June 2016; Moral Perception in the Work of Iris Murdoch, 28 April 2018. The In Parenthesis project has a blog, <http://www.womeninparenthesis.co.uk> (accessed 18 October 2018).
5. Terry Eagleton described MGM as a 'rambling, repetitive ragbag of a book, the philosophical equivalent of Murdoch's devotion to the loose baggy monster of a novel'. 'The good, the true and the beautiful' (a review of *Metaphysics as a Guide to Morals* by Iris Murdoch, *The Guardian*, 20 October 1992).
6. On Tuesday 17 May 2016, <http://www.vogue.co.uk/article/vogue-archive-article-iris-murdoch> (last accessed 20 February 2018).
7. *The Secret Life of Walter Mitty* is a short story by James Thurber which appeared in the *New Yorker* in 1939, and which has been the basis of two Hollywood film adaptations: one starring Danny Kaye in 1947, and one starring Ben Stiller in 2013. Walter Mitty is an ineffectual man who daydreams about himself as a hero in an array of fantastic situations.
8. See for example Renzi and Rainey (2006); Andersen (2014); Smith (2004).
9. It is interesting to speculate which film experts Murdoch might have been aware of in 1956: perhaps British film critics such as Iris Barry, Paul Rotha or Ernest Betts, or perhaps later figures such as C. A. Lejeune. For further reading about this period, see Lowell MacDonald (2016).
10. John Locke (1690) writes about pictures in a dark room resembling the understanding of a man. This is explained and analysed further by Francis J. Broucek (1991: 142–3).
11. Correspondence between Queneau and Murdoch over a period of thirty years is considered in depth by Avril Horner and Anne Rowe in *Living on Paper* (2015).
12. David Morgan was a pupil of Murdoch's at the Royal College of Art in the 1960s. They formed a close and tumultuous relationship, which Morgan sets out in his memoir *With Love and Rage: A Friendship with Iris Murdoch* (2010). This letter is reproduced in Horner and Rowe (2015: 278).
13. Kingston University and Archives Special collections (KUAS) 142/7/51.
14. KUAS 70/1/32.
15. KUAS 100/1/123. The film Murdoch refers to is *Murderers Among Us* (Wolfgang Staudte, 1946).
16. KUAS 142/6/141.
17. KUAS 142/5/176.
18. KUAS 142/6/71.

CHAPTER 2

Film as Art, and Cinema as a Hall of Reflection

> If cinema could do nothing but present faces it would have enough material to be a major art. (OTC): 98)

> A great work of art gives one a sense of space, as if one had been invited into some large hall of reflection. ('Literature and Philosophy' (L&P): 28)

> Good art . . . provides work for the spirit. Of course morality is quite largely a matter of action, though what we look at profoundly affects what we do . . . art remains available and vivid as an experience of how egoism can be purified by intelligent imagination. (F&S: 453)

Before progressing to explore how film can be the type of moral training in which Murdoch considered we are all engaged, I need to tackle a fundamental question: is film the right type of art for Murdoch? By which I mean, when Murdoch speaks about the role that art can play in our moral lives, and describes painting, sculpture, certain novels and moments in nature, could the cinema in general, and an individual film in particular, be the type of art she contemplates? For Murdoch, paying attention to art is a way of training oneself in the objectual attention required to address issues in our own moral thinking about others. But a certain state of mind is required; a certain distance and attention. The photograph in the frontispiece is a light-hearted representation of Murdoch paying attention to art. This chapter will address the question of whether watching and thinking about film can be the type of experience of art which Murdoch envisaged, and I will argue that it is not only a perfect example but also is a more efficacious and affective one than some of the other art forms Murdoch discusses. In order to assess this, we need to turn not only to what Murdoch herself says about cinema, but also what the objections might be to considering film as 'the right type' of art. Clearly the epigraph from Murdoch's essay 'On the Cinema' suggests she considers that film has the potential to be a major art; but has it achieved that potential in Murdochian terms?

WHY MIGHT FILM NOT BE ART?

The principal objections to discussing film as art are mainly to do with a concern that to do so denies, or ignores, the amount of labour that goes into a film, and the cultural and industrial contexts. To call film 'art' might be more consistent with the idea that a genius auteur produces the film rather than it being an industrial product, the existence of which is dictated by a plethora of factors. The other traditional objection to film as art is focused on the way in which it reproduces reality, mechanically and technologically, rather than offers an interpretation by an artist using creative materials. Walter Benjamin's 1935 essay 'The Work of Art in the Age of Mechanical Reproduction' (2007) examines these ideas, and we know that Murdoch read this because her annotated copy is available in the archives.[1] Murdoch has underlined the sentence that notes that photographic reproduction, 'with the aid of certain processes, such as enlargement or slow motion, can capture images which escape natural vision' (Benjamin 1968: 222). Benjamin explores the reproducibility of art, in terms of the loss of what he calls the 'aura' of the original artwork, and the changes in the way people perceive and receive art once it is technologically reproduced. He then attends to filmic reproduction in particular, and observes that 'the painter maintains in his work a natural distance from reality, the cameraman penetrates deeply into its web' (ibid.: 233). Murdoch has underlined this sentence, suggesting that she is interested by the notion of the manipulation and creation of images in the film-editing process. (We know from OTC that she is interested in the juxtaposition of images.) Murdoch also underlined Benjamin's point that film has deepened apperception in society 'for the entire spectrum of optical, and now also acoustical, perception'. Benjamin argues that 'filmed behaviour lends itself more readily to analysis because of its incomparably more precise statements of the situation' (ibid.: 236). This volume of Benjamin's essays, *Illuminations*, was published in 1968, and Murdoch's copy is dated April 1973, some seventeen years after her essay on cinema. All that we can glean from the annotations is that Murdoch retained an interest in film and the type of art that it is, particularly in relation to performance and politics.

Analytic philosophers have long been concerned with the question of film as art, and whether film qualifies to be considered as art at all. Cynthia Freeland develops Benjamin's comparison of cinema to avant-garde art in its ability to broaden human perceptual power in the ways that the surrealists such as Buñuel and Dali had done (Freeland 2001: 180). She also notes Benjamin's approval of the distancing effect of cinematic acting, which he perceived would prevent the absorption of the false reality, as might happen in the theatre; and also his optimism about the democratic nature of cinematic culture. However, Freeland does not share Benjamin's optimism about films in light of the distinction between high and mass art that persists in cinema (ibid.: 181). For Freeland, the nuanced appreciation of great work in cinema is confined to the experts, and 'cinematic features praised by critics and other directors might not be recognised by audiences' (ibid.: 184). She also imposes a reality check on what she perceives as Benjamin's naïvety in relation to cinema's political potential by drawing attention to those who use and control cinema today, and how films are consumed, referring to vast corporate complexes like Time-Warner or Disney-ABC (ibid.: 185). Freeland expects that audiences will be excited by the rape scenes in Kubrick's *A Clockwork Orange* (1971) rather than consider the novel's message of 'how mind control reins in individuality' (ibid.). These low expectations sound elitist. Her distinction between high and mass art cannot prevent serious consideration of a filmic text that might fall in either camp. She cites Benjamin's observation that 'the public is an examiner, but an absent-minded one' (2007: 241), as a reason for concern, saying, 'An absent-minded public is dangerously close to a public with a vacant mind, or a controlled mind' (Freeland 2001: 185). This resonates with Murdoch's comments in *Sartre: Romantic Rationalist* about an 'extreme of self-forgetting' in the cinema; but I propose that this comment is overstated and indeed may be far from the truth. Murdoch writes that, according to Sartre,

> The work of art, depending as it does upon the reader or spectator for its existence, is an appeal, a demand . . . The imagination must be enchanted, but, I think Sartre would agree, not too enchanted. An excessive detachment or suspicion will fail to create the work at all; an excessive self-forgetfulness will break down its objective contours and blend it with private fantasy and dream. In the latter case novel-reading becomes a drug. (It is characteristic of the art of cinema to encourage, by its very form, this extreme of self-forgetting.) Our *delight* in a work of art is our sense of the imaginative activity involved in creating and maintaining it, as it were, just at the right distance from ourselves. (SRR: 97)

The suggestion that cinema may be too absorbing to allow conscious engagement is potentially a stumbling block here if it is to be a form of art that enables the cultivation of Murdochian attention. However, if 'unselfing' is the aim, to be taken out of oneself, then this does not seem incompatible. As Murdoch writes, the film is 'the most natural image for the consciousness', and that its task is to 'delight and enlarge the imagination' (OTC: 98). The suggestions that Murdoch comes up with are in relation to the showing of objects, the human face, and emotions minutely expressed: and the films I am going to explore in this chapter certainly use all of these elements in their film worlds.

For Katharine Thomson-Jones, 'the art status of film has long been secure', but 'there is still a philosophical self-consciousness to the tradition of film studies' (2008: vii). She ascribes this to the role of technology in the art, and how, at its inception, 'film had to earn art status in the face of considerable technophobic scepticism' (ibid.: vii). Such scepticism does still exist in some quarters, and the suggestion that film is art, let alone philosophically laden, does still meet with some resistance. Thomson-Jones conducts an investigation of terminology and concepts in this field, referencing *Seven Samurai* as a cinematic masterpiece that goes to the establishing of film as art. (Clearly Murdoch would have agreed, as her analysis of the film in her article on the cinema demonstrates.) Thomson-Jones examines Roger Scruton's philosophical objections to film as art, based on his argument that photographic reproductions cannot be art and that this applies to film by extension. Thomson-Jones draws on Arnheim's analysis of the limitations of filmic reproduction of reality as an argument for its artistic status. In other words, space, time, perspective, size and many characteristics of the pro-filmic material are distorted by their filmic reproduction, and indeed its exhibition on flat screens limited by the frame only furthers these distortions. And it is of course in editing that the work of distinguishing film from 'real life' becomes most apparent. Although Arnheim was writing about the creation of silent film, these basic elements of difference and creation still apply. Concentrating on what film cannot do is hardly a positive methodology for accounting for its specificity, which should be, according to Thomson-Jones, showing 'that film has its own methods for creating a world on screen for the viewer to enter in imagination' (ibid.: 14). She cites Alexander Sesonske, who observed that, 'when we view a film, our experience of space, time, and motion, differs from any other context of our lives' (1974: 54, in Thomson-Jones 2008: 13). We can jump from place to place and time to time, while remaining in our cinema seats, and editing gives moments and elements particular focus, size, proximity and duration.

When we watch a film, we perform a variety of cognitive functions, such as making sense of narratives, recalling and revisiting earlier information – both intra- and extra-textual – evaluating actions and interpreting outcomes. Cognitivists such as David Bordwell (1989) are concerned with how we understand what we see, and analytic philosophers such as Noël Carroll (2008) are interested in how we categorise and evaluate the films we watch. Victor Perkins proposes that film should be judged as film: we should 'look for coherent patterns of interrelationship', and judge 'on the degree of meaningful interaction within the elements of the film' (Perkins 1972: 193). All these thinkers have demonstrated how the viewer of a film is a thinking viewer, not simply a passive receptacle of ideology as suggested by 1970s apparatus theory. And of course each of us brings our own lived experience to our viewing. We are thinking and feeling viewers, and the field of film phenomenology, including Vivien Sobchack's work on the film body and Laura Marks's discussions of haptic visuality, has enabled a new vocabulary of film interpretation and understanding (Marks 1999, 2002; Sobchack 1992, 2004). Emotional and bodily affect is an integral part of the film experience, and indeed filmmakers appeal to these elements as significant conveyers of meaning, sometimes replacing dialogue and action, as I have considered elsewhere (Bolton 2009, 2014, 2015a). The question of empathy with a character, and identification with them, is an important one in a Murdochian context. There is far more going on in the eyes, mind and body of a filmgoer than a simple 'self-forgetting': for a film philosopher this could not be further from the truth! But do we unself sufficiently? Does Murdoch's concept of paying 'loving attention' apply to the viewing of a film in the same way, or as much, as the making of and looking at a vase or sculpture? And are our responses of empathy and evaluation the type of moral progress that Murdoch says we should be making? If so, then her concepts constitute a significant intervention in film aesthetics and ethics, and open out a new way of conceptualising film's moral and ethical possibilities.

MURDOCH ON ART AND PHILOSOPHY

Martin Puchner observes,

> For Murdoch, the importance of art lay in the fact that it could serve as a symbol of the good. This is so because art as Murdoch conceived of it is primarily antipersonal or, in the parlance of modernism, impersonal or depersonalised. Art, she held, is the most powerful experience we have of being taken outside ourselves. And since the good requires leaving behind individual desires and desire for individual bodies . . . art is the best training for goodness. (2010: 176)

Murdoch not only emphasised the importance of art for ethics but also recognised an artistic dimension in philosophy itself. She discussed Sartre's novels in this light with Bryan Magee, along with works by Tolstoy, Dickens and Shakespeare (L&P: 3–30). She spoke of a dramatic form of thought in philosophy, from Hegel to Sartre, and repeatedly discussed Plato as an artist, using characters, scenes and stories to convey philosophical ideas. One of the questions Murdoch is faced with in most interviews, and something which continues to occupy many scholars, is how her literary works and philosophical works are related; in particular, how intentionally philosophical are her novels (Altorf 2008; Conradi 2001; Forsberg 2013; Leeson 2010). This is relevant here because it probes whether Murdoch sees fiction as a suitable medium for conveying philosophical ideas. Anne Rowe has examined the role of visual arts in Murdoch's novels, arguing that paintings and images in the fiction often function to engender sensory experience. For Rowe, there is a sensory phenomenology demanded by Murdoch's writing, and the visual arts relate to this evocative spirit.[2] For Marije Altorf, there initially seems to be a strong relationship between Murdoch's philosophy and her novels, in that characters in the novels use vocabulary taken from Murdoch's philosophical essays (2008: 1). And Murdoch writes about art and literature in her philosophical essays, demonstrating how important their role is in her moral philosophy. Altorf notes Murdoch's use of the nineteenth-century novel as more able to demonstrate ideas than philosophical vocabulary, and observes that, for Murdoch, 'Art thus indicates what an exemplary state of consciousness can be like, but also shows more common states of mind' (2008: 2). Murdoch remained resolutely opposed to the idea that her novels should be read as philosophy. In conversation with Brian Magee, she argues,

> In general I am reluctant to say that the deep structure of any good literary work could be a philosophical one. I think this is not just a verbal point. The unconscious mind is not a philosopher. For better and worse art goes deeper than philosophy. (L&P: 21)

For Murdoch, art does not need to have philosophy inserted into it deliberately in order to be philosophically valuable: it is by its very nature a philosophical process.

> I think good art is good for people precisely because it is not fantasy but imagination. It breaks the grip of our own dull fantasy life and stirs us to the effort of true vision. Most of the time we fail to see the big wide real world at all because we are blinded by obsession, anxiety, envy, resentment, fear. We make a small personal world in which we remain enclosed. Great art is liberating, it enables us to see and take pleasure in what is not ourselves. (L&P: 14)

For Murdoch, seeing is fundamental to our being as moral agents. Seeing art, attending to art, engenders 'true vision' as it literally takes us out of ourselves and engages us with the world of others. And here, in the presence of art, and, I suggest, in the engagement with a film world, we can understand what

Murdoch means when she says that 'A great work of art gives one a sense of space, as if one had been invited into some large hall of reflection' (L&P: 28). Cinema as a 'large hall of reflection' is a suitably spacious, yet contained, and visually resonant metaphor for the moving images and affective sounds on the cinema screen.

The distinction between saying and showing is pertinent here. Scott H. Moore argues that 'Murdoch believes that fiction can *show* what philosophy can only *say*' (2010: 101). Moore is writing about the lives of fictional philosophers in Murdoch's novels as conveyors of what Murdoch calls 'philosophy, as such' (in conversation with Jack I. Biles, in Dooley 2003: 58), and is exploring how these fictional lives put Murdoch's moral philosophy into action in their daily lives (or fail to!). For Niklas Forsberg this distinction prompts the question 'how can a piece of language – be it a philosophical text or a literary one – carry enough sense so as to show something that cannot be said?' (2013: 53). Forsberg ventures to develop the role of language and speaking in fiction when he considers *The Philadelphia Story*, and he analyses the complexity of communication in the film, concluding that 'it is not merely a question about what is being *said*, but it is also about what it means to listen' (ibid.: 141). The medium of film matters here, as Forsberg explains, because 'we learn this by watching a movie rather than by reading arguments and theses' (ibid.). Forsberg argues that we know a great deal about Tracy and the men who love her, and how they all see her, because we have experienced the full film. Forsberg observes that Tracy's situation is 'in a sense, unique or particular', and without knowing all about her situation the ideas expressed in sentences alone would not have had the same meaning. So, Forsberg proposes, and we cannot but agree,

> this is one reason why philosophy might do well in going to the movies . . . If the philosophical point lies in the artwork as a whole, then the watching of the film or the reading of the book are philosophical activities in their own right. (2013: 141)

Although there is so much scholarship on the philosophical content of Murdoch's novels, it seems in keeping with her philosophical intentions that the two should also stand apart, so that the philosophy can be kept discrete. Murdoch's play 'Art and Eros: A Dialogue about Art' (A&E), is a discussion between Plato and his friends who have just come from the theatre. They consider the merits of art, with Plato maintaining a quiet distance. They discuss the role of the audience's imagination, how the audience is moved, and the purpose of theatre, wondering can it just be fun? They also discuss different types of art, and Socrates wonders 'if sculpture is a better art than painting' (A&E: 469). They consider the idea that art is simply copying reality. Acastos says, 'good art is deep wise thinking. And bad art is bad because it's stupid or depraved thinking ... I'm sure good art *tells* us something. It isn't just a dose of emotion. It's like vision – insight – knowledge –' (A&E: 472). Socrates says

> Isn't it the nature of art to explore the relation between the public and the private? Art turns us inside out, it exhibits what is secret. What goes on inwardly in the soul is the essence of each man, it's what makes us individual people. The relation between that inwardness and public conduct *is morality*. How can art ignore it? (A&E: 475)

Plato, by contrast, keeps his counsel. He is quiet and withdrawn, until he mutters 'Art is lies, it's fantasy, it's play, it's humbug, it's make-believe, the theatre is rubbish, it's . . .' (A&E: 484). Plato argues that art makes people believe they have understood something when in fact they haven't gone deep enough; it is deluding. He talks about living in a cave, with people living their lives in darkness, 'seeing nothing but flickering shadows and illusions, like images thrown on a screen' (A&E: 488). Socrates persists in defending art and says that 'the language of art is the most universal and *enduring* kind of human thought' (A&E: 493). Plato, as Murdoch writes him here, is an artist: he is writing poetry and trying to be a great poet, and, Socrates says, he speaks with 'poetic eloquence' (A&E: 494).

Murdoch mentions Plato's concerns elsewhere, when considering the dangers of art. She refers to Plato's cave story as 'instructive *pictures*' (MGM: 10), but acknowledges the dangers of becoming 'lazy sentimental spectators of fictional dramas' (MGM: 13). This view of the possible dangers of art leads her to distinguish between what she considers to be good and bad art. While writing about the use of the visual arts in Murdoch's novels, Anne Rowe notes that, for Murdoch, celebrating art is only part of Murdoch's perspective: 'art must work, too, by being difficult, deliberately incomplete and imperfect; it must defy any consolatory function and present an unflinching picture of evil' (2002: 19). Rowe continues, 'whilst readers watch characters undergo a spiritual experience, they undergo one simultaneously by being shown the utter particularity of another consciousness, and by being experientially induced to feel love and tolerance for it' (ibid.: 23–4). This, writes Rowe, is how 'characters and readers alike participate in salvation by art' (ibid.: 24). This notion is pertinent to my consideration of how a film can simultaneously work as an engaging story, causing immersion in, and reflection upon, the particularity of another's consciousness and moral vision, and at the same time affect our own consciousness and moral vision, submitting us to a personal, ethical experience.

GOOD ART AND BAD ART

Murdoch frequently refers to art as being either good or bad, and it is important to address this issue before examining specific films. In conversation with John Haffenden in 1985, Murdoch responds to the questions of what she thinks is the true function of art: is it consolation, education or pure pleasure?

> The phrase you've used – pure pleasure – is good, I think. One should live with good art and not get addicted to bad art, which is demoralising and disappointing. Good art is a pleasure which is uncontaminated, it's happiness. One also learns a lot from art: how to look at the world and understand it; it makes everything far more interesting. It's a mode of reflection, and this is why it's a terrible crime for totalitarian states to interfere with artists . . . Art is a great hall of reflection . . . It's a mode of thought, a mode of knowledge. Good art can't help teaching you things but it mustn't aim at teaching. (Dooley 2003: 137–8)

It sounds rather pious to prohibit art from intentional didacticism, particularly as it is the aim of many artists to be provocative and encourage reflection. But the emphasis on learning how to look is vital to the understanding of film as Murdochian philosophy: it is a focused, attentive looking and experiencing, and the description of this as a 'mode of thought, a mode of knowledge' conveys the idea that it is a sustained practice, not a brief exposure or reaction. This is not a matter of a one-off or instantaneous response, but rather a state of being that a film can engender and encourage, both within the cinema theatre as 'a great hall of reflection', and beyond as we carry our experience of the film out into our contemplations, our conversations and our worlds.

In another conversation, with William Slaymaker in 1985, she says:

> I think art is good for people. Good art is good for people because it takes them away from themselves, and enables them to see many aspects of human life in detail, and all kinds of particular things, instead of being trapped inside their own fantasy, which is one of the opposites of freedom. (Dooley 2003: 141–2)

This idea again lends itself to the cinema, as two hours experiencing an engaging, challenging film does indeed expose us to scenarios and worlds that are not our own, but which offer the opportunity to see stories and exchanges that might challenge and develop our thinking. Murdoch concedes, 'we can also understand why Plato was suspicious of art, because art is a great place of illusions and magic as well as a place of liberation' (ibid.: 142). What Murdoch means by good art is art that does not console us. She explains this repeatedly across the body of her work, but makes it crystal clear here: 'Good art accepts and celebrates and meditates upon the defeat of the discursive intellect by the world. Bad art misrepresents the world so as to pretend there is no defeat' (MGM: 88).

The danger of art is consolation and fantasy. This will be explored in the chapters that follow, but it is important to note here that for art to function as Murdochian moral philosophy there needs to be sufficient distance for observation and contemplation, and the experience of the art should not be deluded consolation. Returning to the Sartre quote about the 'self-forgetting' encouraged by the cinema, it is useful to consider Thomson-Jones's analysis of the cognitive and emotional work done by viewers. It is not so that all films blend with our private fantasies. There are of course films that are founded on fantasy. Perhaps one might fantasise of being able to fight like Lorraine Broughton (Charlize Theron) in *Atomic Blonde* (David Leitch, 2017), but a character such as Jenny Davin (Adèle Haenel) in *The Unknown Girl* (Jean-Pierre Dardenne and Luc Dardenne, 2016) commands attention, evaluation and empathy, as will be examined in Chapter 7. The films I analyse in this book are examples of contemporary films that provoke, unsettle and challenge us to examine ourselves: they are far from consoling fantasies.

In 'The Sovereignty of Good', Murdoch speaks about the need to pay a 'patient loving regard' to the other, and how both nature and art can work to get us thinking like this. Her most famous example is of the kestrel:

> I am looking out of my window in an anxious and resentful state of mind, oblivious of my surroundings, brooding perhaps on some damage done to my prestige. Then suddenly I observe a hovering kestrel. In a moment everything is altered. The brooding self with its hurt vanity has disappeared. There is nothing now but kestrel. (SGC: 369)

Here, nature can bring us out of ourselves and we find the possibility of a focus on something else, which dilutes our ego and improves our vision of the world. Art also can act as practice in this way: in other words, we can hone our moral thinking through art as a type of practice.

Murdoch's article on the cinema shows that she saw particular abilities and qualities in film, but the article itself and her later comments in correspondence as recorded in Chapter 1 suggest that she felt not *all* cinema was significant in this regard. Her prime interest is in a vision resembling a dream, or 'emotional vision', as she says, 'After all, this is a form of *Art*': 'A film should show us a strange and startling world, disintegrated and distorted, and full of dramatically significant objects' (OTC: 98). And the prime object is us – human beings – our bodies and our faces, which she sees as being able to be expressed and depicted in the most minute emotional detail. Rudolf Arnheim wrote about the place of the human body among cinematic objects in *Film as Art* in 1957:

> A broken windowpane may be as good as a quivering mouth, a heap of dead cigarette stubs as the nervous drumming of fingers. Once again the classification – so characteristic of film – of man as one among many objects is plainly revealed. The traces of human strivings are as visible on inanimate objects as they are on the body itself. (Arnheim 1957: 121)

Arnheim draws on similar films to those referred to by Murdoch in *Vogue*, such as Cocteau's *Blood of a Poet* and Chaplin, in a consideration of visual perception and close attention to form, including how it can distract as well as inform. Film possesses the ability to close in on an object using the close-up shot, which, as Mary Ann Doane writes, 'has inspired fascination, love, horror, empathy, pain, unease' (2003: 90). Doane cites Epstein's essay 'Magnification', which, as she puts it, 'verges on the obscene' in the way he writes so intensely and hyperbolically about the human face in close-up (ibid.). Doane also cites Hugo Münsterberg from 1916, where he aligns the close-up with 'the mental act of attention' (ibid.: 91), thereby naturalising it rather than reifying it as Epstein does with his focus on its cinematic specificity, describing it as 'the soul of cinema' (Epstein 1977: 9). Doane focuses on the significance of the cinematic face, and how it is transformed by the close-up into something gigantic, monstrous and overwhelming (2003: 94). Doane highlights the phenomenological experience of the close-up as being both a presence and a sign demanding to be read, which she sees as 'inside or outside the cinema, the inevitable operation of the face as well' (ibid.: 94). It is, as Doane notes, 'barely possible to see a close-up of a face without asking: what is he/she thinking, feeling, suffering? What is happening beyond what I can see?' (ibid.: 96). These assessments of the close-up face recall Murdoch's interest in film's abilities, as they gesture towards what she was concerned with: the focus of attention, the intensity of experience, but also the realisation that there is work to be done by us when we look at the close-up on the human face. It is difficult to be an absent-minded spectator in the face, literally, of such a shot.

How does film make an object, or a face, appear in this way, so laden with meaning? There are a couple of examples that are instructive here. Firstly, the scene of emotions 'made minutely concrete' on the face of Anna (played by Nicole Kidman) in *Birth* (Jonathan Glazer, 2004). In a simply constructed scene, Anna is watching the orchestra playing Wagner and yet we are watching her face, as conflicting emotions of shock, fear and hope, play out across her features in a close-up that zooms in and is held for two minutes (Figure 2.1). Secondly, in *Innocence* (Lucile Hadzihalilovic, 2004), there is a moment where two of the schoolgirls, Bianca (Bérangère Haubruge) and Iris (Zoé Auclair), are

Figure 2.1 Anna's (Nicole Kidman) complex emotions on display, in *Birth* (2004), directed by Jonathan Glazer.

walking through the forest and they come across a fawn. This moment can be likened to Murdoch's kestrel, in that it halts us – and them – in our tracks and challenges our thought. We have been absorbed by the menace and the peculiar threat of the film's woodland *mise en scène* and tinkling piano music. When the girls pull up with a start we expect a sight of something horrific or frightening; in fact it is a spectacle of something gentle and delicate. This image interrupts our perception and confronts us with our assumptions. However, with Anna's face in *Birth*, the effect is less equivocal. The scene focuses our close, and patient, attention on this particular face, evidencing the complex emotions that she is experiencing in light of her extraordinary circumstances (a young boy has appeared in her life claiming to be her dead husband in some way, and is convincingly accurate about intimate details).

This close-up compels our attention, and draws us in to her consciousness and the complexity of her emotions as she begins to wonder if the boy's story could possibly be true. In both of these examples, the Murdochian resonances with emotion and attention are clear, but the ethical lessons require explication. Surely the position of these moments in the narrative of the film is significant, and how we analyse the experience of the character, and our experience of either the same spectacle that they see (the deer or the concert), or of them regarding the spectacle. There may be a moment in the film that is just for our eyes, not for the characters. Clearly performance is integral to the image, and our relationship to a star face is mediated by the extra-textual elements of that star's image. We might think of Cate Blanchett as multiple characters in

Manifesto (Julian Rosefeldt, 2017), or Jake Gyllenhaal and Amy Adams as Tony and Susan in arrestingly beautiful close-ups over the dinner table in *Nocturnal Animals* (Tom Ford, 2016). These star faces, along with Kidman's in *Birth*, raise the question of how the film world can be interrupted by the spectacle of a familiar star face. In his famous essay 'The Face of Garbo', Roland Barthes writes

> Garbo still belongs to that moment in cinema when capturing the human face still plunged audiences into the deepest ecstasy, when one literally lost oneself in a human image as one would in a philter, when the face represented a kind of absolute state of the flesh, which could be neither reached nor renounced. (1993: 56)

Discussions of Murdoch alongside Barthes, Benjamin and Epstein might suggest that her thinking about film belongs to their earlier era. However, Murdoch's approach to film is not naïve, or founded in awe of the medium. She is interested in human faces, not 'vacuous regular faces', but the place where 'we can find tragedy and comedy made minutely concrete in the movement of a muscle, and human character on display at the point where spirit and matter are most intensely fused' (OTC: 98). Murdoch is looking for meaning in the faces, not bathing in their aura or stunned by their mechanical reproduction.

In the second half of this chapter, I will discuss films that relate to Murdoch's ideas about film as art: the significance of the face, the question of distance and fantasy, and the importance of sound. Firstly, I will examine the ideas expressed by Murdoch in relation to the human face and what it is able to convey by looking at *Jackie* (Pablo Larraín, 2016). Then I will examine the way in which we can be engaged in a film and yet kept at a distance, unsure of what to believe, by *Stories We Tell* (Sarah Polley, 2012). And then I will look at how film can make objects look and sound strange, including the human face and the world around us, in *Under the Skin* (Jonathan Glazer, 2013).

THE FACE OF *JACKIE*

After the production company motifs, the screen is black, and we hear an extraordinary dropping, sliding note, conveying the sinking into darkness and destruction of a mood. The film's opening shots are a close-up of Natalie Portman, her shoulders and head, as we acclimatise ourselves to seeing her as Jackie Kennedy. The soundtrack's sliding note climbs up a little, conveying her attempt to 'pull herself together' for the interview to come. This drooping, sinking sound is repeated throughout the film's score, written by Mica Levi, and powerfully conveys the falling heart and stomach of the grief-stricken, as the recollection of loss hits her again and again. These close-ups are interesting in relation to the star face, as we are so familiar with Portman's tense face and tearful eyes from the relentless intensity of her other performances, notably in *Black Swan* (Darren Aronofsky, 2010). That performance was highly praised and rewarded with awards, and her face has become a striking image from the film's poster and artwork, adorned as it is with exquisite stage makeup and ballet costume-jewellery. Here, Portman's face is familiarly tense and tearful; her delicate bone structure and symmetrical features lend themselves well to the period makeup of the 1960s, and her dark eyes and bouffant hair recall the iconic trademarks of Jackie Kennedy without being a distracting imitation. She is clearly Natalie Portman, performing Jackie Kennedy, and the emphasis from the outset is on this character's state of mind, grief-stricken and burdened with the public nature of her family tragedy. An intertitle then tells us it is Hyannis Port, Massachusetts, 1963. Her tiny figure, silhouetted against a huge leaded-light window, sees a taxi pull up the drive, and a reporter (Billy Crudup) get out. Their terse exchange on the doorstep, filmed in stark shot reverse shot, sets up the duel that is to come. This is to be Jackie Kennedy's assertion of her version of what happened.

Portman's voice seems peculiarly sing-song, but this is a necessary evocation of Kennedy's vocal intonation and delivery. This is made especially evident in the recreation of the tour of the White House documentary, containing footage from the actual film, as well as recreations using Portman.[3] The soundtrack appears to be, at least partially, that of Kennedy's own voice from the 1962 film. There is a contrast between the nervous artifice and self-consciousness of Kennedy's performance in the documentary, and her sure-footed confidence with the journalist. Here she is very confidently beginning the story that will come to be the history of the Kennedys, or what she will name as Camelot.

An earlier classical music concert in the White House focuses on the presiding image of the immaculate Jackie, flanked by brothers Bobby and Jack, as the shot slowly closes in on her satisfied, almost transported face; confident that – as the voiceover of the documentary has established – everything in the White House is the best. Flashbacks to the day of the assassination show the amount of work and preparation that Jackie put in to her public events, practising greetings and preparing her appearance. Their arrival is greeted by huge crowds, and a tight close-up on her face shows her being slightly overwhelmed by the noise and activity on all sides. Cutting back to her face as she recounts what happened to the journalist in the present, her ability to recount the gory details of what happened when her husband was shot (a piece of his skull in her hands, blood and brains in her lap) is captivating. Her breathy, strange voice is strong and deliberate as she crafts the narrative that will be committed to history, even though she says 'don't think for one minute that I'm going to let you publish that'. She describes how his head and his mouth were beautiful, and his eyes were open. In extreme close-up we see Jackie's face after the assassination, as she gasps with tears and wipes splatters of thick dark blood from her face. She is looking at herself in the mirror as she does so, but we are tightly close in on her face. The most striking thing is that she is alone. She has nobody really close to help her. She is still splattered with her husband's blood as Lyndon B. Johnson is sworn in as President. Her face is dazed and silent, watching these emergency proceedings. In a strikingly realistic gesture, as Jackie turns away from the swearing-in party, she looks perplexed and amazed, and, as the repeated sinking musical swoon conveys her falling insides, she jumps: this conveys a jolt of reality as she is sidelined and the next presidential couple are feted. She sits alone on the plane back to Washington, but then she begins to try to discover as much information as possible, asking about the size of the bullet. She is determined to be present and visible, not brushed aside, but the strength of her voice and attitude appears awkward because of her diminutive size compared to the tall uniformed men standing around her, who find it so difficult to look her in the eye.

An extreme close-up on Bobby Kennedy's (Peter Sarsgaard) face as they ride with the casket shows he is upset but also concerned about Jackie's persistent questioning of the driver and the nurse in the car about what they remember about presidents who were assassinated. In her room, in private at last, she removes her suit, her stockings, all covered in blood, and close-up shots enable us to see this in detail. We hear the sound of her crying and breathing, and we see the sight of her husband's blood: she has to scrub her nails, and shower it off her. She looks very thin and small. There is a tight close-up on her face as she plans the funeral. She says with conviction, 'Must get this right – it has to be beautiful.' As she is challenged about things such as the guest list, a close-up on her tense face captures her awareness of the magnitude and complexity of what is happening.

Throughout the film, Jackie is constantly linking herself and JFK with history, especially Lincoln, but she is also worrying about needing to sell furniture to put John and Caroline through school. She speaks harshly about her own life, saying, 'Nothing is mine, not to keep anyway; a first lady must always be ready to leave the White House, it's inevitable', as she smokes cigarettes and defiantly utters her self-penned 'script' to the journalist. She's determined to march with the coffin at the funeral for eight blocks. She persuades Bobby, she fights for it. But she is shown as being very alone, as tracking shots follow her walking though the high-ceilinged cavernous White House, looking at all the ornaments, photographs and furniture, and putting on the record 'Camelot', sung by Richard Burton.[4] We follow her small body, in a familiar Jackie-style shift dress, and see her trying on her different dresses, drinking, taking pills, rearranging photographs, and then sitting, looking into the distance, crying, with 'Camelot' playing. We see her horror at having to pack all her clothes and belongings, to tape them up in boxes. She struggles to remove her wedding ring, looking at herself in the mirror, as if looking at how she appears to the outside world, or trying to work out if she looks different.

This is an emotive concoction of images, objects, sounds, music and references, which serves to create an intimate encounter with a cultural personality during a defining period in US history. In her discussions with the family priest, close-ups on her face combined with her recounting of mixed-up memories, about herself, and her marriage, convey an emotionally complex state. Speaking to her friend Nancy (Greta Gerwig) in an intimate conversation, she wonders if Nancy had been jealous of her, and what they will both do now. Jackie here is tearful and confessional; and yet there is an iron will on display too, fuelled, it seems, by anger at the destruction wrought upon her family by the presidential office. She demands that photographs taken at the funeral 'should record the truth – two heartbroken fatherless children are part of that'. She wants to ensure that there are 'children on full display for the world to see'. A striking close-up of her looking out of the car window, with the crowds reflected in her face, captures not just the character of Jackie Kennedy, but her public office too (Figure 2.2). By this stage in the film, the presence of Portman has been overtaken by her performance of the embodiment of Jackie. The close-up on her face, so recurrent and affective, accompanied by intense,

Figure 2.2. Jackie Kennedy (Natalie Portman) sees the crowds lining the streets, in *Jackie* (2016), directed by Pablo Larraín.

emotive music, depicts a powerful woman surrounded, at this particular period in her life, by men who are not fully free to fight her as they might wish to because of her circumstances, which are both uniquely tragic and uniquely privileged.

She explains to the priest, 'I never wanted fame, I just became a Kennedy.' She asserts that she can remember everything, and there is a close-up on her face as she recalls being driven at speed to the hospital, with her dead husband's head in her lap. She tells the reporter that every night she prays to die: 'Oh God let me be with my husband.' Just as she is consciously recounting how she wants this period to be remembered, so the *sympatico* reporter reassures her, 'You left your mark on this country the last few days. Decades from now people will remember you.' It is then that she instils in him the idea of Camelot, thus creating a cultural legend out of her personal tragedy. She creates a family grave, which includes their babies who died, but she is shown still to be solitary. The film ends as she is driven through town and she sees shop models going into the store window with her fashion 'look'. She sits back a little, and her face settles into a look which may be one of satisfaction, but certainly conveys a mixture of emotions. She will indeed be remembered. The film's final shots are as she recalls happy times with her husband, dancing in the White House. Jackie's face has dominated this film, capturing conflicting emotions, but also fusing spirit and matter with nerve-jangling intensity.

ART AS UNTRUTH: *STORIES WE TELL*

Sarah Polley's film is a moving and personal investigation of her family history, which interrogates the way in which we use images to concoct our own stories of our past, even relying on them as evidence for our imaginations. Through the use of actual footage and staged recreations – and the withholding of disclosure of the difference – the film provokes us to question our belief in what we see and the role of artistic representations in the formation of our thinking. It also gives the lie to the idea that watching film is an easy experience of 'self-forgetting' or 'absent-minded' examining. This film undercuts our comfort and our trust in what we see and believe both on-screen and about ourselves.

The film begins with a sweet and simple piano melody, redolent of a child haltingly playing a tune, and footage of a train travelling through snow, featuring a woman on the train looking out of the window, and a man's voice telling us that 'when you're in the middle of a story it isn't a story at all . . . it's only afterwards that it becomes anything like a story at all, when you're telling it to yourself or someone else'. We are looking at what appears to be home movie footage of a family, in the kitchen, at parties, and the images and sound appear to be linked, as if the man is giving his opinion on the stories we are going to hear. Then we are shown that his words are a quote from Margaret Atwood's novel *Alias Grace*, not a homily of wisdom straight from the speaking man himself.[5] A hand scribbling notes on paper, followed by the film's title 'Stories We Tell' in Courier font, looking like typewritten words, establishes that the film is to be about memoirs. The director, Sarah Polley, is then shown setting up microphones with a series of interviewees, who are her family members, including her elderly father Michael who is in a recording studio, and her siblings Joanna, Susy, Mark and Johnny. We are shown black and white footage of her beautiful mother Diane, before Polley asks each interviewee to tell 'the whole story, from the very beginning to the very end, in your own words'. They all react with surprise at the extent of the task. One of the sisters, says, 'who cares about our stupid family?' They begin recalling their mother, saying how enthusiastic and fun she was, how vivacious, how loud, and how productive she was too. We see footage of her as people remember her, running ahead of them, fooling around, working and acting. There is footage of her father and mother meeting as young actors, and we are told how her father bought a Super 8 camera to record family life. The scene is set for us to watch the family footage and learn from it, as it seems contemporary and intimate.

As the interviews progress, and the circle of interviewees widens, discrepancies creep in to people's accounts of Diane. One person says she was secretive, another says she was not at all private. The marriage to Michael is revealed to have had its problems. One of the sons says that his father told him that his mum wanted to have sex a lot more than he did. Michael says he was good at contributing, and providing, but not good at loving Diane. One of the sisters says Michael did nothing to care for the kids or around the house and that Diane was frustrated by his wasting his talent for writing and acting. When Diane got an offer to do a play in Montreal, she accepted it, and Michael says he was secretly ecstatic to have a break from each other. We then see footage of the play and the group of actors, and her friends, all working and socialising in Montreal. Michael goes to visit her, and the absence has reinvigorated their sex life so that they have a romantic weekend. She returns to Toronto, and discovers she's pregnant, at the age of forty-two. She thought she should have an abortion because there were risks of Down's syndrome. She arranged to go to the hospital for an abortion, but changed her mind on the way there. Then Sarah is born, with a surprising shock of red hair.

The interviews then turn to Diane's illness and death from cancer. Some say she and the whole family knew she was dying, others say 'she never fully realised'. Her female friends say how much she fought, and break down in tears. Michael says 'she didn't know'. The siblings say that they think Michael became depressed after Diane's death, and he sat around smoking and playing solitaire. Michael then talks about this as becoming a 'great period in my life', due to the concentration of his relationship with Sarah, as it was just the two of them living in the house for four or five very close years. We then start to look back over what happened around Diane's pregnancy with Sarah. Footage of Diane on the telephone which we have seen before is now replayed as the eldest son Johnny describes how he overheard her on the phone crying, saying she was pregnant and that she didn't know who the father was. So we wonder then whether that footage was of something Johnny actually saw, and we now see it in a different light. It then emerges that Johnny managed to get the information about their mother having had an affair years later from her friends.

It emerges that the identity of Sarah's father began to come up as a family joke: they all used to say she looked nothing like Michael, and play who could her father be? They would take guesses as to which of the three actors in the play in Montreal it could be: Tom, Wayne or Geoff. Most people, it seemed, thought it was Geoff Bowes, so Sarah decided to investigate a bit more, telephoned him and they met. We see him interviewed, as Sarah in voiceover says she felt he was hiding something, by saying he and Diane just had friendship. Another contact said that Sarah might want to meet up with producer Harry Gulkin, who knew her mother at that time, so she contacted him and they met. Sarah and Harry are shown having coffee, as we are told that they got on well, and she felt so comfortable with him that she asked him if he knew whether her mother had an affair in Montreal, and whether somebody else could be her father. He said 'it's possible it's me'. We see this conversation on-screen, so clearly it is a re-enactment. Then we see footage of him much younger, in an astrakhan hat, and it looks like him, but we are perhaps puzzled as to how this footage of them meeting exists, and how Sarah has it. Harry tells of how he developed huge passion for Diane, and asked her to move to Montreal and bring her children. We then learn that Diane was married before Michael, and we see footage from that wedding. We hear about how controlling her first husband was, and then how she fell in love with Michael and left her husband; and how she went back for the children the next day and the husband had changed the locks. He applied for custody, and the court ruled in his favour. Her desire to escape from her husband, and to pursue her career, cost her dearly. At this point, the adult sibling interviewees all become distressed, mainly because they recall seeing their mother only once a month, and having successive horrible stepmother characters who hurt them. We see footage of her apparently at the time, acting, but looking sad, as we hear that this must have made her sad every day. The inference is clear: here she is, at that time, looking serious. Do we assume she is feeling sad about her children?

Harry talks about how she felt guilty over the loss of her children, and says that she was thrilled at being pregnant by him. He says their affair was 'pretty open'; her friends say it was secret. We return to footage of Diane's funeral, but now see that Harry was there – did we miss him the first time round? Sarah watches a documentary about Harry, and we see footage from the film too. Then we also see footage of the family at Michael's house, conjuring up the same family vibe as the older home videos. Sarah and Harry conduct a DNA test and it proves that Harry is her biological father. He is delighted. Sarah continues to call Michael 'dad'. Sarah meets her half-sister Cathy, and we are told that they share the same gummy grin, which we can see too as they are both shown smiling. Although initially only telling her siblings, and not Michael, she does eventually have to tell him because a journalist is threatening to publish the story. All three sisters got divorced following the revelation, whereas Mark, the younger son, started his own family. Mark admits that he was critical of Diane's irresponsibility in terms of birth control, but older gay son Johnny is not critical at all.

We see Sarah visit Michael, who has shorter hair than in the supposedly 'current' footage, and we see her mouthing the words to him about her paternity. Again, it is hard to believe that this is the actual footage of Sarah telling Michael that he is not her father. Sarah is seen to say, 'It doesn't make any difference, does it?', which is what Michael is recalling that she said. So here we have information being conveyed by a voiceover, and being ostensibly supported by images, but the provenance of those images is at best questionable. Who was filming this conversation? Michael's reaction is that he thought it was a great story, and he says that it awoke an obsession in him to tell the story to anyone who would listen. We see him writing, getting thoughts down on paper. He is concerned that Diane should not have any blame, revealing that he'd always told her to take a lover at any time she felt he was inadequate. Michael entertains the possibility of having lived with the ambiguity of Sarah's parentage had Diane told him about her affair. We see Diane sitting on a bed, as if talking to Michael, who says 'Why do we talk and talk but not say what we're really like?'

It emerges that Harry also wanted to write a memoir of what he considered to be a strong story that could be told in many different ways. Sarah suggested they each write up their own versions, then show them to each other. Harry writes it up and wants to publish it, which upsets Sarah greatly. Harry says 'I felt constrained in my relationship to you, because of the private way you were dealing with it.' He felt that 'the atmosphere got a little heavy' and he backed off. All these different takes on the ownership of the story are emerging, and Sarah then says she wants to document it through filming everyone's point of view. We see Sarah filming. She asks Harry, 'What do you think of this concept of giving everyone's point of view equal weight?' Harry replies, 'I don't like it.' He says it is woolly, and 'we can't touch bottom with it'. He sees all narratives as being shaped by people's various interests and loyalties, and he declares that the crucial function of art is to find the truth, to tell the truth. What this means, in practice, is that he just wants to tell his story! Michael also raises the issue of truth, saying to Sarah that they are engaged in a 'farcical theatrical exercise', and that her selection of moments and excerpts is part of editing the truth. He claims that if she had just let a camera run and record it all, that would be closer to truth: 'But your editing of it is turning it into something completely different.' Of course, any filmed footage has creative decisions that prevent it from just being a simple recording of 'the truth', but what seems to bother Michael and Harry is that theirs won't be the only version.

The eldest brother Johnny seems to be serious when he asks Sarah what she would say this documentary is really all about. Sarah says memory and the way we tell the stories of our lives. He interrupts by saying, 'Is this a good angle for me?' making her laugh and call him an asshole. So, he interrupts the seriousness that he seemed to seek from Sarah, and she has chosen to leave it in: this serves to highlight the multiple perspectives and investments in the film. One of the main focuses is the discrepancies, how similar stories can have large and small details that vary. Where is the truth if we are all recalling different details and asserting them as facts, and how are we as viewers of this film to react to the plethora of perspectives and opinions on display?

At this point, we are shown that Sarah has been recreating the 'siblings' around the dining table using actors; we see young 'Harry' in makeup, and 'Diane' being directed. These people we have been watching have been played by actors. But not always: there is some real family home movie footage too. Sarah's sister Joanna says that those memories, of what kind of person their mother was, are just illusory. Harry declares that only two people can tell the essentials of what took place (although of course this is only what took place that involved him). We continue to see Sarah filming on her hand-held camera.

Harry announces that 'The story with Diane, I regret to say, is only mine to tell, and I think that's about it; my recollections may be faulty at times but I'm not gonna lie.' Joanna says she was really happy to hear about her mother's affair, that she found love from Harry, and had been loved that much, even though it was Michael she really wanted the love from. Michael comes across as an unemotional man, withdrawn and self-contained. He questions Sarah's motives, and her need to make the film. Sarah says, in voiceover,

> Every time I feel I have my footing I lose it. Have I totally lost my mind trying to reconstruct the past from other people's words? Trying to form her? Is this the tsunami she unleashed when she went, and all of us still flailing in her wake, trying to put her together in the wreckage, and her slipping away from us, over and over again, just as we begin to see her face?

Figure 2.3 Footage of Diane Polley from *Stories We Tell* (2012), directed by Sarah Polley.

This is clearly a personal voyage into loss and a degree of trauma for Sarah Polley, but these words resonate with anyone who has lost a loved one. We might envy her all this real video footage of her mother, or find some of the recreations somewhat peculiar, but the experience of loss is acute for all the family. Sarah cuts to the bone when she asks her father what he said to Diane at the very end. Accompanied by colour footage of her sunny, swimsuit-clad mother heading into the sea, Michael is heard to say, 'What?' in response to Sarah, as Diane turns round and mouths 'What?' at the camera (Figure 2.3). This is a visual and visceral fusing of Michael and Diane and their shared experience. Michael says in a slightly offhand way, 'Dunno, probably that I would miss her, that we loved her, we'd never forget her – that's about all.' He fights crying, but finally Sarah has broken Michael down and he shows emotion as he confesses that when somebody 'has given your life much of its meaning for twenty-five years . . . it's awful hard to lose them'. Shots are then held on each family member in turn, then friends, as they think about Diane at the end, and they are emotive and revealing of a truth: the pain of their loss. Michael immediately tries to lighten the mood, by saying to Sarah, 'That's a dire line of questioning, you must find a way of making it more funny. What are you, some kind of sadistic interviewer?'

There is then some footage of a student film that Sarah made, where she asked Michael to submerge himself in a freezing cold swimming pool, wearing a dinner jacket. He recalls, 'You see what a vicious director you are?' Here, the memory, a less emotive one, and a more humorous one, is indeed captured on film, and the event is beyond question: it is evidenced by the film. Regarding

Sarah's paternity, Michael concludes that the whole question has become an unimportant part of the past for him. He says, 'so don't feel sorry for me. If you have pity have some for Harry, who loved and lost Diane.' This is potentially remarkably generous, but then Michael can afford to be in a way as Diane stayed with him. In another gesture of seemingly extreme generosity, Michael thanks Harry for loving Diane, as Sarah would have been different if she had been his: and the one she is, is the one he loves.

As Michael is reading these emotional words in the recording studio, from his own notes, Sarah asks him to stop and go back over a really emotional line. The apparently genuine emotion is interrupted: Michael quips, 'I was being so real; I completely convinced myself.' Once again, humour has undercut apparently sincere emotion. This looks like making a revealing comment on the filmmaking process, or Sarah's emotional resilience, but this is hard to be sure of. How general a point is the film making about the sharing of emotions with others, and the possibility of having distance from even intense emotions about love and loss, and how specific is it to this family and these individuals? Michael says that he wrote this story because it really says so many interesting things about the human condition. But then concedes 'perhaps deep inside I suffered more of a shock than I would openly admit. Something inside has for the rest of my life changed: a certain cord that runs between Sarah and me has been severed, and I am powerless to join it together.' Ultimately, Michael says the final revelation and its aftermath brought Sarah and him closer together, and resulted in him writing volumes, as Diane always wanted him to. It has given him a new lease on life. He appears to have the final words, when he asserts, nobly, 'Never ask why Michael – just accept the sentence. I will go on. I will go on.' The image fades to black, as if it is the end, and all the secrets are out. A honky-tonk version of 'Ain't Misbehavin'' gets going, and the credits roll, but then we see a cut back to the interview with Geoff Bowes. We see Sarah telling him that actually Harry Gulkin was her father, but she found it puzzling that so many people thought it was him. Bowes says, 'Well, I'll have to tell you that we did sleep together once.' So, even in the interviews, face to face and on camera, there is no guarantee that 'the truth' has been told. Perhaps Bowes was anxious about being named as Sarah's father, and didn't want to reveal it until he was sure that wouldn't happen. But in any event, when he said that he and Diane had had a 'friendship', and Polley included that footage in the film, he wasn't being completely truthful. Casting a light over the preceding film, the credits read 'Michael's narration, written by Michael Polley'. There is very little of Sarah's own story, remembered by herself, in there, and we have indeed been taken on a puzzling visual, aural and sensorial journey into the realm of images and personal memories. We have seen emotions minutely expressed on many real human faces, not star performers or masks, and we have been profoundly challenged to assess the veracity and value of what we have seen and heard. This film is a documentary about personal fantasy in some ways; pitched as being about how we tell 'different' stories, there is evidence of self-delusion on-screen. When Harry recalls attending Diane's funeral, he tells of how he went to embrace Michael, to comfort him, and Michael stiffened, leading Harry to conclude that Michael knew about the affair. When Sarah puts this to Michael, he is surprised to know Harry was even there, and has no recollection of him at all. One of them has constructed a consoling fantasy for themselves.

This challenging film creates a viewing response of assessment of truth and wondering about different people's perspectives almost throughout. The sight of Sarah's filmmaking work, her camera and her booms, keeps us aware of the project she is carrying out, but the footage constantly shows us a mixture of possible recordings of reality, actual footage, and illustrations of memories. It is not an option to be an absent-minded spectator, but rather a great deal of imaginative activity is involved in immersing and reflecting on the status of the images we are shown, and the emotions behind the stories we are told.

'A STRANGE AND STARTLING WORLD, DISINTEGRATED AND DISTORTED': *UNDER THE SKIN*

In Jonathan Glazer's uniquely shot film from 2013, the camera is akin to an alien eye, viewing the world around it from a non-human perspective, which in turn creates a morally challenging disconnect from the film world for the spectator. This calls attention to the specificity of our human ethical view, which is evoked through the film's formal and artistic mode. There are moments in the film of shock, horror and beauty, and the challenge of the film is that it demands a degree of callousness on our part but refuses to allow us to consider it as such. The film's confrontational stance asks us to view humans with a non-human eye. Glazer has stated how he attempted to convey an alien view on the world – that's how he chose to make a film of the book – and he does so in a profoundly affective way (Leigh 2014). In Michel Faber's novel *Under the Skin* (2000), the reader follows protagonist Isserley as she picks up hitchhikers and despatches them for extra-terrestrial purposes. As the novel progresses, we realise that the humans are actually being farmed: they are mutilated and turned into distended, butchered, nameless beings that are processed into prime cuts of flesh and more dubious minced products, and shipped off to be alien cuisine. The book subversively reproduces factory farming as an industry that you as a reader could fall foul of. It renders human beings disgusting, and suggests that humanity is repugnant and callous. Jonathan Glazer distilled the novel and bravely leaves many questions unanswered. He uses cinema's ability to affect our senses and bodies, and to confound our thoughts, in order to convey the experiences and impressions of his earthly looking unnamed alien, played by Scarlett Johansson. As the alien moves through the streets of Glasgow in her white van, or through the forests and the beaches on foot, it is the film's depiction of sounds and sights that enables the viewer to encounter her chillingly observational perspective, on a world full of objects and people 'made strange'.

Johansson casts her eyes over a bustling ant in the same way as she takes in the image of a baby facing death (and who she could easily rescue). The colour palette and sound design ensure this film's landscapes and soundscapes are not human-centric. The sound design is by Mica Levi, composer of the affective and emotional score for *Jackie*. In *Under the Skin*, the musical score is both eerie and unnerving, as upward intonations seem to ask questions about what is being shown, undercutting confidence in our understanding. Sounds seem to be of equivalent volume and detail, speech does not dominate, and people are seen as inhabitants of the urban and rural environment, singular but not noteworthy, sometimes in faceless groups. Skin is the currency of this film in several ways. Laura Marks's work on intercultural cinema is a way of approaching this inter-species film. Skin, between the alien and the human, is similar to what Marks describes as 'an interstitial space of the fetish' (2000: 90). And this interstitial space is also between the film and us. The fetish space is created by the encounter between two, and is built on incomprehension. We are confronted by what it is for our skin to be a commodity. There is tactile experience of skin here, but it is all jarring. Marks talks about memory being awakened by the feel of fabric or image of skin (2000: 112). This film fetishises skin as an object but not in a way we can affectionately relate to. We see skin under water, or ripping apart on the aliens's body, or we have an image of the famously desirable body of Johansson completely naked in a way that could be described as flagrant, even forensic. The perspective on skin is not a familiar or reassuring one. This creates the difficulties of relating the spectator's eye to the protagonist's eye when that eye is not human.

There are various ways to approach the film: a feminist analysis of penetrability and power of the female body, with questions of allure and entrapment, tapping into the conventions of the femme fatale. Or a star-based analysis centring on the impact of the naked star body of 'Scar Jo' – it is quite strikingly deployed and has a currency that lends the film extra-textual elements. There are naked male bodies of unnamed characters, with erect and flaccid penises, so the significance of the star body becomes even more pronounced. We could approach the film as post-human, or ecological, possibly even post-colonial (featuring the viewpoint of a predatory, exploitative species); or in terms of production, as so much of the filmmaking was essentially guerrilla-style, with cast and crew capturing events that were not staged, enticing passers-by into scenes where they did not know this was happening. What is important for this Murdochian perspective is the film's creation of an alien view on our world, the objects within it and the affective experience of it. The film means to disconcert as it confounds the humanity of our phenomenology of the film: so how is the alien's view created?

The film begins with a point of light in the centre of the screen, and then circles and discs of light appear around it, that construct an eye; at the same time the soundtrack is a voice learning vowel sounds and enunciating consonants: 'fail, fails, sell, sells'. So the camera begins inside the eye of the alien and hearing vocal chords inside its head. We then see an earthly landscape that looks strange, as night-time shots of running rivers cut to similarly shaped but man-made zig-zagging roads. The images are accompanied by sounds, like harsh violin strings and electronic pulses, not music and not recognisable noise. A motorcyclist collects a girl's body and slings her over his shoulder. We next see a totally naked Scarlett Johansson on all fours clambering around the girl's prone body, stripping the clothes off her. Johansson's body is lit harshly in an almost blue and very revealing light, in unflattering motion as she crawls around the girl, her breasts swaying. We see Johansson dress in the girl's clothes and stand over her, vaguely appraisingly. A tear roles out of the girl's eye: she is not dead. She is paralysed in some way, and we don't know how this happened or what her fate is. Then Johansson finds the ant crawling in the girl's belly button. She picks it up on her finger and twists her hand and wrist to follow the ant's bustling progress, more transfixed by this little creature than the living, weeping body at her feet.

What the film is creating here is the perspective of a non-human, on humans. A scene where this perspective is chillingly conveyed is when the alien sees a baby crying on a windswept beach as its parents are drowning. The baby sits and cries, now orphaned and most likely about to be swept into the ocean, but the alien passes the child as she secures the object of her desire, the young fit body of the surfer who attempted to rescue the parents. As the alien crushes his skull with a rock, and leaves the terrified baby to its imminent death, the point is driven home that human beings have a particular value to this creature, and we do not know what it is. The motorcyclist comes to the beach that evening to collect a piece of evidence left behind, seemingly clothing. The baby is still sitting on the beach, crying. The motorcyclist pays it no attention at all, and leaves it there. The emotional value we attribute to the screaming orphaned baby is not felt by the alien. To further emphasise this, we see the alien reminded of that baby's cry by a cry emanating from another baby in the car next to her in a traffic jam. But no sooner is this slight recognition evident than the sound and image of an aeroplane overhead and a nearby car horn take precedence. No significance is given to the alien's association between the crying of the two children; there's no realisation that the sound might be linked to distress. But we are aware of the connection made, through the film's immersion of us in the series of shots which reveal the connections made by the learning – if not feeling – alien.

The alien drives around Glasgow in a white van and picks up single men. The camera surveys a range of men walking around the city. These sequences offer a gaze on anonymous men as prey that is appraising and a very unusual on-screen sight. She offers lifts, asks questions, enquires where they are going, whether they have a girlfriend waiting for them, establishes whether they are suitable for her purposes, then says 'I have a place a few miles away.' When they arrive, the alien does a slow striptease as she walks into the house, the entranced men following her. The alien turns towards the men and audience, backing away in her underwear. As she walks across the glistening floor, the men step down through the floor into a black, treacly enveloping fluid until they disappear. The unearthly soundtrack accompanies the surreal image, as the men do not panic or protest but simply submerge.

One scene takes place under the surface, and it is a sensory immersion into a realm of annihilation. The sound design here is such that it combines the silence of being underwater with the sounds of the movement of fluid, but also with a sound of cracking and breaking under pressure, as if you can hear your own bones squeaking and disintegrating. A shape that was a person but which appears to be in a state of melting or emptying moves towards the more recently submerged man. They touch hands, and the more deformed shape, whose skin we now see is loosening, is extinguished in the visual equivalent of an underwater 'pffft'. The emptied skin floats like a plastic bag. There follows a shot of a slow moving conveyer belt covered in thick blood-coloured matter moving towards a trapdoor of some kind. This is pure cinematic horror: by this I mean that the connections between the images and sounds that we experience could not be conveyed with such economy and such physical, sensorial impact in any other medium. Rationale is not made explicit, but rather we are faced with a watery realm in which we would be out of our element, unable to move, speak or react as we would in our normal environment, being sucked of our innards, reduced to a membranous epidermal sack.

This sequence reminds me, perhaps surprisingly, of Woolf's 1926 essay on cinema (Woolf 2009). In this precise and thoughtful engagement with the specific experience of cinema, Woolf discusses her experience of seeing *The Cabinet of Dr Caligari* at the cinema. Describing a moment where a black shadow creeps across the screen, she says 'for a moment it seemed as if thought could be conveyed more effectively by shape than by words. The monstrous quivering tadpole seemed to be fear itself, not the statement "I am afraid"': terror, for Woolf, 'burgeons, bulges, quivers, disappears' (2009: 174). This is affective cinema, then, and it invites analysis in terms of skin, touch, sound, humanity and inhumanity. But I suggest there is even more going on than this, requiring analysis from a Murdochian perspective on the appearance of objects and attention to another.

A few things begin to make the alien aware of what is under skin: she pricks her finger on a rose, drawing unexpected blood, then she picks up the young man David (Adam Pearson), who is facially disfigured. She encourages him to touch her face, then her neck, and says he has beautiful hands. He descends into the fluid depths, but is spared from the watery death for some reason: we do not know if she pities him, or if he is rejected. She looks at her face intently in a mirror, and then releases David, and goes out into the world again. She tries to eat human food – a piece of cake – but retches and has to spit it out. These experiences suggest that she is becoming interested in humanity, and is also exposing her vulnerability. She sets off on her own, walking the countryside. She is not aware of her own violability. She begins to make love with a caring man who has offered her shelter and taken care of her; but as he attempts to penetrate her she leaps out of bed to examine her genitalia, having not experienced that feeling before or indeed been aware that there was an orifice there. It is after this that she roams off into the forest, where she is brutally assaulted by a forest worker, and as she escapes her assailant she essentially begins to disintegrate. Her alien body is revealed, as her skin tears, and her assailant sets fire to her. Images of her burning body are incorporated into shots of stunning natural beauty, conflating ash and smoke with falling snow. These shots are poetic and metaphysical, blending visions of the earthly world with elements of fire and water, with other-worldly images of the alien looking at her earthly face, which still blinks and shows life (Figure 2.4). As the burning alien runs and falls to the snowy ground, the smoke from her burning body rises, as snow

Figure 2.4 The alien looks at her own 'human' face: Scarlett Johansson in *Under the Skin* (2013), directed by Jonathan Glazer.

falls down, and they meet somewhere in the middle. The film shows us images that perplex and mystify: what is the relevance of this physical disintegration to our understanding of the film?

Sarah Cooper discusses the concept of the soul and its presence throughout a century of film theory (2013). Many of the thinkers mentioned earlier, such as Epstein, Arnheim, as well as Woolf and indeed Murdoch, have wrestled with defining the ineffable element of the art of cinema. In one passage, about the films of the Lumière brothers, Cooper considers Edgar Morin's thinking about the soul in relation to objects in the cinema, and this resonates with the world of *Under the Skin*. Rather than maintain the ideas of Balázs, Epstein, Pudovkin or René Clair, that the capturing of objects in film imbues them with 'atmosphere' or 'soul', Cooper explains how Morin identifies the role of spectatorial response in this creativity. For Morin, writes Cooper, 'the soul sits thus on the boundary between the interior and the exterior, between object and subject, image and spectator, emotion and its transfer onto the contemplated object as the viewer watches the film' (2013: 92). Cooper writes that, by the mid-1920s, 'cinema itself becomes what Morin terms the apostle of animism' (or the idea that non-human objects or entities can have souls). Morin writes, 'Inanimate objects, now you have a soul in the fluid universe of the cinema' (Morin 2005: 227, cited in Cooper 2013: 92–3). As Cooper explains, here, 'the soul is set up as a semi-fluid, semi-reified residue of the magic of cinema' (2013: 93).

There is physical affectiveness in *Under the Skin*, and also an interest in kindness and glimpses of transformative encounters, perhaps encapsulated in the swift moment when David, having been asked by the seductive alien if he wants to come back to her place, secretly pinches the skin on his hand to see if he is dreaming. *Under the Skin* depicts alien distance in its perspective on the human race, but through its flickering fascination with the mutability of human nature, and its celebration of the earthly natural world in a painterly, occasionally surreal, style, the film creates a particularly confounding cinematic encounter that just might be elucidated by a consideration of its soul.

Examining *Under the Skin* in terms of its alien phenomenology paradoxically highlights the humanity of the film. The alien's face is a complex mixture of familiarity, masquerade, flirtation and impassivity, as it makes its way around the city hunting for prey. But the vulnerability and humanity on its face in the film's final sequence begins to display the risks and frailties of being a woman (Osterweil 2014: 50). Murdoch's views on the emotional complexity of the human face might be confounded by the alien who we view, and whose eyes we view the world through, but in fact they serve to draw our attention to the humanity missing at the alien heart of the protagonist, and enable us to be keenly aware of how gestures towards humanity begin to build and lead to the film's violent conclusion. It is perhaps the development of a moral vision, aroused by David, which leads to her flirtations with humanity. Although the protagonist is not a person building their moral vision, they do perhaps come to be what Murdoch might consider a moral agent, albeit at an early stage. The alien certainly comes to know the reality of kindness and cruelty before her earthly time comes to an end. In the next chapter, I will demonstrate how Murdoch highlights the ways in which stories, and pictures, can function to assist us in the development of our moral vision, and argue that cinema powerfully involves us in this process.

NOTES

1. Murdoch's copy of Benjamin's essays, *Illuminations*, is in the Iris Murdoch Library held at Kingston University, reference IML 494.
2. Rowe writes, 'paintings, images, tableaux, and aesthetic and synaesthetic narrative strategies, can be analysed for the way they encourage character and reader to perceive reality more accurately and, on the reader's part, the moral evaluation of the repercussions on character becomes, somewhat paradoxically, a valid mode of moral/aesthetic criticism of her novels' (2002: 15). See also my interview with Anne Rowe (Bolton 2017d).
3. The film is called *A Tour of the White House with Mrs John F. Kennedy*, and was broadcast on 14 February 1962 on CBS and NBC. The film is available on YouTube: <https://www.youtube.com/watch?v=9myrArq-1h8> (last accessed 1 January 2019).
4. Richard Burton sang this version in the original Broadway production of the Lerner and Loewe musical Camelot in 1960. Jacqueline Kennedy invoked the comparison between Camelot and the Kennedy presidency in the 1963 interview for *Life* magazine on which the film *Jackie* is based. See Oline Eaton (2017).
5. The line from *Alias Grace* is 'When you are in the middle of a story, it isn't a story at all, but only a confusion' (Atwood 1997: 345–6). Polley discusses her use of this quote in light of her production of a mini-series based on the novel (*Alias Grace*, TV mini-series, directed by Mary Harron, Canada: Halfire Entertainment, 2017) (Onstad 2017).

CHAPTER 3

Film as a Moral Fable

> That moral improvement involves suffering is usually true; but the suffering is the by-product of a new orientation and not in any sense an end in itself. ('On "God" and "Good"' (OGG): 355)

> We need more concepts in terms of which to picture the substance of our being; it is through an enriching and deepening of concepts that moral progress takes place. Simone Weil said that morality was a matter of attention, not of will. We need a new vocabulary of attention. ('Against Dryness' (AD): 293)

In this chapter, I will explore Murdoch's thinking about art as morally instructive, and the idea of the morally relevant fable, as opposed to a fable that is merely decorative. The three films I will focus on in depth are *Margaret* (Kenneth Lonergan, 2011), *Blue Jasmine* (Woody Allen, 2013) and *Compliance* (Craig Zobel, 2012). Moral thinking is really the driving force behind most of Murdoch's philosophical work and so I will draw on a wide range of her writings. It is important to address the matter of terminology here: morality, moral philosophy and moral thinking – why not ethics? Film philosophy has talked mainly about ethical relationships (Downing and Saxton 2010), exploring ethics through film (Teays 2012), the ethic of the image (Wheatley 2009) and cinematic ethics (Sinnerbrink 2016). Dan Shaw's book *Morality and the Movies* is subtitled *Reading Ethics through Film* (2012). For Peter Singer, the words 'ethics' and 'morality' can be used interchangeably: he also notes, however, that 'some people think that morality is now out of date' (Singer 1979: 1).

> They regard morality as a system of nasty puritanical prohibitions, mainly designed to stop people having fun. Traditional moralists who claim to be defenders of the morality, when they are only defending

> one particular moral code, rather than morality as such, have been allowed to pre-empt the field to such an extent that when a newspaper headline reads BISHOP ATTACKS DECLINING MORAL STANDARDS we expect to read yet again about promiscuity, homosexuality, pornography and so on, and not about corporations bribing government officials, or the puny amounts we give as overseas aid to poorer nations. (Ibid.: 1–2)

Singer is writing in 1979, and the attitude towards morality has developed to the extent that contemporary concerns are more to do with the treatment of minority groups, the use and abuse of animals, particularly how they are farmed for food, questions concerning the end of life and voluntary euthanasia. Alasdair MacIntyre examines the development of morality and ethics in his influential book *A Short History of Ethics* (1998). Singer himself has developed his work on animal rights and global poverty. However, there are still groups and communities where questions of sexual practice are regarded as moral issues, especially same-sex marriage and parenting, and the question of legal abortion is still part of contemporary public moral debate. Singer usefully asserts what ethics is not. Firstly, he argues, it is not a set of prohibitions concerned with sex: 'sex raises no special moral issues at all' (ibid.: 2). As Singer sets out, there may be questions of honesty, probity, concern for others or self-care that are raised by sexual behaviour, but no more than – to use Singer's example – by driving a car, which in fact raises more serious issues to do with safety and the environment. Secondly, ethics is not an ideal system, but more a case of ethical practice: this is a question that concerns Murdoch fundamentally. Thirdly, for Singer, ethics is entirely independent of religion. Murdoch is deeply concerned with the tenets of Christianity and Buddhism, but her moral thinking does not depend upon either religion for its concepts or its practice. And fourthly, Singer denies that ethics is relative or subjective. For him, 'Ethics takes a universal point of view' (ibid.: 11). Murdoch does not argue for universalist morality. For Murdoch, the notion of practice, of attending to others and growing in understanding of one's own moral vision, is at the heart of moral philosophy, rather than the proscription of judgements from which we can extrapolate universal rules.

Murdoch sets out some of her arguments on these points in 'Vision and Choice in Morality'. The most pertinent idea for film is that of Murdoch's thinking in relation to a fable that can be 'morally relevant' and not simply 'morally decorative' (VCM: 85). Analysing the films in this chapter will investigate how we may actually learn about our personal moral vision through experiencing a film, and may in turn take that moral learning or changing into our interactions with the world around us. For example, the moral discombobulation caused by the experience of *Margaret* leads us to realise the complexity of the questions asked by the film and forces us to resist making moral judgements of the characters. In turn, do we then think about our neighbours and our family with more tolerance? Does the way in which *Blue Jasmine* offers us the option to view Jasmine with some sympathy enable us to change our mind about how we judge her? And does *Compliance* challenge us not simply to be drawn into a 'what would you do' conundrum, but actually think through the stage at which we would intervene, or in other words how strongly developed our moral vision is in relation to others?

Murdoch's moral philosophy is concerned with the individual and with individual consciousness. She is opposed to the idea that morality is something that can be decided upon in isolation from the real world and the real people in it. Murdoch argues that facts are decided upon within the framework of the individual consciousness of the moral being. So 'morality is bound up with our deepest conceptual attitudes and sensibilities about the world, which determine the facts from the very beginning' (Antonaccio 2000: 38). As Murdoch writes, 'We differ not only because we select different objects out of the same world but because we see different worlds' (VCM: 82); and seeing our moral world 'should be the prime task of the individual moral agent' (Blum 2014: 307).

Now, this idea of seeing different worlds, and the way in which Murdoch describes this, provides a link to the way in which films can offer visions of worlds in which moral journeys take place. Not simply engaging narrative arcs, but transformative moral experiences: for the characters within the diegesis, usually, but also for us as we experience the film. What I am doing here, then, is drawing upon Murdoch's analysis of moral visions in my analysis of film, and then extending this to the relationship that we might be able to understand having with the film world and the real world around us. In *Cinematic Ethics*, Robert Sinnerbrink considers film as a medium of ethical experience, and argues that 'this ethical potential is important to recognise if we are to appreciate why cinema matters today' (2016: 185). For Sinnerbrink, film 'is a medium with the aesthetic power to evoke ethical experience – through affective response, emotional engagement, and cognitive understanding – that invites, indeed in some cases demands, critical and philosophical reflection' (ibid.: 185). This book is developing a similar perspective on film following Murdoch's reflections, and the films in this chapter do indeed provoke such an ethically challenging response. In the next section, I will bring together Murdoch's moral philosophy with the moral agency of Lisa in Kenneth Lonergan's 2011 film *Margaret*, in an investigation of how film can be a moral fable that is relevant to our understanding of the development of another's moral vision, and how it inculcates moral development in us.

'THE WORLD AS I SEE IT': *MARGARET*

Teenage protagonist Lisa (Anna Paquin) has a very certain view of the rights and wrongs of her melodramatic world. When faced with the ramifications of a tragic accident, Lisa is forced to realise that the question of what is right is not as simple as she thinks. Through the unfolding of the film's narrative and its formal entanglements, we are also forced to appreciate the complexity of Lisa's – and perhaps our – moral world. *Margaret* was shot and completed in 2007, but was not released until 2011 due to legal disputes with the studio, Fox Searchlight and the producers. It was originally conceived of as a three-hour film, released into cinemas as a two-and-a-half-hour cut, with the extended cut available on the DVD (Gardner 2014). Joel Lovell of *The New York Times* described it as 'a big, messy, problematic film' (2012), and Peter Bradshaw of *The Guardian* called it 'a sprawling neurotic nightmare of urban catastrophe' (2011). Many critics and bloggers refer to the film as being operatic, and this impression is plainly founded on the highly charged emotions of the central character, as well as the somewhat overdetermined operatic soundtrack. Lisa wrestles with the dramas and demands of being a teenager with divorced parents, living in New York City and going to an exclusive high school. Following a road accident for which she is partly responsible, Lisa holds a severely injured woman during the last minutes of her life, coming face to face with the imminence and immediacy of death. The rest of the film is concerned with how Lisa resumes life after this incident: the decisions she makes to tell certain untruths, her pursuit of particular people in order to resolve her confused and conflicted feelings, and the volatile, self-centred maelstrom of emotion that surrounds her. The film explores Lisa's attempts to make good choices, and the reasons why she might be considered to make bad ones.

The film gives us an experience of the lead-up to the accident that aligns with Lisa's perspective. Lisa is out shopping for a cowboy hat to wear on a horse riding trip which has been promised to her by her absentee, unreliable father. While looking in shop windows, Lisa spies a cowboy hat such as the one she wants on the head of a man driving a bus. Lisa runs alongside the bus, trying to get the driver's attention, and he flirts with and teases her, repeatedly taking his eyes off the road ahead. He points to his hat and laughs at her. While doing so, he misses a red light and runs down a woman who is crossing the road in front of him. Their flirtatious encounter has resulted in the woman being killed. The death scene is one of the most traumatic and distressing death scenes I have ever seen on film. As Lisa holds the woman in her arms, we and Lisa realise that parts of her body are left under the bus in the middle of the road, that she has no chance of survival, but she is not yet dead. We are confronted with the last moments of her life. The woman speaks: she asks if her eyes are open or closed; she mistakes Lisa for her daughter; she is filled with panic and confusion. Lonergan says of the scene:

> that single incident drives the entire film and drives the entire journey of Anna Paquin's character, and it's a long film. And I knew that if that accident wasn't extremely awful – as awful as humanly possible – then there'd be no movie. You don't see any flashbacks of it. It's got to stay in your mind the way it stays in the character's mind. (Lonergan 2012)

This is an acute instance of the need for the impact of an incident on-screen to have an effect on the viewer. The impact of witnessing this death creates a gut-wrenching connection with the magnitude of Lisa's situation and the severity of the fear of the consequences that might ensue from her cheeky exchanges with the driver. On the spot of the accident, as they are being interviewed by police officers, the urge to cover up their innocent but reckless complicity is excruciatingly intense (Figure 3.1). The driver looks over at Lisa with terror-stricken eyes. Was the light red or not? Was it the pedestrian's fault or the driver's? The police report hangs on Lisa's word, and she covers up for the driver. She says 'I guess it was green.'

Lisa returns home, covered in the dead woman's blood, and washes herself clean. Her life resumes, in all its melodramatic intensity, as she argues with her classmates, clashes repeatedly with her mother, engineers the loss of her virginity and seduces her teacher. As her days pass, she becomes increasingly

Figure 3.1 Lisa (Anna Paquin) looks at the driver and says 'green', in *Margaret* (2011), directed by Kenneth Lonergan.

concerned to connect with the dead woman's past. She introduces herself to the woman's best friend and tries to build connections and community with the woman's life. As a result of this, her perspective on the accident shifts, and she decides to speak to the bus driver about what happened. It seems she is seeking a more honest account of the blame for the accident. We set off on the journey with Lisa in her operatic bubble of personal quest, and it appears understandable that she should want to speak to him to help her ease this nightmarish guilt and pain she is suffering. Only they – and we – know what happened at the scene. But the film challenges our conviction that she is doing the right thing. As Lisa emerges from the subway, we enter the Italian district; we see families going to mass, in a more densely packed and lower-class neighbourhood than Lisa's. We see the stars and stripes flag outside the driver's door, we see his house – his home. When we arrive, alongside Lisa, we see a woman answer the door, look puzzled, and invite Lisa in. A crucifix hangs on the wall behind the door. We hear his children playing noisily, we are confronted by his family domesticity, and we realise what he has to lose. Through her conversation with the driver, we learn what he has been through since the accident, and what the ramifications might be – both in that room and in the light of the wider institutions and networks that govern their lives – if he admits a different version of the accident, and we – like Lisa – falter. He is angry to be contacted by Lisa, he flatly denies her account of them looking at each other, and he demands her phone number. The situation becomes quite hostile, and we wonder what his perspective might be, realising that this is not all Lisa's to dictate. Perhaps she needs to leave him alone. In this scene, Lisa confronts the realities and complexities of the issues surrounding her seeking acknowledgement from the bus driver about what she considers 'really happened': and our appreciation of the rights and wrongs of this situation – already uneasy – is now confounded.

This is the way the film works to unsettle our moral certainty. Lonergan has stated that he wanted to make a film about the way teenagers transition into an adult world. The film is called *Margaret* after a poem called 'Spring and Fall' by Gerard Manley Hopkins (1880). This poem is about a young girl's realisation that the passing of things is sad: in the poem this is the fall of leaves from a tree and the onset of autumn. The poet observes that the girl is realising the sadness of death and will come to understand mortality and loss. The film, then, is partly the telling of Lisa's existential lightning bolt and her realisation that the world around her is too tired or resistant to bother with her concern about the truth. But it also works as an obstacle course of moral reasoning and analysis for the spectator, and it is here where I turn to Murdoch.

In 'Vision and Choice in Morality', Murdoch is teasing out the position of her contemporary moral philosophers and where they locate the material for their moral philosophy. For Murdoch, moral philosophy can be seen as 'a more systematic and reflective extension of what ordinary moral agents are continually doing' (VCM: 83). What she means is that universal rules and models are not suited to understanding the complexity of everyday life and the inner lives of individuals. Under objective models, questions such as 'what is my morality?' and 'what is morality as such?' are addressed by descriptions of choices expressed in specific language. 'On this view', she says, 'the moral life of the individual is a series of overt choices which take place in a series of specifiable situations' (VCM: 77). Moral concepts are 'roughly an objective definition of a certain area of activity plus a recommendation or prohibition' (VCM: 77). For Murdoch, this objectivity is a problem. She is concerned with the 'inner life', which she clarifies as 'in the sense of personal attitudes and visions which do not obviously take the form of choice-guiding arguments' (VCM: 80). She asks us to consider 'moral being as self-reflection or complex attitudes to life which are continuously displayed and elaborated in overt and inward speech but are not separable temporarily into situations' (VCM: 81). Murdoch thinks about moral differences not as differences of choice, but rather differences of vision. She writes, 'We differ not only because we select different objects out of the same world but because we see different worlds' (VCM: 82). A term such as 'good' cannot have the simple empirical meaning, Murdoch argues, as does 'red'. There are more complex regions that lie outside actions and choices, and we need to attend to these areas or visions, which we may not always be able to understand. In this way, we can see more clearly what she means by saying that moral philosophy is 'a more systematic and reflective extension of what ordinary moral agents are continually doing' (VCM: 83).

This discussion, of how moral insight differs from moral performance, links clearly with Lisa's situation in *Margaret*. Lisa comes to see how a moral life is far more complex than whether one traffic light was red or not. Even though the ramifications of this event may be far-reaching, the morality of the surrounding circumstances cannot be dictated by one objective act. It is not as simple as saying that her decision to lie was wrong and her decision to come clean is right. She cannot console herself by deciding to give a different account of the accident now. Lisa's moral maze can be seen as creating a filmic moral philosophy along the lines Murdoch describes: a vision of the self-reflection Lisa has to experience in order to come by her own vision of a moral world. This moral world is created by what happens to her and what she chooses to do, but far more than this, it is also affected by the behaviour, choices, problems, conversations and happenstances that circulate around her and satellite off in different directions. The film conveys this through unfinished conversations, snippets of overheard dialogue, unresolved ambiguities and unsatisfactory non-conclusions.

Murdoch can help us further in understanding how the film might contain or convey moral philosophy by her consideration of the value of a moral fable. She asks, does a morally important fable always imply universal rules? And how do we decide whether a fable is morally important? Murdoch talks about two types of moral fable: the one that is morally relevant, the other that is purely decorative. (This idea seems to exist at the heart of the question of the significance of the film and its status as film philosophy: is film simply an illustration of an idea or can it actually be philosophical?) Murdoch talks about parables of widely held religions, which have the concreteness of personal fables, but which may have universalisable implications: that is, always do this in these circumstances. Is this then the test for value, that such a fable should have universal reasoning? For Murdoch, personal reflection is morally important in that it constitutes a person's general conceptual attitude and day-to-day 'being', which in turn connects in complex ways with their more obviously moral 'acts': including a person's meditation upon their own lives, such as that which lies ahead of Manley Hopkins's 'Margaret' or Lonergan's 'Lisa'. I want to take this a step further and consider whether *our* experience of the film *Margaret* can be considered to be Murdochian moral philosophy. Is the film a morally important fable, without being a universalisable model, or is it simply a purely decorative moral tale?

Again Murdoch helps us, as she moves on to consider the relationship between art and morals. For Murdoch, 'a moral agent may explore a situation imaginatively and in detail and frame a highly specific maxim to cover it, which may nevertheless be offered as a universal rule' (VCM: 87). This would suggest that the experience of watching – or exploring – a film such as *Margaret* might well be sufficiently universalisable to satisfy the more behaviourist moral philosophers among us. After all, one can meditate and explore the 'mysteriousness and inexhaustibility of the world, but meanwhile one has continually to make judgements on the basis of what one thinks one knows, and these, if moral, will claim to be universal' (ibid.). But, Murdoch argues, 'why should we blot out as irrelevant the different background of these choices, whether they are made confidently . . . or tentatively?' (ibid.: 88) Might not attending to the details, and inexhaustibility of them, induce humility rather than induce paralysis? (ibid.) And, she argues, this needs to be done in ways other than in language. She considers the limitations of language when it comes to serving us creatively, and that 'the task of moral philosophers has been to extend, as poets may extend, the limits of the language, and enable it to illuminate regions of reality which were formerly dark' (ibid.: 90). Calling for 'not a renewed attempt to specify the facts, but a fresh vision which may be derived from a "story"' and which 'represents a "mode of understanding"' (ibid.: 91), Murdoch suggests that moral freedom 'looks more like a mode of reflection which we may have to achieve, and less like a capacity to vary our choices which we have by definition' (ibid.: 95).

Experiencing the long, tormented and disturbing three hours of *Margaret* creates a fresh vision derived from a story, but also from the very cinematic telling of that story. To return to the scene at the bus driver's house, the sight of the wife and the sound of the children convey the bus driver's home situation in ways that force *us* to make the realisation that he has a lot at stake. The come-down from the set-up of Lisa's operatic quest, accompanied by *La Traviata* and images of post-9/11 New York City, brings us sharply down to earth too: we do not expect him to put up such a brick wall of denial. We gather the information that there have been disciplinary proceedings and no finding of fault. In the context of the film we are unnerved by the conversation that fails to deliver the atoning liberation Lisa craves, and proceed to be challenged at every turn by the quandaries and frustrations Lisa creates and confronts: befriending the dead woman's family, seducing her teacher, fighting with her mother, dealing with her disappointing father. The web of individuals with their own inner lives and moral frameworks is complex and connected, and not only through the main narrative events. This complexity, as well as the film's long duration and slow pace, afford unusually multi-layered engagement with events on-screen, and the truly traumatic early accident serves to sustain the attention required in order to experience the moral discombobulation that the film inflicts.

By bringing Murdoch and *Margaret* together in an exploration of the moral decision making of the film's protagonist and our assessment of her choices, we can learn more about the idea of film as a morally important fable rather than a fable that is purely decorative. Vitally, we do not have to learn a universalisable lesson from watching the film. Neither do we have to decide whether Lisa did – or did not do – the right thing. The film thwarts our attempts to identify 'the right thing' on-screen – it cannot be reduced to the red light – and instead creates a maelstrom of people making moral decisions tentatively, confidently, against a range of backgrounds, many of which are suggested, without being developed, serving to stress the multitude of moral agents with their own inner lives. As Lisa arrives at a state of distressed but reflective realisation of the uncertainties and brutalities of social living, then we – as distressed and hopefully reflective participants in the film's moral philosophy – cannot help but recognise a moral fable that constitutes what Murdoch might call 'philosophical pictures of morality' (VCM: 98). *Margaret* shows how film can do more than just tell a story – a moral story – and can create an experience that is relevant and affects us as moral beings. But can it also affect our judgement of another?

'LOOKING THE OTHER WAY': *BLUE JASMINE*

Jasmine (Cate Blanchett) is portrayed as selfish and morally corrupt, but I suggest that by Murdoch's notion of paying 'loving attention' to Jasmine's experience and countenance, we are able to appreciate the suffering and torment that Jasmine feels, thereby adjusting our judgement of her to be more compassionate. *Blue Jasmine* is about a woman who lived a very affluent life married to a property broker who has turned out to be crooked. They lost all their money, her husband was convicted and hanged himself in prison, and her stepson no longer speaks to her. With nowhere to go, she turns to her working-class sister Ginger (Sally Hawkins), who willingly takes her into her home. Jasmine and Ginger are sisters but not related by blood – they were both adopted. They state this a few times, and their differences are very marked, not only in terms of aspiration and education, but also passions and desires. Ginger always says that Jasmine had the good genes. Jasmine is a shocking snob and bore, who drinks too much and despises her sister's entire life – her choice of man, her children and her home. Ginger works in a supermarket, loves her home, and has a steady boyfriend, Chili (Bobby Cannavale). Jasmine makes it clear that she despised Ginger's ex-husband, as well as her new boyfriend, sees them both as losers, and thinks her life and home are dreadful. Ginger is tolerant and caring, and receives her sister's acerbic criticism with indulgent good humour. She defends Jasmine to others and does her best for her.

It emerges through a process of flashback and dialogue between the sisters that Jasmine's husband lost the lottery winnings of Ginger and her ex-husband by persuading them to invest in a dodgy deal. We also see flashbacks of Jasmine talking derisively about her sister and dreading her visits – she describes Ginger to her friends as not very smart, and makes up excuses to not have to see them or have them stay at her house. In the present day, Jasmine is trying to improve her current prospects by taking a course in computing, and getting a job as a dentist's receptionist, a job she considers terribly demeaning and for which she lacks the skills. She and Ginger go to a party, where they both meet men: Ginger meets a seemingly middle-class man who pays her lots of attention and seems to fall for her hard; Jasmine meets a smooth operator with political ambitions who believes Jasmine when she tells him she is an interior designer (which is what she is actually hoping to become). The relationship proceeds on this deceit, and gets more serious, leading to a proposal of marriage. Ginger discovers that her new lover is in fact married, and when Jasmine is spotted on the street by Ginger's still furious ex-husband her duplicity is revealed to her staggered fiancé. So once again Jasmine's world is in ruins, and now she's lost the support of her sister due to her derision of sensitive working-class Chili who is now back on the scene.

There are several factors that determine the way in which we might judge Jasmine. Firstly, in a flashback we see that it was news of her husband's infidelity that prompted her, in a rage, to make the phone call to the FBI that turned him in, suggesting that she must have known of, or been wilfully blind to, the illegality of his business while enjoying the riches he produced and fleecing her sister of her winnings. Secondly, we see Jasmine come across her estranged stepson, Danny (Alden Ehrenreich), working in a second-hand musical instrument store. He has got his life together, come off drugs, has a girlfriend and loves his job – and hates Jasmine. He tells her as much and says he never wants to see her again. Within the parameters of the snobbery, deceit, self-centredness and avarice that we have seen Jasmine operate, these final revelations confirm her as a person perceived by many as beyond the pale. The film ends with her sitting on a bench muttering to herself, with nowhere to go.

Now, some of the film's moral messages are clear, if not overdetermined: relationships based on deceit will founder; financial irregularities will catch up with you; a simple honest life is the key to happiness. But the character of Jasmine is not entirely unsympathetic, and this suggests that another view of her might be possible. This is what I want to explore in relation to Murdoch's notion of 'loving attention', but we need to take care to understand why we might have sympathy for Jasmine, which could be for very cinematic reasons. Firstly, she is played by Cate Blanchett who gives a fabulously sensitive performance, with humour – almost slapstick in the dentist's office as she wards off his unwanted advances – and desperation. Blanchett's star turn was rewarded with award after award for best actress in a leading role, including the Academy Award, the Golden Globe and the BAFTA. Secondly, there is the resonance with Blanche Dubois (Vivien Leigh) in *A Streetcar Named Desire* (Elia Kazan, 1951), which was noted by many critics at the time (Chagollan 2014; Feinberg 2013; Handy 2013; Pinkerton 2014). Disturbed, vulnerable and desperate, living in a fantasy world of halcyon days that were in fact founded on deceit, she cuts an almost mythic tragic figure.

Woody Allen describes Jasmine as having a tantrum when she makes the FBI phone call (Shoard 2013). The view of Allen, and the journalist interviewing him, Catherine Shoard, is that she brought it on herself. Shoard writes that *Blue Jasmine* 'is a bruiser of a movie, a Greek tragedy that dispatches a Park Avenue princess with a massive slap' (2013). Shoard sees the film as a character assassination, pivoting on what Allen describes as Jasmine's 'tantrum'. He says

> she could have gotten a divorce, forgiven him, had a talk with him, moved out of the house. But she just hit the ceiling blindly and went on a rampage that brought destruction upon her whole household. She never stopped to think about the consequences of her raging moment. (Shoard 2013)

This is a staggeringly one-sided view of the film. Another view is that Jasmine gave up her anthropology degree to marry Hal, she supported his career through her wifely devotion, she loved him; and he has not only repeatedly slept with many women of their acquaintance to the knowledge of everyone except her, but now proposes to leave her for the teenage French au pair. Jasmine has a panic attack, she cannot breathe, and is clearly suffering from an acute stress reaction, facing the prospect of – yes, her high-class life – but also her marriage to the man she loves, being in ruins in a desperately painful and humiliating way. So, she turns him in to the authorities, and that phone call is followed by his arrest, their financial ruin, his suicide and her desperate state. But, it wasn't her phone call that caused that: it was Hal's illegal business affairs. And despite Jasmine displaying offensive snobbery and callous self-centredness, I suggest that it is possible to see her in a more compassionate light.

This is where Murdoch's metaphor for generous thinking comes to my mind. In 'The Idea of Perfection' from 1964, Murdoch writes her most famous philosophical parable about a mother and a daughter-in-law. A mother, M, feels hostility towards her daughter-in-law, D. She finds her quite a good-hearted girl, but that she lacks refinement and is somewhat unpolished. D can be juvenile and brusque, and M doesn't like how she dresses. Basically M feels that her son has married 'a silly vulgar girl' (IP: 312–13). M is a very 'correct' person and behaves beautifully to the girl throughout, not allowing her real opinion to surface. And in order to ensure we consider that what Murdoch is concerned with is what is happening in M's mind, she says we may now assume that the couple have emigrated or even that D is now dead. As time passes, M could settle down with a grievance. But, Murdoch says, M is an intelligent and well-intentioned person, capable of self-criticism, and of giving careful and just attention to an object that confronts her: 'M tells herself, "I am old-fashioned and conventional. I may be prejudiced and narrow-minded. I may be snobbish. I am certainly jealous. Let me look again"' (IP: 313). M then reflects deliberately about D, until gradually her vision of D alters. The change is not in M's behaviour, but it is in M's mind: 'D is discovered to be not vulgar, but refreshingly simple . . . not tiresomely juvenile, but delightfully youthful, and so on' (IP: 313). Murdoch explains that M might be moved by various motives, such as a sense of justice, attempted love for D, love for her son. Some may say 'she deludes herself', others may say she was moved by love or justice. M's motives and actions don't matter; it's all about how she perceives. We could be hypothetical, as in, if she were to speak her mind to D now it would be different. But in the interim she has been active – what Murdoch calls, 'morally active' (IP: 313–4). M is attempting 'not just to see D accurately but to see her justly or lovingly' (IP: 317). There is a necessary fallibility built into this idea – it is potentially an endless task.

This is where Murdoch uses the word 'attention', which she says she is borrowing from Simone Weil, to express the idea of 'a just and loving gaze' directed upon an individual reality: 'I believe this to be the characteristic and proper mark of the active moral agent' (IP: 327).

> As moral agents we have to try to see justly, to overcome prejudice, to avoid temptation, to control and curb imagination, to direct reflection. Man is not a combination of an impersonal rational thinker and a personal will. He is a unified being who sees, and who desires in accordance with what he sees, and who has some continual slight control over the direction and focus of his vision. There is nothing, I think, in the foreground of this picture which is unfamiliar to the ordinary person. (IP: 332)

She describes this outlook as a sketch of a metaphysical theory, a kind of inconclusive non-dogmatic naturalism, and she says it must be judged 'by its power to connect, to illuminate, to explain, and to make new and fruitful places for reflection' (IP: 336). It demonstrates Murdoch's thinking about inner vision, not action, and the emphasis on focusing our vision in order to see in a more moral way. This is something we all do: moral philosophy is the stuff of our everyday lives. Being terribly English, M's actions towards D don't change. She's always polite. But her inner view changes. Now, sadly, the parable does not apply directly to Jasmine in the film. In fact the reverse happens to Ginger as she comes to see Jasmine in a worse light by the end of the film. Jasmine fails to make any effort to improve her own moral vision; her values are all about her status.

But what about us? At its most simple, our actions can't change: we either keep watching the film, or we turn it off, or walk out of the cinema. But we do assess Jasmine from a moral perspective. The film is a profoundly relevant contemporary morality tale, calling attention to illegalities in high finance, in a world post-Bernie Madoff and other high-profile, white-collar criminality over the last few years. But the film is far more than this, and the concept of Murdochian attention can help us to identify how. The following five scenes call for our attention and develop our view of Jasmine.

First, the discussion of Hal's death. It has been strongly suggested in the film that Jasmine either knew of Hal's illegal business or was wilfully blind. Similarly, she seems laughably blind to his organising of his infidelities. But it is the film that knows all this – Jasmine does not appear to. She says to Ginger (who has seen Hal kissing Jasmine's friend), 'Oh Hal's not the roving type.' Ginger says of her sister, 'When Jasmine doesn't want to know something she has a habit of looking the other way.' Well, this delusional state is shattered by Hal's death in his cell, which Jasmine describes in frank and brutal detail. When Chili and his friend ask what happened, and suggest that death by hanging results in strangulation, Jasmine puts them straight. She says, 'No, no, it wasn't strangulation; when you hang yourself your neck breaks ... a lot of people are under the misapprehension that you strangle, but your neck snaps.' This scene shows how Jasmine's delusional state is shaky, and that what happened to Hal has forced her to confront something truly awful that she may consider to be the consequence of her action. This burden must be an unbearable one, and offers a glimpse of the true trauma that Jasmine experiences, rather than simply the loss of her jewellery and fine lifestyle. It also conveys the effort involved in her artifice, and that there may be more effort on show than delusion.

The next scene to consider is when the dentist makes a pass at her. Jasmine has been working in the dentist's office, and, while not doing a brilliant job, she is trying and learning. The dentist scolds her for reading her college work on the job, forcing her to apologise and promise not to do it any more, and then declares his lust for her. He says he finds her clothes arousing and congratulates her, saying that she should be happy she's made a conquest. This shows some of the problems that a woman in her current position might encounter; Jasmine is probably not used to the power imbalance in this situation, or the arrogance of the dentist and his assumption of power over her. She resists, so she loses her job.

Thirdly, there is the scene when she receives the phone call from her potential new beau, Dwight (Peter Sarsgaard). In this scene, the importance of the call from Dwight is heartbreakingly but subtly illustrated. We can see how Jasmine is entirely obsessed with Dwight's phone call, as she commands the use of the telephone in Ginger's apartment. We also see the level of artifice that goes into the conversation and the arrangements, as she lies about being busy having meetings and injects deliberate pauses as if she is checking her diary, and then we see the vulnerability and relief once she puts down the telephone (Figure 3.2). The camera lingers with Jasmine long enough once the receiver has been replaced to see the exhalation after the effort it has taken to conduct that phone call. This also conveys how significant the opportunity is for her, and how much she is depending upon this new man to rescue her.

In another scene, Jasmine reveals her history of mental health problems. When babysitting Ginger's boys, and a few martinis to the wind, Jasmine describes her history of psychiatric treatment, including electric shock therapy and drug therapy. This shows her as a person with vulnerabilities, dating back into her past, and it sheds light on her reaction when told about Hal's infidelities, her need to self-medicate with martinis and Xanax, and the toll that her

Figure 3.2 Jasmine (Cate Blanchett) breaks down after Dwight's call, in *Blue Jasmine* (2013), directed by Woody Allen.

experiences have taken on her. Importantly, being told about this involves the viewer without any attribution of blame: we can only think of her rather than assess whether or not she 'deserves' to suffer in this way. After all, she says, 'There's only so many traumas a person can withstand until they take to the streets and start screaming.'

The final scene I want to focus on is the conversation with Danny, which does several things. It shows how, perhaps unfairly, she has received more vitriol than Hal from Danny, and this is particularly interesting in light of how women often seem to receive extra or misdirected fury (Downing 2013: 58). It also shows how Jasmine's values have not changed: she sees money and position as the desirable outcomes and any other source of satisfaction is inconceivable to her. And it shows how she has nobody now from her own family unit: she had no child of her own, and Hal's son blames her.

There are many more such elements and moments in the film that call for our attention, such as the relationship with her parents, with her old so-called friends, and more painful and brutal exchanges with Ginger. Like her cinematic predecessor, Blanche Dubois, in her exchanges with the men her sister introduces her to Jasmine is quite tough and resilient, displaying a steeliness and worldliness that show her to have backbone combined with independence. This suggests either that it is only now that these qualities are being called upon, or that she is transforming, developing harder layers, and moving further and further away from the social butterfly she once was. By paying attention to Jasmine we see more, and Murdoch might propose we 'grow by looking': for example, at the scenes where Jasmine is crippled with shame and horror at herself, not just her economic and social situation, but her place as the bearer of all the blame for Ginger and Augie's lost money, and the death of Danny's dad. And, indeed, she assumes this guilt. After the confrontation with Augie in the street, when Dwight is raging at her lies, seeing his political prospects tumbling around him, she says, 'I brought it on myself again.' Here is a woman who talks to herself, holding the conversations she wishes she had been able to have, saying the things she wishes she had been able to say, but couldn't for various reasons. She's left sitting on the bench, talking to herself, berating her dead husband for sleeping with the au pair, conceding that even the lyrics to the song that was playing when they met – 'Blue Moon' – are now 'all a jumble'.

If I am M, and Jasmine is D, my time with D is over once the film is over, and I can choose to condemn her as the prevailing opinion of many will do, or I can look again, and pay attention to all that is there, not just the cut-and-dried legal or even moral framework of the film. I can try to think about the options that Jasmine has had available to her, the specific realities of her mental and emotional life, her vulnerabilities and her choices, and pay what Murdoch might call 'patient attention' to lead me to a view of 'just discernment'. This might not be accurate, and this need not be complete, but it may come close to what Murdoch might consider 'goodness by proxy' (SGC: 371). Murdoch also writes about how, pursuant to Weil's commitment to attention, 'moral change comes from an *attention* to the world whose natural result is a decrease in egoism through an increased sense of the reality of, primarily of course other people, but also other things' (MGM: 52). This is something that we can all do and in Murdoch's opinion should be doing:

> We do not have to have a theoretical interest in morality. There is indeed a kind of (instinctive) orientation or certainty which is rejected if we emphasise free will and individual decision. Are there however some ways in which, if we reflect about moral value, we cannot properly avoid picturing the world? (MGM: 55)

Murdoch here means that we can go about our daily lives without thinking too much about our choices and what we should be doing, because, if we have been paying attention to reality in a Murdochian sense, we are probably fine to follow our instincts. But, if we do examine moral value – the things we consider to be right and wrong – we must look at the way the world is and how people live in it. Murdoch was concerned to argue that the distinction between fact and value, as propounded by her predecessor G. E. Moore, was abstract and erroneous. She saw this as stripping metaphysics out of ethics, suggesting there was no naturalistic or metaphysical structure: 'it is presented simply in terms of exhortations and choices defended by reference to facts' (M&E: 63). As Cora Diamond notes,

Murdoch argues that oversimplification in moral philosophy derives not only from the philosophical will to impose a rational unity but also from the force of our own particular moral pictures, which she sees as leading to an overemphasis on the role of choice in moral life and a denial of the significance of vision and understanding. (Diamond 2010: 53)

Diamond highlights Murdoch's point that 'Moral concepts do not move about *within* a hard world set up by science and logic' (IP: 321). It isn't that Murdoch is not concerned with action, but rather that 'she took action to come out of true and just vision' (Diamond 2010: 66). The role of attention, then, is in continuous work on our individual moral vision, which equips us for taking the right action when the time comes. Here, again, Murdoch indicates how fictional imaginings or scenarios may inform our moral vision: 'Man is a creature who makes pictures of himself and then comes to resemble the picture. This is the process which moral philosophy must attempt to describe and analyse' (M&E: 75). The role of pictures and images here is clearly so important, as language has been used by the linguistic philosophers around her in such a reductive way. Murdoch is interested in a broader spectrum of values and behaviour:

> We were too impressed by words when we assumed that the word 'good' covered a single concept which was the centre of morality. We were not impressed enough when we neglected less general moral words such as 'true', 'brave', 'free', 'sincere', which are the bearers of very important ideas. (M&E: 73)

It is in these other concepts and values that Murdoch sees the richness of our individual moral visions and the range of possible differences. The concept of 'good' may be less difficult to share or explain than others, for example,

> the concept of 'truth' . . . contains tangles and paradoxes the unravelling of which would show us really interesting features of the modern world. It is in terms of the inner complexity of such concepts that we may display really deep differences of moral vision. (M&E: 73)

And 'to analyse and describe our own morality and that of others may involve the making of models and pictures of what different kinds of men are like' (M&E: 74). This concept of a range of values, and range of different moral visions, is explored in the third film in this chapter, which is certainly a contemporary moral fable.

HOW FAR IS TOO FAR? *COMPLIANCE*

In this affective and shocking film, based on true events, a prank call to a supermarket leads to one of the employees being poorly treated, assaulted and sexually abused by co-workers, who comply with the instructions of the caller believing him to be a police officer. The film disquiets the viewer through disbelief and revulsion and then implicates us in the process of questioning how we would behave in this situation. This raises the question of moral strength, which the film depicts so painfully in its collective weakness.

The film begins with these words on the screen:

In 1961, a psychologist carried out the now-renowned Milgram Experiment: a study that proved people behave immorally if instructed by an authority figure.

From 1991 to 2004, people's compliance with authority was exploited multiple times with disturbing consequences. The following story is so shocking, it's hard to believe it's true.

Nothing has been exaggerated.

Then, in screen-filling capital letters, to drive the matter home, 'INSPIRED BY TRUE EVENTS'. The film begins with a bad-tempered encounter between the regional manager of an outlet of the fictional fast-food chain, Chickwich, and her delivery driver. The manager Sandra (Ann Dowd) has had to order in extra bacon, because somebody failed to close the freezer door properly, and the delivery driver is very angry and critical of her. She says she doesn't appreciate being spoken to like that, and he reveals that his kid has 'a big game tonight' and he's fifty miles away, so we start from the point of view that everyone has their own concerns going on that day which affect how they see the world.

We then see a man shouting into a payphone. This man will go on to play the driving role in the film, but we are quickly returned to Chickwich, and the camera passes over all the paraphernalia in such a chicken food store, then to the staff in uniform, awaiting briefing for the shift. The manager tells them about the freezer door, and says, 'We've gotta be by the book tonight; we potentially have a franchise quality control person coming, a secret shopper': so everything has to be just right in terms of portion sizes, the order of assembly, and 'clean, clean, clean'.

Some of the staff are chatting about boyfriends, and one says that another has 'got like three dudes'. Sandra looks a bit put out, and joins in the conversation, saying, 'My man sexts me sometimes – he knows what to do to get me worked up.' When she leaves them, the others exchange comments and laugh at her, which Sandra overhears. So some tension is established between Sandra and the younger staff, especially the women. Sandra is shown discussing their milkshakes with the caretaker, Harold (Stephen Payne), and stresses proudly there is a lot of choice, displaying herself to be a 'company person'. The film takes some time in order to show that the food is highly processed, repetitive and unnatural: close-up shots of the ends of fries in cartons, burned and orange, shards of breadcrumbed chicken pieces put in paper cases, fizzy drink coming out of the pump and spraying all over the hand. This is not attractive food. But at the same time, there are shots of ordinary people sitting and eating, chatting with their friends and families, enjoying this food. So the set-up is established as very workaday and unremarkable.

Then Sandra receives a telephone call from a man who claims to be a policeman called Officer Daniels. He asks for the manager's name and says he has the regional manager with him. He begins to ask about a young blonde woman who works for her, and Sandra says, 'Who, Becky?' She thereby provides the name of her employee to this man, who goes on to say that he has a customer with him who says Becky (Dreama Walker) stole some money from her.

Sandra says she finds it hard to believe, but instantly accepts that she must do what 'Officer Daniels' tells her to. She takes Becky out to the back into the storeroom. The Officer says he has a woman who describes her exactly, and that it is backed up by surveillance. Becky denies it. Following the officer's instructions, Sandra searches Becky's pockets and handbag. She holds Becky's arm in a slightly restraining way. Sandra says, 'If you did I'm going to have to fire you on the spot.' When Becky denies it, Sandra says, 'Then why do I have a police officer calling me, telling me your name, telling me you stole from a customer?' It was Sandra who provided Becky's name, but that has slipped her mind.

The man tells Sandra she is going to have to keep hold of Becky until he can get there. He cajoles Sandra by saying he needs her to assist the authorities, and that 'Wouldn't it make sense that she would try to hide it from you?' Appealing to Sandra's 'jobsworth' character type succeeds in getting her to follow the instructions, and when he asks to speak to Becky his tactic is to wear down her resistance. He threatens Becky and diminishes her power in the situation, saying, 'I'm gonna need you to address me as sir or officer understand? You don't realise what kind of trouble you're in' (Figure 3.3). Through this technique of cajoling Sandra and threatening Becky, he gets Sandra to strip search Becky, check her underwear, remove her clothes and handbag and take them to the car in the car park, leaving her naked in the storeroom. The caller's next step is to ramp up the seriousness of the alleged crime, by saying they are investigating Becky and her brother, and her clothes could have forensic evidence.

Figure 3.3 Becky (Dreama Walker) knows there's nothing she can do, in *Compliance* (2012), directed by Craig Zobel.

The soundtrack music is steady and slow percussion, then choppy cello notes, slightly comic in tone, but also ominous.

Sandra's attention is returning to the running of the business now, and she agrees to the caller's suggestion to get a male employee to watch the naked Becky. Cut to chips frying furiously with a rumbling, thunderous soundtrack. We now see the parallel activity: a muffled male voice on the phone, a pen nib making notes, toying with a cigarette, the back of a man's head on the phone. We become aware that there is a man conducting this phone call, and he does not look like a policeman. Sandra says to Becky's friend and co-worker Kevin, 'There's some upsetting news about Becky. She stole from a customer and she may be in some trouble with her brother.' He doesn't believe it, and refuses to accept what the caller says, especially when he is told he will have to inspect her body. He leaves, saying, 'You can't make me do that. Becky is my friend. When the cops come I don't want anything to do with it.'

We now see the caller making a sandwich, squirting mustard, and blatantly lying about being a police officer not able to spare one officer to come out to Chickwich. He cajoles Sandra into talking about having a fiancé and to ask him to come by and help, saying, 'It would really help me out.' Two shots of ice and snow break the stress briefly, but then Sandra's fiancé Van (Bill Camp) arrives. We see a full restaurant outside, with people eating, burgers being made, the till collecting all the money. Sandra tells Van that he has to watch Becky, and he says, 'Do we really have to do this?' to which Sandra replies, 'Honey it's not up to me.'

The caller speaks to Van, now left alone to watch Becky, and establishes some details about him, then tells him he is going to have to inspect Becky's body: 'You believe everything a thief says? You think a naked girl doesn't have a place to hide money?' Again, the caller intimidates Becky too, saying, 'You're the one that is causing all the problems. Allow the person that I authorised. You can go to jail or you can let this guy inspect you.' When he tells her to give the phone back to Van, he is laughing to himself, presumably at the ease with which he is succeeding to control them, and he asks Van to describe what her chest looks like, the size of her nipples, to know identifying marks. He then gets Becky to turn around and bend over, for a 'standard cavity search', and then to do jumping jacks 'to shake it out'. Van looks up her vagina with the torch on his phone, and then spanks her for disobedience, until the caller persuades Becky to 'Do something nice for him', and perform oral sex. The sordid nature of these events is bolstered by close-up shots of dirty sink water, and a visual double-entendre of a dog-leg in a plastic drink straw. Becky's lower legs and feet contort on the floor, as she is clearly kneeling in front of Van. Throughout this excruciating episode, Van's face has been hard to read. He does not appear lascivious, he is hesitant, but embraces the opportunity to act in this way. When asked to place the telephone close to the spanking so that the caller can hear, he comes up with the idea, 'You want me to lay the phone on her back?' This is followed by a cut to the caller laughing in disbelief at Van's enthusiastic acquiescence.

There are fleeting close-up shots of the plastic straw, globular chicken, gnarly fries and a disgusting sink. Kevin reveals that he has texted his friend and Becky's brother isn't even in town. Sandra is rude and dismissive to Becky by now, telling her not to talk to her. Van leaves quickly, clearly disturbed, and calls his friend to say, 'I did a bad thing.' Several people now clearly disagree or suspect, but they all fail to intervene or make efforts to protect Becky, who is by now dazed and simply staring at the CCTV. When Harold the factotum comes back to the store and asks what's going on, Sandra says to him, 'Becky stole something, we had to strip search her': she entirely accepts the allegation and legitimacy of the consequent actions. She enlists Harold to watch Becky now, and passes him over to the caller, who begins his line of instruction again. Harold, however, is having none of it. He says to the caller, 'I don't know who you are but I don't think it's right to see a lady like this in the buff.' When the caller says that the decision is not up to Harold, he replies, 'I'll be damned if it isn't.' He then tells Sandra this is not right, 'This is not policemanly.' Sandra checks and finds that the regional manager was off sick today, not sitting alongside the fictitious Officer Daniels. Sandra realises he was not real, and falls silent. Kevin calls the police.

The truly agonising previous hour and twenty-five minutes has been an escalation in outrage, veering between disbelief, fury and dismissal for the spectator. We cannot help but be incredulous at the ways in which Sandra complies with the caller, and critical of the fact that none of Becky's friends and co-workers intervenes to protect her. And yet, the film tells us, these events happened not once but seventy times between 1992 and 2004. Assurance of basis in fact is often a technique used by filmmakers to bolster the impact of on-screen events, and such an assertion needs to be handled with care as the veracity of events can vary greatly from their 'real world' inspiration. However, some superficial internet research swiftly confirms that *Compliance* is indeed based on almost identical events in a McDonald's restaurant in Kentucky in 2004 (Koehler 2012: 55).

Hannah McGill observes how, 'As can so often be the case, real life here supplies extremes of human behaviour that might well be thrown out of a fiction-film script meeting for lacking credibility' (McGill 2013: 82). The film attracted a lot of critical attention after it was shown at the Sundance Film Festival in 2012, with Laura Kern (2012) calling it 'the most polarising film' of the festival, and Amy Taubin considering it to be 'the most abhorrent, classist, sexist movie of the festival' (Taubin 2012: 62). As Kern observes,

> it's one squirm-inducing viewing experience . . . And every time you think there's no way this could ever happen – and that thought most certainly pops up a lot – just remind yourself that a similar incident actually did take place (more than once!). (Kern 2012: 65)

This basis in truth does not let director Zobel off the hook in Taubin's eyes, however, who still criticises his specific script and casting choices in relation to his deployment of the 'gullibility and moral failure of an overweight, middle-aged woman who's been stuck in a shit job in a fast-food restaurant for her entire working life' (2012: 62). For Taubin, the casting encourages a sense of superiority in the viewers who she takes to be 'a lot of upper middle class white guys' (2012: 62). I think Roger Ebert's review is closer to the mark, however, when he observes that one of the reasons for the film's effectiveness is because 'we feel we know people like this' (2012). For Ebert, when addressing the fact that people were seen to be walking out of the film, these walk-outs 'aren't because it's a bad movie, but because it's all too effective at exposing the human tendency to cave in to authority'. As Ebert observes, 'If the stunt worked seventy times, they must prove something – perhaps that we are afraid of authority' (ibid.). As Robert Koehler writes, *Compliance* 'contains within it the most profound questions generated by the largest human tragedies of the twentieth century . . . What makes a decent and generally intelligent person obey an authority to commit evil?' (2012: 56). For Koehler, this Chickwich is a 'human hell', staffed by a range of people, who each have their moment to make a stand and choose whether to comply with the caller's instructions, or to act in a different way. This is perhaps what is most striking about the film: that not one of them actively intervenes. The challenge to us as viewers then, is not simply to think 'what would I do?' or 'what should they have done?', but *at what point* would I actively intervene? This is the unusual moral challenge of this film, that sets it apart from the more straightforward moral conundrum movies such as *Indecent Proposal* (would you let your wife sleep with Robert Redford for a million dollars?), *The Box* (would you accept a million dollars if the price was that somebody you didn't know would be killed?) or *Good People* (would you keep a bagful of cash you found left behind by your old tenant, even when it is clearly ill-gotten gains?).[1] It is more than a universalist assessment of right and wrong in this situation, as it compels us to question our tendencies to susceptibility and to assess qualities such as strength of character, care for another and fearlessness, which Murdoch would undoubtedly call moral qualities (see again her thinking on 'brave', 'true' and 'free' at M&E: 73). These are the character traits that go towards what 'in the ordinary sense, a person "is like"' (VCM: 80). The range of very ordinary people, just like us and people we know, makes the magnitude of these questions acutely relevant. Also, the dynamics of the relationship to the characters compels us into a similar impotence to that of Becky: neither of us can escape this situation, except – as apparently many did – by walking out of the cinema. It demands a thoughtful response of not just what one might do but precisely when: at what point does one's moral responsibility require one to take action on behalf of another?

Murdoch insists that we are compelled because 'at crucial moments of choice most of the business of choosing is already over' (IP: 329). The work we do on our moral vision and our moral thinking means that we come to decisions on the basis of this ongoing work. And art is part of this work. Art contains 'moral insight' and represents 'moral achievements' (IP: 332). And it is in terms of vision that Murdoch conceives this perspective: 'true vision occasions right conduct' (OGG: 353). As Michael Schwartz writes, 'for Murdoch, great art allows us to see things as we had never perceived them before' (2009: 320). He draws attention to Murdoch's belief that 'freedom is not strictly the exercise of the will, but rather the experience of accurate vision . . . [as] . . . by the time the moment of choice has arrived the quality of attention has probably determined the nature of the act' (OGG: 354). Art is therefore a place of 'fundamental insight' (OGG: 360). In MGM, Murdoch writes that, for Plato, 'value is everywhere, the whole of life is movement on a moral scale' (MGM: 56). This idea of a moral scale is apt for approaching the range of responses to Becky's situation in *Compliance*. As Elizabeth Dipple notes, discomfort 'is part of (Murdoch's) moral thrust' (1982: 90); and the discomfort we feel while watching this film compels us to assess our very particular set of priorities and weaknesses, and how much we value the experience of Becky, or Sandra, or Van.

Having examined the ways in which film can act as a moral fable, which challenges our tendencies to judge and simplify, as well as to examine our own moral vision, in the next chapter I will analyse three protagonists whose varying qualities of attention prepare them for different moral choices in very particular ways.

NOTE

1. *Indecent Proposal* (Adrian Lyne, 1993); *The Box* (Richard Kelly, 2009); *Good People* (Henrik Ruben Genz, 2014).

CHAPTER 4

Film and the Existential Hero(ine)

One might say, broadly, that the logical analysts describe ordinary language, and behaviour so far as it illuminates this, the existentialists describe a range of psychological phenomena connected with private personal experience, and the Marxists describe man's behaviour as a social being. ('The Existential Political Myth' (EPM): 132)

I agree that what the age requires is a refurbished Marxism. Existentialism has perhaps some contribution to make. But its *appeal* as a philosophy is at present through its most non-Marxist aspects – its dramatic, solipsistic, romantic and anti-social exaltation of the individual. ('Existentialist Bite' (EB): 153)

Sartre's man is still at the stage of thinking perpetually of himself. (SRR: 134)

It has been assumed that moral argument always takes the form of pointing to facts, rather than the form of analysing or explaining concepts . . . But our freedom is not just a freedom to choose and act differently, it is also a freedom to think and believe differently, to see the world differently, and to see different configurations and describe them in different words. (M&E: 72–3)

This chapter will engage with Murdoch's work on existentialism and her analysis of Sartre in a consideration of how films address the question of what gives life meaning, how free we are, and where characters turn to find guidance about the right way to live. The three chosen films explore how characters develop their rationale for living when they have either lost something that defines them, or are faced with a dilemma that will have lifelong repercussions for themselves and others. At that moment of solitary decision making, where does a character turn, and how does film convey the isolation, desperation and significance of these decisions and these lives?

Actress Maria Enders (Juliette Binoche) in *Clouds of Sils Maria* (Olivier Assayas, 2014) faces a professional opportunity and a personal loss that throw her life into crisis. She turns to others and to memories of her younger self, but these serve her unreliably. *Once Upon a Time in Anatolia* (Nuri Bilge Ceylan, 2011) takes place in the bleak Anatolian landscape as a group of policemen drive a captured killer to find the body of the man he has admitted to killing. The men experience different emotions and conflicts on the journey, culminating in an unforeseen dilemma for the doctor who carries out the autopsy on the victim. In *Graduation* (Cristian Mungiu, 2016), a father tries to do what he thinks is best for his daughter, but his choices lead to complication of his already messy life. Approaching these three protagonists from the perspective of Murdoch's analysis of the existential hero enables us to see how their difficulties arise and to assess the values and visions that guide their choices and actions.

MURDOCH AND EXISTENTIALISM

Murdoch's relationship with the existentialist movement is lengthy and fluctuating. As stated in the introduction, her first book was on Sartre, in which she critically analyses his novels and assesses his approach to consciousness and freedom. While clearly welcoming and respecting the emphasis on the significance of the individual consciousness, Murdoch finds that Sartre fails to account for, or even be interested in, the variety of human existence. Murdoch does not mince her words: 'The rationalism of Sartre is not geared on to the techniques of the modern world; it is solipsistic and romantic, isolated from the sphere of real operations' (SRR: 106).

Murdoch appreciated how brilliantly Sartre understood 'the psychology of the lonely individual' (SRR: 106), but solipsism made the characters in his novels, and the Sartrean existentialist thinker, egocentric, and ultimately consoling for the thinker and the reader:

> It is patent that what many readers of Sartre find in his writings is a portrait of themselves. A likeness is always pleasing, even if one is not handsome; and to be told that one's personal despair is a universal human characteristic may be consoling. But this is not to say that what we are offered here is nothing but an irresponsible caricature of a modern mood. (SRR: 111)

Murdoch's encounters with existentialism occur throughout her philosophical writings, and have occupied many scholars who have teased out her adoptions and rejections of various tenets and notions. Maria Antonaccio explains how Murdoch 'developed an ethics of vision built on the fundamental analogy between art and ethics, where moral rationality is more like the perceptive vision of the artist than the rational objectivity of the scientist', and how this undermined one of the cornerstones of analytic ethics – its assumption of logical and ethical neutrality (2012: 161). Although Murdoch's opposition to the linguistic analytics was overt, as Antonaccio asserts, 'no serious reader of Murdoch's philosophy could deny that existentialism was one of her "principal opponents"' (2012: 164). Antonaccio suggests that Murdoch's attitude toward existentialism remained ambivalent (2012: 164).[1] She understood the appeal of existentialism to a devastated post-war Europe, questioning what gives life meaning and who to turn to for guidance:

> the heroic consciousness, the individual self, inalienably and ineluctably free, challengingly confronted the "given", in the form of existing society, history, tradition, other people. The war was over, Europe was in ruins, we had emerged from a long captivity, all was to be remade. (SRR: 9)

This was a picture that resonated with many people in Europe in the aftermath of the war, such that 'Existentialism was the new religion, the new salvation' (ibid.: 10). Murdoch was, however, acutely aware of its limitations.

Peter Conradi writes that both existentialism and Anglo-Saxon philosophy came to seem 'equally facile' to Murdoch, because both 'evacuated inwardness through dignifying a romantic voluntarism or cult of the will' (Conradi 1994: 332). He writes how Murdoch's philosophy and fiction was 'in strong revolt against this world-view and of the popular "hero-of-the-will" to whom Existentialism had given birth in mid-century fiction' (ibid.: 333). Murdoch, as we have seen, was turning to Weil, who was helping her deepen her understanding of Plato. Conradi explains that Weil also drew on the Christian mystics and on Buddhism, and 'saw morality as a form of un-selfing through the discipline of attention' (ibid.: 333).[2] Conradi explains that Murdoch's reinterpretation is that

> human beings inhabit a cloud of egoistic fantasy, designed to protect the psyche from pain ... The power of imaginative attention alone can – albeit with difficulty – cut through this fantastic reverie and start to reveal the world and its inhabitants more accurately. (Ibid.: 333)

So, unlike the existentialist hero, occupying a world of his own and choosing whatever he wants, real freedom is 'the total absence of concern for Self, the energy of which is burnt up in its strenuous effort to proceed towards the Good, which is to say the Real' (ibid.: 333). The transcendent good will be looked at in detail in the next chapter, but here it is vital to note the difference between Murdoch and Sartre's existentialist project in this respect. As Ana Lita writes, Murdoch 'wishes to renew our sense of the difficulty and complexity of the moral life in dealing with particular persons' (Lita 2004: 1), whereas Murdoch's understanding of Sartre's existentialism pictures 'the fearful solitude of the individual marooned upon a tiny island in the middle of a sea of scientific facts, and morally escaping from science only by a wild leap of the will' (IP: 321). This description stresses isolation, reliance upon science, and freedom to charge off in any direction desired. This is not the kind of individual that Murdoch believes we are. For Murdoch, we are far more situated and embedded in relation to others: 'The individual life must be shown to be related to its historical surroundings, by a continuous to and fro *mediation* by various paths between the general and the particular, which would reveal the place and nature of free choice' (SRR: 27). Murdoch is concerned with an individual who is in relation with others, but who is decentring. As an example, Murdoch favours the idea of 'de-individualised individual of Buddhism or mystical Christianity' (MGM: 352). As Julia Meszaros explains, in Kierkegaard, Murdoch finds 'a particularly formative and existentially relevant conversation partner' (Meszaros 2016: 41). Meszaros continues,

> His insistence that thought must serve life, and that we cannot speak of faith (or, in her case, goodness) in impersonal terms, is close to her own concerns. By his life and art, Murdoch finds, Kierkegaard is an *example* – outdone only, perhaps, by Simone Weil. (Ibid.: 42)

This is indicative of the complex situation of the Murdochian individual: she or he is historically and socially situated in relation to others and their times, but is selfish and deluded. This delusion, however, can be overcome by following the path to the 'true and full selfhood' through the relation with the transcendent Good – with which we are already in relation (ibid.: 44). Our freedom, therefore, is related to our obedience to the transcendent, and our moral lives occur and develop in the actions of waiting and attention, as emphasised by Murdoch repeating Weil's claim that 'we should pay attention to such a point that we no longer have the choice' ('Knowing the Void' (KV): 159). Murdoch argues that 'until we become good we are at the mercy of mechanical forces' and that 'we make advances by resisting the mechanism: but there is no reward' (KV: 158). She directly adopts Weil's notion of attention and hence of love as 'an orientation, a direction of energy, not just a state of mind' (Meszaros 2016: 52).

It is important to appreciate that Murdoch does not adopt Weil wholesale. She distances herself from the 'extremism' that Weil practised in her own life (MGM: 247). Murdoch writes that the personality which emerges from Weil's writings 'is not always attractive, but it compels respect' (KV: 159–60). As Sabina Lovibond notes, Murdoch is 'well disposed towards a notion of rights' (Lovibond 2011: 34), whereas Weil rebukes the notion of rights (Weil 2002a: 4). Weil was committed to solidarity with the poor and the afflicted, but Murdoch was also concerned about happiness. Murdoch believed that 'There are worse ends than the pursuit of an unexacting happiness' (MGM: 86). And she described how 'a Benthamite utilitarian conception of happiness must not . . . be eroded by high-minded considerations about quality of happiness or by theories which make happiness invisible' (MGM: 483). As Meszaros notes, then, 'despite her great respect for Weil, Murdoch thus ultimately senses the need to balance Weil's understanding of love as selfless attention with a greater and more worldly concern for the individual, and his needs, desires, and happiness' (Meszaros 2016: 53). Meszaros continues,

> Murdoch carves out a path between Sartre and Weil that avoids the one-sided extremes of both. Arguing that we best affirm ourselves by loving the Good, she rejects Sartre's notion that we can affirm ourselves single-handedly. Yet she does so without uprooting erotic desire from the human person and her love, and without devaluing the human self, its individuality, and its potential for personal growth. (Ibid.: 176)

So, although not seeking reward, or attaining reward from others, 'selfless love may in fact build up the self' (ibid.: 176). This objectual attention, or direction of thought towards the other, in our daily lives and complex social networks, thereby enables the recognition of the other as they are, and with respect. As Murdoch writes,

> This picture of cognition which 'favours the object' also favours conceptions of truthfulness, of sacredness, of respect and duty and love which belong to ordinary traditional morality and might be more clearly expressed (as they are by Simone Weil) in ordinary-language reflections without the compulsory use of Hegelian-Marxist terminology. It suggests a philosophy better suited to a world in which respect for rights (human rights, rights of citizens, rights of blacks, rights of gays, rights of whales) has made innumerable places for the meeting of theory and practice. (SRR: 37)

This is old-fashioned language perhaps, but it demonstrates the contingency and variability of Murdoch's moral thinking about our lives as individuals and our duties to others in their variety. This in turn signals the contemporary relevance of Murdoch's thought, and the possibilities for it as a mode of ethical looking at contemporary films. Lovibond highlights the fact that a central idea in Murdoch's thinking is that 'we have to work at *removing the impediments* to correct thinking, these impediments arising from an improper influence exerted on judgement by "the appetitive part of the soul"' (Lovibond 2015: 243). Murdoch writes that 'in the moral life, the enemy is the fat relentless ego' (OGG: 342), and moral philosophy is concerned with its defeat. Lovibond summarises thus: 'This is a freedom that moves towards the ideal limit of *perfect* responsiveness to reality, and hence, paradoxically, of "obedience" (to the objective requirements of one's situation)' (ibid.: 244). This is encapsulated in Murdoch's pronouncement, 'If I attend properly I will have no choices and this is the ultimate condition to be aimed at' (IP: 331). We will now think about how making such moral progress, or remaining a fat relentless ego, can be seen in cinema. Murdoch describes a particular hero that we are all familiar with:

> We know this novel and its hero well. The story of the lonely brave man, defiant without optimism . . . whose mode of being is a deep criticism of society. He is an adventurer. He is godless. He does not suffer from guilt. He thinks of himself as free. He may have his faults, he may be self-assertive or even violent, but he has sincerity and courage, and for this we forgive him. (D. H. Lawrence, E. Hemingway, A. Camus, J. P. Sartre, K. Amis . . .). (E&M: 225)

For Murdoch, this is the hero of the existentialist novel. She distinguishes him from the hero of what she calls the mystical novel:

> Whereas the existentialist hero is an anxious man trying to impose or assert or find himself, the mystical hero is an anxious man trying to discipline or purge or diminish himself. The chief temptation of the former is egoism, of the latter masochism. The philosophical background or protective symbolism is fairly clear in each case. The first hero is the new version of the romantic man, the man of power, abandoned by God, struggling on bravely, sincerely and alone. This image consoles by showing us man as strong, self-reliant and uncrushable. The second hero is the new version of the man of faith, believing in goodness without religious guarantees, guilty, muddled, yet not without hope. This image consoles by showing us man as frail, godless, and yet possessed of genuine intuitions of an authoritative good. (E&M: 227)

These two types are helpful for teasing out the elements of the journey of a protagonist and what the source of their moral vision is, as well as the values that guide their choices. Elsewhere, Murdoch differentiates between 'ordinary language man' and 'totalitarian man'. For the former, 'a man is what he observedly does' ('The Sublime and the Beautiful Revisited' (SBR): 268), and for the latter, virtue is 'the unillusioned exercise of complete freedom' (ibid.: 268–9). Both of these figures are solipsistic: 'Neither pictures virtue as concerned with anything real outside ourselves. Neither provides us with a standpoint for considering real human beings in their variety, and neither presents us with any technique for exploring and controlling our own spiritual energy' (SBR: 269). For Murdoch, this is 'an empty lonely freedom' (IP: 321). This type of hero, which Murdoch is identifying mainly as being in novels, is not an example for us as they are not what we are like: 'what place, one might ask, is left in this stern picture of solitary all-responsible man for the life of emotions?' (SGC: 366). Our emotions are significant and important to understand as potential impediments to just thinking: 'We are anxiety-ridden animals. Our minds are continually active, fabricating an anxious, usually self-preoccupied, often falsifying *veil* which partially conceals the world' (SGC: 369). The classic existential hero of film noir has survived across the decades in many forms, and indeed, in 2015, Rowan Righelato declared that an existential hero comeback was in full swing in the hands of filmmakers such as Michael Mann, Paul Schrader and Sean Penn (2015). The three less conventional film protagonists I am going to consider contain elements, in various configurations, of all the heroes that Murdoch outlines. I want to argue that the films enable us to see how they construct their moral worlds and to come to understand, through our close attention and understanding, how they make the decisions that they do. In this way, the films not only illustrate some of Murdoch's ideas, but the protagonists act as objects for us to learn from. Through the ethical challenges presented by these individuals to us, we are able to reflect upon the bases for their actions, and the principles that guide them. This in turn may affect or develop our own moral contemplations.

A FAT RELENTLESS EGO: *CLOUDS OF SILS MARIA*

Maria (Juliette Binoche) is a successful actress, who is self-centred, temperamental and a demanding employer of a long-suffering personal assistant, Valentine (Kristen Stewart). Her journey, as such, is not one from self-centred egotism to decentring; rather the film acts more as a morality tale about remaining on a cloud of egoism. The protagonist therefore more resembles Murdoch's understanding of a fat relentless ego, veiled and impeded from thinking of others, than a straightforward existential hero or heroine. The film opens on a train, with Val on the telephone managing Maria's work arrangements, making apologies for her, liaising about diary commitments and divorce papers: in other words, fielding Maria's stressful encounters, and having stress of her own with poor mobile reception. Val buys her coffee and water, so is caring for her personal needs too. She enters Maria's train compartment, and Maria instantly says, 'Did you read this article about Google and how it uses private information? It's disgraceful, they're too powerful.' She is relaxing and thinking about world events, while her assistant manages her life. She is rejecting action roles, saying she doesn't want to do any more 'hanging from wires and acting in front of green screens – I've outgrown it'. She checks arrangements for an interview, but barely bothers to remember the interviewer's name. She is happy with her agenda, but she wants to run through the first draft of her speech. It is about her old friend and mentor Wilhelm to be given at an awards ceremony for him, but also about her and his importance in her life. He gave her the famous role of Sigrid in the play and the film, and 'everything she needed to build a career on – my career'. She wants help from Val, but she does say, 'It is my tribute to him I have to find my own words.' Then she agrees to take a phone call from her husband's ('Creep's') lawyer about her divorce. While she is speaking, Val takes another call. She looks worried and goes to find Maria, who won't talk to her; the call is to tell her bad news. She shows Maria a sign saying 'Wilhelm has died'. So, the celebratory event will now be very different. Val says, 'Who could do him justice better than you – you love him'; Maria says 'I love him. I know so little about him.' Rosa (Wilhelm's widow) calls, and she tells Maria they think it was a heart attack. We see the frozen body being loaded into an ambulance. As Maria arrives at the station she says she is going to head right back to the hotel, as she says, 'I have to think it over, everything is hitting me at once.' As she arrives in the hotel room she sits down and manages the room without doing anything herself: 'Can we turn this off, and no fruit thank you.' This is a woman who is used to telling people what she wants and expects to get it. She does not ask after other people, or consider the needs of others; rather she expects attention and to be the focus of the situation.

We see Maria picking out jewellery and clothes for a fashion shoot, as we see Rosa leave the morgue on her own, arrive home on her own, and burn notebooks from Wilhelm's desk. Their experiences of this man's death are very different: Rosa is having to think of Wilhelm; Maria needs only to think of how the man's life and its loss relates to her. When they speak, Rosa tells Maria that Wilhelm had an illness, and so he killed himself.

Maria arrives at the tribute event. Her ex-lover Henrik is going to be interviewed about his plays before he will also pay tribute to Wilhelm. Maria is angry with him because they had an affair when she was eighteen and she didn't hear from him again until she was famous. We see Maria follow Henrik on stage to applause, say thank you, and then we cut to Maria arriving at the post-event reception. She gets out of the car (ignoring the person who opens the car door for her), and says coolly but charmingly to the host, 'It's great that you celebrate his work, especially today.' There is a new director here who wants to persuade Maria to play a role to which she has already said no. Val asks permission to go and meet the photographer from the shoot, which is met with gentle teasing by Maria.

Klaus (Lars Eidinger), the new director, wants Maria to act in the play that she did for Wilhelm when she was eighteen years old. The play is about two women, the young Sigrid, and the older Helena who falls obsessively in love with her. Maria played Sigrid when she was eighteen, and says, 'In some way I am still Sigrid . . . Sigrid is free, beyond everything, and . . . destructive, unpredictable, and right or wrong, I've always identified with that freedom – it's a way of protecting myself.' Now, Klaus wants her to play the older woman, Helena. Maria says, 'Helena is forty, she runs a company, she falls head over heels in love with a girl who doesn't love her and drives her to suicide – yes, she's completely the opposite.' Maria concedes that she is Helena's age, but that doesn't mean she can play her: 'Time's gone by and she can't accept it – me neither I guess.' For Klaus, however, 'Sigrid and Helena are one and the same person. That's what the play is about. Because you were Sigrid only you can be Helena now.' A young actress, Jo-Ann Ellis (Chloë Grace Moretz), who is a scandal-hit A-list celebrity, apparently admires Maria and is willing to pull out of other commitments to play the role. Maria answers, 'I've listened carefully. But to be honest, the role scares me. Helena scares me. I'm in the middle of a divorce, I'm vulnerable – probably too vulnerable to do this.' The director Klaus tries emotional blackmail, saying that not playing it will be a missed opportunity, 'especially for Wilhelm'. But Maria also has another reason. The actress who played Helena opposite her Sigrid died in a car accident a year after, and she admits she is superstitious about it. Klaus brutally says, 'Her conventional style of acting highlighted the modernity of your performance; you should be grateful to her.' Klaus is unsentimental, and clearly determined to persuade Maria to play the role in his production. At dinner, her ex-lover Henrik, who she has tried to avoid, is seated next to her. He also discusses the role of Helena and has some insights, but Maria disagrees with him. She says the play is about what attracts the women to each other, and that the impossibility of their relationship is as cruel for Sigrid as it is for Helena. Henrik insists that Helena is not used to being turned down: 'She discovers her own frailty and she can't accept it.' Maria is clearly beginning to consider playing the role. Henrik strokes her hand and asks her if she wants a nightcap, but she laughs at him. As they part, however, she gives Henrik a piece of paper with her room number and he looks surprised. Back in her room, she drinks miniatures from the minibar and she searches for Jo-Ann Ellis on Google, so we know she's hooked.

An intertitle announces this is 'PART TWO', which is set in the Alps. Maria has a short cropped haircut. Val is driving, as Maria has her eyes shut. They pull into a garage, and Val fills up the car with petrol. Maria wakes up, and Val apologises for the fact that she went wrong on the journey, but Maria is lost in herself. Maria says she had a dream, they were 'already rehearsing, the past and the present were blending together'. So she has clearly accepted the role, but she is already saying, 'I shouldn't have said yes to Klaus.' Val says, 'He is a sick director, Jo-Ann's a superstar. It pays well'; she responds, 'I don't need the money.'

The Alpine scenery is exquisite, and they arrive at a beautiful house, meeting Rosa there. Of course, Val handles the bags. Rosa likes the fact that Maria is working on the role of Helena here in Wilhelm's house, which is where it was written. As they walk in the mountains, they emerge as small figures within hills, before the lake where Rosa tells Maria that this is where Wilhelm killed himself, saying, 'but that stays between you and me'. This is the Maloja Pass, and they discuss the snake-like cloud formation that apparently foretells bad weather. Then, back at the house, we see a film of the Maloja Snake from 1924.[3] As they watch it on the television, Rosa says Wilhelm was fascinated by this film, and that the true nature of the landscape revealed itself in these images. For Maria, however, there is a block between her and the film. She says that the black and white creates a distance, which says the passing of the time. Rosa says it is almost a century old, that actually it comes from very far away, and that that is the beauty of it. Rosa then leaves them at the house, and gives Maria something that belonged to Wilhelm.

Val and Maria get drunk over dinner, and Val grills Maria as to whether anything happened with Wilhelm. Maria says he chose her for the part so he must have felt something but it remained unspoken. Maria says it isn't important, and laughs, as Val says, 'If that isn't important what the fuck is important.' This is peculiar, as, outside Rosa, Wilhelm and Maria, it really doesn't seem that important. This shows how much Val is part of the circle surrounding and supporting Maria, shoring up the sense of her importance. As Val pushes her, Maria concedes that she 'was attracted to Wilhelm but it's normal. I was fine with just feeling attracted and with the intimacy.' When Val says she was in love with him, Maria replies, 'Stop oversimplifying, it was less than that . . . maybe I only remember what I want to remember.'

Val goes through Maria's work offers which do not sound like a range of great roles: opening a shopping mall, modelling eye glasses (only in Latin America, she says), playing a mother superior in a Spanish horror film with werewolves; an interview with an Italian magazine tackling 'active women's seduction after forty', on the cover, shot by Mario Testino. Maria is not interested in any of them. Jo-Ann Ellis wants to meet and so they discuss her celebrity and reputation: stories about getting wasted, having a gun, shooting up her boyfriend's place, needing to be subdued. As Maria says, this is 'not exactly how Klaus described her'. It seems she has been to rehab to get out of going to prison: Val says she has a theatrical background, but jumped off the rails and went wild. Maria says to Val that she could have told her, but Val says, 'I love her, she's not completely antiseptic like the rest of Hollywood.' Maria can't see her cigarettes even though they are right in front of her, and Val hands them to her. They argue about Jo-Ann, until Val says she's probably her favourite actress, which brings Maria up short: 'Ah, you mean more than me.' Maria is offended. She sulkily challenges, 'I'm more conventional, boring, I can't reach her intensity.' Val says she didn't say that, but Maria goes to bed and watches videos of Jo-Ann on YouTube. These videos show her in a press conference saying in an offhand but malicious way that she's in a play with Maria Enders, who plays the older woman and 'I'm the younger woman who drives her to suicide' with a sadistic grin. Maria roars with laughter at the girl's attitude, suggesting shock but also confident amusement.

The next day, Maria and Val begin rehearsing the play. Maria makes a mistake and has a crisis, saying there are too many memories of Susan Rosenberg, the woman who played Helena opposite her, and the disgust she feels 'as she was slipping into the skin of this defeated woman'. Maria feels that everything in the play is weighted to make Sigrid look good. Val reassures her, saying, 'I didn't read it like that; I see her arrogance, her cruelty, and Helena's humanity; she's able to talk about her own pain, it's moving.' Val acts as an interpreter of the play, but also a coach and a conscience.

When Val wants to go to meet Burt the photographer, she worries about whether Maria will be alright alone. Maria, in turn, worries that Val will be safe on the mountain roads at night. Val says Maria is jealous, of her thoughts and her time. Maria says that is not the case and that she is glad she has a boyfriend, as there haven't been that many and she burns through them pretty fast. This relationship is increasingly blurred in terms of the boundaries between employer and employee, co-workers, friends, even parent and child. When Val goes out, Maria runs upstairs and watches her drive away. Then we see her spending some time on her own. She writes 'Maloja Snake' on a pad. Then we see her FaceTiming her agent complaining about the play, saying she cannot play Helena, because, 'I wanna stay Sigrid'; he says 'Sigrid is twenty.' She asks her agent to get her out of it and he says it won't be cheap.

As Val is driving home in the daybreak, accompanied by a Primal Scream track, 'Kowalski', she pulls over to the roadside and vomits. She smokes, and she's distressed: she clearly has not had a good date. At this time, we are treated to a vision of the Maloja Snake. To the same incongruous music, we see the cloud formation wind its way through the pass, the 'head' of it rearing up, the 'body' moving through in a stately, stunning, formation of natural wonder. This scene is for us alone. Val is hastening home, hungover and miserable, Maria is undoubtedly asleep back at the house. So, as film viewers, we are treated to this spectacle; and it works to take us out of the hothouse of Maria and Val's relationship, and the self-centredness of Maria's concerns, and shows us, and involves us, in this moment of exquisite natural beauty. This is the film's Murdochian 'kestrel' moment, and I will return to discuss its role more fully at the end of this section. Back at the house, we see Maria's feet creeping down the stairs to see Val crashed out on her bed.

The next day Maria and Val go to see Jo-Ann's latest film, which is a science fiction adventure. They go to a casino afterwards, have a few beers, and discuss the film. Maria says she could feel her brain cells dying, and it's such a stupid character. Val says she's fascinating, and begins to talk about the character's superpowers, at which Maria bursts out laughing. Val tries to convince her of the merits of the film, but Maria can't stop laughing at Val's argument, so she gives up. At the gambling table, they relate more like a couple, as Val queries, 'All of it?' when Maria puts all her money down. And then outside, as they drive away, Val crashes into a car: they are both drunk, and Maria says, 'Go, go, go!' They make it home and Maria forces Val to discuss Jo-Ann. She wants to know what she has to do to make Val admire her more: clearly the comment still rankles, as a slight to Maria's ego. We might be reminded of Murdoch's 'damage to my prestige' that she is resentful about before she is taken out of herself by the kestrel (SGC: 369). Val says that you can't be as accomplished as Maria is and still hold on to the privileges of youth, to which Maria replies, 'So I'm allowed to not be old so long as I don't wanna be young, is that it?' Val says, 'Yah, I don't know, I guess so, totally, well put', and goes to bed. Maria wants to carry on talking, and to hear about the date with Burt, but Val says she does not have the energy. There is increasing evidence that Val is growing tired of the egoflattery that Maria demands. Maria seems to be clinging to her own past, the past of the play and the role she played in it, and her stature as being at the top of her profession. She does not want to admit that these are in the past now, and seems to struggle with the idea of ageing and that older things, like the Maloja Snake film, are of value.

The next day the pair walk in the Alps, rehearsing a scene. They sit in the spot where Wilhelm killed himself. Their conversation has some echoes of their relationship, crossing over between their job and their personal life, but there is no suggestion of sexual attraction between Val and Maria. Val knows the role and has brought sandwiches; she physically teases Maria with the sandwiches by holding them out and pulling them back, like one might do with a child. Maria complains that she doesn't believe the scene; it is too theoretical and phoney. Val offers her interpretation, but Maria does not agree. They fall asleep, and are woken by a goat! They need to head off, as the sun is going down. Maria says she knows a steep way, Val disagrees, but Maria takes no notice and keeps going. Relations now appear to have deteriorated between the two. Val says,

> You don't have to keep me on if you find my ideas simplistic . . . If you find my point of view uninteresting, I don't know what I'm doing here . . . you hate the play, you hate her, you don't have to take it out on me. I'm just doing my job.

They travel back on the bus without speaking. They have more rehearsals and discussion of the character, but they continue to disagree, and Val has had enough of Maria's intensity; she says she has her own interpretation of the play which is just confusing things. Maria asks her to stay and hugs her, but she says no.

In the next scene, we see Jo-Ann and her boyfriend at a music recital in a high-class hotel, before they meet up with Maria and Val. Jo-Ann says things to Maria such as, 'I don't think you know how much this means to me' and 'I'm incredibly intimidated to take on your role'; she also says it is incredibly brave of Maria to take on the role of Helena. Jo-Ann drinks chamomile tea, is dressed in a demure outfit, and seems sweet and respectful. Maria is totally won over by the flattery, and says to Val when they leave that she thought they were really nice. Val observes, 'They spent the whole evening flattering you', to which Maria says, 'That has nothing to do with it', and Val replies, 'Of course not.' However, Val has seen the obvious display, and Maria has been blind to it, believing the flattery, because it is precisely what she wants to hear.

The next morning they are up at daybreak in the snow to see the Snake. As they walk, they argue about the meaning of the play, and Val says, 'The text is like an object; it's going to change perspective depending on where you're standing.' They climb up to see the Snake, but Val doesn't appear to make it. Maria is there on her own, straining her eyes looking for the Snake but she sees just mist, then she thinks she sees the Snake, then she's not sure. For the first time in the film she calls her assistant by her name, and says, 'What the hell are you doing?' She goes shouting after her, but Val has gone (Figure 4.1). Val and Maria both miss the Snake. We, however, see the Snake's majestic progression, to the suitable crescendos of Pachelbel's Canon.

Figure 4.1 Maria Enders (Juliette Binoche) realises Val has left, in *Clouds of Sils Maria* (2014), directed by Olivier Assayas.

The next intertitle announces it is the 'EPILOGUE', in London a few weeks later. Maria meets Klaus, and there is a big drama because Jo-Ann's boyfriend's wife has tried to kill herself. Klaus says he has had a long conversation with Wilhelm's widow, Rosa. He's seen Wilhelm's last texts, which puts a new spin on the play, and he wants to update the play, 'to think like Wilhelm'. Jo-Ann comes, and Chris the boyfriend arrives too, so their celebrity scandal totally takes over the meal and Klaus hurries them out to a waiting car. Their car is all set to leave without Maria, it seems, but she runs round to the other side and gets in. She is certainly the least important person at the scene. Next we see her back at her hotel, with a new assistant running her schedule. Maria has the offer of a new role – the lead – of a hybrid, set in the twenty-third century. Surprisingly, Maria says she's interested. The new assistant offers to rehearse with her. She says of the play's new scenes – which she's had for two weeks – that she wants to keep them spontaneous. It's how she prepared twenty years ago as Sigrid: 'If he asks you, tell him I think they're very good.' This suggests he has not asked Maria what she thinks of them, because it does not matter to him.

At the theatre, Maria speaks to Jo-Ann and asks her to pause for a second in the play at a certain point, and Jo-Ann replies, brutally and with relish, 'No one gives a fuck about Helena at this point right? I mean it's pretty clear to me this poor woman's all washed up, I mean your character, not you . . . I think they want what comes next.' Maria says, 'I think I'm lost in my memories . . . you think you've forgotten your old habits, but they come back . . . I have to break them.' Jo-Ann says patronisingly, 'I guess you do', in a way that shows she really doesn't care at all. She has shown herself to be far more like the girl in the online press conference than the demure flatterer at the hotel meeting.

In her dressing room, Maria sees the new director about the part of the hybrid. She says to him, 'When I read it I imagined someone much younger, maybe me younger, but you're seeing me in movies that were made years ago – I've changed.' He says of the character, 'She has no age, or, she's every age at once, like all of us.' Maria says, 'Can I be frank – I was thinking about Jo-Ann – she's modern'. The director says his character isn't modern, but outside time, and that he doesn't like his era. Again, the words of professional flattery seem likely to work on Maria.

The final scene of the film is as the play is about to start, with Maria sitting in her on-stage office as Helena. She sits still, breathing, waiting to start. Maria arrives at the end of the film in some ways in a different state from what she was at the beginning, being able to make comments about her age and perspective with some insight, but it is hard to tell how much she has changed. She has a new assistant, a replacement Val, and she appears to be acquiescent with her colleagues. Jo-Ann has confronted Maria with her lack of respect for Helena, and by extension Maria herself, saying, 'They want what comes next' – which is her, Jo-Ann. Because we see Maria in character as Helena in the final shot of the film, it is difficult to assess her state of mind, but we see from her conversation in her dressing room with the new director that she realises she has changed. The progress of the film, and Maria's journey, recalls Murdoch's analysis of Sartre's heroes. Murdoch writes, 'Sartre takes his heroes up to the point of insight, realisation, despair – and there he leaves them. They may fall back, but they do not know how to go on' (SRR: 60).

What sort of journey has Maria been on during the film? Has she deepened her vision and pierced the veil of her fat relentless ego? On top of the mountain at Maloja Pass, crying out for Val, Maria is in a state of despair, and the film leaves her there, for that section. She is looking for the Snake but cannot see it. She has been oblivious to the presence of Val to the extent that she does not even realise that she has left her. Maria is an image of isolated self-absorption: with little insight into her own vanity and without the ability to pay attention to others. Her love for Wilhelm remains focused on the role he played in her life, choosing her for the role of Sigrid, setting up her career, and her distaste at playing Helena reflects her unwillingness to confront ageing and vulnerability. Her pique at Val's admiration for Jo-Ann reveals her competitiveness and her jealousy, and her response to Jo-Ann's flattery reveals her willingness to be consoled. Maria is Murdoch's description of a Sartrean hero(ine): 'The individual is the centre, but a solipsistic centre. He has a *dream* of human companionship, but never the experience. He touches others at the fingertips' (SRR: 63). The companionship Maria has with Wilhelm is like a dream, and that with Val is like touching at the fingertips. There seems to be a bond with Rosa, but she says she may not come to London to see the play, and also shows Wilhelm's last texts to Klaus, not Maria. So that relationship is not as close as perhaps Maria dreams it is. The scene where they all watch the film of the Maloja Snake is telling, as Rosa is sharing this favourite of Wilhelm's with Maria, who can only comment upon the distancing effect of the black and white film, rather than the majestic, timeless majesty of the Snake, or the fact that Wilhelm loved it so much. This suggests her concern remains preoccupied with a dislike of 'old things' and an inability to see beyond her own discomfort and interrupted vision. So, Maria does 'fall back' and 'go on', unlike Murdoch's expectation of a Sartrean hero, but there is little evidence that she knows how to do so differently. It has taken an offensive and dismissive insult spoken directly to her face by the current incarnation of her younger self to make her show some humility about needing to break old habits: but whether she will, or whether she can, is left to be explored beyond the film's closure.

A FREEDOM TO CHOOSE AND ACT DIFFERENTLY: *ONCE UPON A TIME IN ANATOLIA*

This is a film that demands effort and attention from the viewer, showing us scenes where unselfing does not occur, and where egocentric solipsism reigns. The film also demands that we pay attention to the plight of another, Dr Cemal (Muhammet Uzuner), and develop a moral view that strives to understand the decision that he takes. The film begins with a direct focus on obscured vision: looking through a window onto the life of others, perhaps in a cell, certainly a scruffy room. A television casts a blue light in the corner, traditional Turkish music can be discerned, three men clink glasses and eat together, drinking raki. It looks convivial. In fact this encounter will end in the murder of one of the men, and we next see the hunt for the body.

    A long-distance establishing shot shows a still landscape interrupted by looming car headlights, glowing like bulbs on a string, or glow-worms. The cars pull up, as we will see them do several times over the course of the next three hours, and thus begins the challenging, repetitive search in this barren, unforgiving and featureless landscape for the site where the killer has buried the body of the man he killed. The film is a police procedural, but not a whodunit – we know this from the outset – rather it is more of a 'wheredunnit'. Along the way, the group of men – for on the surface the film is almost exclusively about men – negotiate their roles in the drama, and disclose their visions and values.

    The scenes inside the car establish the men's roles and places in the systems of local law enforcement and civil service. There are four men involved in the conversation, in the course of their duties, two in the front, and two in the back. Their tone is quite light and workaday; but between them on the back seat is the gaunt criminal, the killer Kenan (Firat Tanis), hardly able to keep his eyes open with exhaustion and horror. He has dark circles, a gash on his face, and sits hunched and haunted. The camera moves in slowly, almost imperceptibly, on this figure, as he struggles to stay awake, while the others talk about cheese and yoghurt, and possible prostate problems, and how often they urinate.

It emerges that Kenan cannot remember where he left the body because he was drunk and also because the landscape is so featureless, especially at night. The quiet, observing, Dr Cemal is emerging as a slightly separate character. He smiles along with the chit-chat, but stays behind the group at the scenes where they look for the body. He has authority on the medical matters clearly, and the others are identified as the prosecutor, Nusret (Taner Birsal), as well as the policeman, Commissar Naci (Yilmaz Erdogan), local police and others from the village, and the suspects. This is a gruesome journey, but there is humour here too. When the policeman's phone rings, his ringtone is the theme from *Love Story*, and on the other end is his angry wife shouting at him, who he calls 'sweetie'. There is also banality, interspersed with moments that might appear surreal or poetic. As Dr Cemal urinates next to a rock, there is a lightning flash that illuminates a vast face carved in the stone right next to him. It is an incredibly surprising moment, which shocks Cemal and us, and its meaning is unclear. Is the suggestion that with light you see what is really there? Or that the past is always present in your life and will outlive you? The troop certainly contemplate their place in time on their journey, comparing themselves with Solomon who lived for 750 years, considering the recurrence of the rain, and reflecting on how short life is. And they discuss how things change, including the idea that these events with which they are now concerned will become a story, saying, 'You can tell it like a fairy tale' (consistent with the film's title). There are intimations, therefore, that this is a story for the ages, not just of this particular time and place.

There are slow-moving shots of extreme long-distance beauty, such as when a train of lights passes across the desert, and exquisitely pictorial shots of the vast landscape; but there are also small moments of contemplation seemingly unrelated to the film's main action. A beautiful apple rolls off a tree, bounces down the hill, and floats along a stream, bobbing, then joins others caught up on the rocks that are simply rotting. Is this an overdetermined metaphor? It is certainly a shot that commands attention and it takes us out of the immediate situation. Perhaps is it a comment on randomness, or the fate of an individual; perhaps it is an observation on loss of hope, or that everything is heading towards death as soon as it is born.

The party stops in a village overnight and shares dinner with the locals, hearing about the villagers' problems, their worries about money, and marriages. The mayor of the village has a young daughter, who silently serves the men tea. She has a profound effect on each of the men, variously elicited by her youth, her proximity, her silence and her beauty. This is an uncomfortable and telling sequence, drawing attention to the repression and exploitation of this young woman. As the prosecutor says to the doctor: 'She'll fade away in this godforsaken place' – like the apple perhaps? Meanwhile, Commissar Naci is effectively torturing Kenan by sleep deprivation. This whirling windy little village takes on the appearance of an existential maelstrom, or a long dark night of the soul. Prosecutor Nusret tells Dr Cemal a story about a woman he knew who predicted when she was going to die. He spent hours, he says, trying to get to the bottom of why 'the gorgeous woman' who had predicted her death did die when she said she would. This supports the idea of women as mystical, tragic and dangerous, which the film projects. The doctor asks rational, scientific questions: 'Why was there not an autopsy? No one dies because they say they will.' The prosecutor says there was nothing suspicious, so 'Why carve up a beautiful young woman for no reason?' This story will be returned to later.

The next morning they discover the body, and now everybody starts to play the role they are employed to: practicality reigns. The prosecutor observes, photographs are taken, they dig up the body, which has been hogtied. Naci becomes angry with Kenan, and calls him a 'sadistic shit'. He shouts at Kenan that he is not human, and that he deserves to be tied up like the body. Dr Cemal is called upon to comment for the crime scene report. The prosecutor says the corpse looks like Clark Gable. He looks up and giggles, others join in, and he says to the clerk, 'Abidin, you got that?' The clerk says, 'You know you look a bit like Clark Gable, Mr Prosecutor?', and the prosecutor relays how he was called Clark at college. He loves this recollection, and strokes his moustache, indicative of his moment of vanity. This is one of the moments that, as Florence Jacobowitz writes, 'evidences the filmmaker's aesthetic of humanist art' (2012: 61). Commissar Naci says, 'Whenever you find a can of worms, look for a woman', and Dr Cemal looks at him disbelievingly. However, it emerges that the altercation leading to death happened because Kenan, the killer, is the real father of the victim's son. This is the revelation that leads to change in the moral picture of Dr Cemal's world.

They get back to town and as they arrive there is some disorder. Kenan sees a woman and a boy, who throws a stone at Kenan's face. This is Kenan's son, who believes Kenan has just killed his father, Yasar. The boy's face is a picture of rage and pain, and his mother puts her arm around him, looking Kenan in the eyes. We then move away from the main business of the film, to spend some time with Dr Cemal in his office. He turns on his computer, and images fill the film screen: his ex-wife, him as a student with friends, as a boy by the sea, then we see that he is looking at a bundle of photographs of the people in his life. He looks out of the window at a cat, foraging around near a bin, then he gets up to go over to the wardrobe. He looks up, and suddenly looks us straight in the eye. The film breaks the fourth wall, in a direct and stunning facial close-up. This is a gripping connection with this character and his contemplations. He is looking directly at us, and he frowns slightly

Figure 4.2 Dr Cemal (Muhammet Uzuner) looks us straight in the eye, in *Once Upon a Time in Anatolia* (2011), directed by Nuri Bilge Ceylan.

(Figure 4.2). What does he see? He has seen his life captured in a few images, moments, relationships. The look at us challenges us to think about his lot, but also ours: what constitutes our life, what do we value?

Naci comes in for a prescription for his son, and reiterates that it looks like Kenan is the boy's father. He says to Cemal, 'It's the kids that suffer in the end. The kids pay for the sins of the adults.' Cemal goes to a hammam, wiping his eyes, and peering through the steam. He watches people in the village, sweeping the street, passing the houses. He sees smoke coming from a chimney, indicative of domestic activity, and birds nesting in a gutter: he pays attention to the world around him and is moved by it. He seems to have status among the locals, and he speaks to some in a café about the case. This sequence has conveyed Cemal's reflection upon the case, his efforts to see clearly, to 'really look', and the report he must file. Back at the hospital, he peeks in the kitchen and sees the boy eating, so the chef has given him breakfast. Yasar's wife is sitting outside in the corridor, and her foot is bouncing with agitation: she is on edge, but nobody speaks to her other than to get her to identify the body as her late husband. So what we are seeing here is aligned with Cemal's perception of the situation.

The impending autopsy weighs very heavily on Dr Cemal and Nusret: but so does the death of 'the gorgeous woman' whom the prosecutor spoke of earlier in the village. Nusret cannot believe how 'sceptical' the doctor is, but it emerges, as the story develops, that the woman had caught her husband with another woman. Nusret asks, 'Would a person kill themselves to punish another person?' Dr Cemal replies, 'Aren't most suicides to punish another?' The prosecutor says calmly, 'Bravo. That's what I thought.' It was, of course, Prosecutor Nusret's wife, and this conclusion makes him weep. He has been consoling himself with the idea that these events were mystical: that the woman possessed some special metaphysical power to ensure her death at the hour she predicted. In fact, Dr Cemal has confronted him with the probability of his wife's suicide. Their world views were opposed, like Murdoch's existential and mystical heroes. The prosecutor's vision of his own role in his wife's suicide is still obscured, as he says the infidelity was nothing, and that 'some women can be very ruthless'. The film has, however, drawn attention to his process of self-delusion, his role in the harm done to another and his refusal to accept blame for the suicide of his wife. But the film is not suggesting that the scientific, medical mindset has all the answers.

The final sequence of events in the film concerns the autopsy. The mortician complains about his equipment, saying he has recently seen another hospital that has a fabulous morgue with great autopsy instruments, such as an electric rechargeable saw. This demonstrates his workmanlike view on matters and lack of emotional investment in the job at hand. They begin the dissection of Yasar's body. They cut off his clothes, which are described in complete detail. He is not wearing underpants, and the mortician and the clerk crack a joke about him being 'ready for action', but Dr Cemal expresses his disapproval. The sounds of the body being dissected are viscerally realistic, with loud cracking and squelching noises. There is intense medical detail concerning the process, the thorax, taking the heart out, and then they find dirt in the windpipe. This suggests he was buried alive.

The doctor looks out of the window and considers his report. He says, 'No abnormalilties.' The mortician queries him, and exchanges a look with the clerk, but Dr Cemal insists. They move on to dissect the stomach, and blood spurts onto the doctor's face. He is thereby affected by the dead man's state directly and physically. He watches the boy out of the window, kicking a ball back to other children in the playground, with Yasar's blood on his face, who the boy assumes to have been his father. He studies the boy, contemplating his future as he walks away and starts to run, and the doctor appears confident he has done the right thing. The final shot ends on the window catch – open – a permeable boundary between the boy and Dr Cemal. The story is unfinished. But we finish the film transformed by the impact of Dr Cemal's choice. Its effects reach into the future. As things stand, his report will not lengthen Kenan's sentence for murder with the aggravating factor of this even greater sadistic act; he has prevented making the boy's future even more difficult by knowing – as he surely would – either that the man he believes to be his father suffered so terribly, or that his real father committed such a sadistic murder. That detail – the burying alive – will be omitted from the boy's future, and Cemal has taken that decision upon himself.

As Florence Jacobowitz writes, 'The film demonstrates that codes cannot always perfectly accommodate human frailties. Life is not clear cut and a certain amount of generosity and empathy is necessary to temper the rigidities of every system' (2012: 59). There are other such moments where Kenan is shown kindness, offered a cigarette or a share of food, and given tea by the young woman, which leads to his breakdown and the revelations about the paternity of his son and what led up to the murder. But the significance of Cemal's decision is that he reaches beyond science, duty and procedure to make a moral decision on the part of another.

Murdoch cites the enemies of love as social convention and neurosis (S&G: 216). The characters in *Anatolia* show both of these through their procedures, hierarchy and self-delusion. The film, however, does not. As Nancy E. Snow writes,

> When we look intelligently at art . . . we learn to focus and direct our gaze in ways that heighten sensitivities. We become more aware of the nuances of good and evil, of human weakness and strength, and one hopes, our attention becomes informed and guided by compassion. Murdoch, after all, thought that moral refinement of attention resulted in a 'loving' gaze, a gaze which scrutinized the world with kindness. (2013: 21)

The implications of this notion of loving attention for the film are not only a deeper understanding and appreciation of the form and style of the film, the need for humanism and realism in the unfolding of the worlds of these various characters, but also a fuller understanding of what leads Cemal to decide to lie, and perhaps a broader consideration, beyond the film, of circumstances in which telling the truth is not the right thing to do. We are left to assess this moral decision, made in the film's closing sequence, which comes at the end of a lengthy filmic journey through the moral visions of several men. The film operates as Murdochian moral realism, not only as art, on-screen, as Cemal feels compelled to act in breach of his professional codes of conduct, but also as an exercise in unselfing for us as we are compelled to recognise Cemal as a centre of moral meaning, and to see the world that he comes to see. The film denies us consolation and fantasy, and acts as a transformative ethical experience through its challenge to pay attention to Cemal's inner life. It is also an instance, perhaps, of true vision occasioning right conduct. When Cemal arrived at the moment of choice, the quality of his attention had determined the nature of the act. This is conveyed by the measured, contemplative character of Cemal, the time taken to reflect upon the case and his life, and the inclination towards thought for others, be it Kenan, Nusret or the boy. In the next film, however, it is the quality of the protagonist's self-centred attention that leads him to make a different sort of decision, for more questionable reasons.

AN ANXIOUS, SELF-PREOCCUPIED, FALSIFYING VEIL: *GRADUATION*

The film begins with an establishing shot of an austere Romanian housing estate, and then inside a family apartment. A brick comes crashing through the window, and a man emerges from the right of the frame with his toothbrush in hand. He goes out of the flat to see who did it, but finds nobody. The man, Romeo Aldea (Adrian Titieni) lives with his wife, who appears to be unwell, and his daughter. He drives his daughter Eliza (Maria Dragus) to college, and at one spot on the journey he hoots his car horn a couple of times, for no apparent reason, but which we later realise is a signal to his mistress, Sandra (Malina Manovici).

As Romeo and Sandra caress on the bed, it appears that she may have been a patient of his: he looks at her scars and says that one has faded, and she says, 'Is this standard treatment?' He gets a telephone call to tell him that Eliza has been attacked. We see that he is a doctor at the hospital, and that his wife, Magda (Lia Bugnar) seems mentally foggy; she is also clearly suspicious of Romeo's whereabouts. Colleagues at the hospital are very helpful regarding calling his 'friend in the police', asking about Eliza's bank cards, and trying to help. Magda asks the staff to leave them alone as she holds Eliza tightly and comfortingly. In the corridor, Romeo and Magda sit far apart, so clearly they are not close to each other and do not comfort each other. The outcome of the assault is that Eliza has sprained her wrist. The examining doctor says that no semen was found, as it seems the assailant did not get an erection. This mentions for the first time that the assault was an attempted rape. The doctor tells her father that she has lost her virginity, and 'not recently'.

In the next scene, Eliza is with her father at the police station, looking at photographs of suspects. Her statement is taken but the policeman dictates it for her. He says that a man held a knife to her throat, and said he would kill her if she did not have sexual intercourse with him. The chief inspector (Vlad Ivanov) takes her father out, saying, 'She's a grown up', and then says to him, 'Don't worry we'll catch him.' The father says, 'Do you think that's all I care about?' and the police say, 'Well that's all we can do.' The father wants Eliza to get to Cambridge University no matter what happens. He says it is more civilised 'there' – in the UK – and that 'Stuff like this happens all the time here.'

The police artist who is called in to do the photofit sketch of the attacker asks whether the doctor could put a word in for his godfather, Vice-Mayor Bulai, at the hospital. Bulai needs a liver transplant, there is a national waiting list, and the chief inspector asks Romeo to call a man in the ministry to 'bump his name up the list'. The chief inspector says he'll die if the doctor doesn't help, and that his godfather, Vice-Mayor Bulai, has always helped everybody. So the doctor says he'll see what he can do.

He brings Eliza home from hospital in the car. Eliza is wondering who broke their window, and then the car hits a wild dog, who seems to run off, but Eliza is shaken up and breathes heavily. There seem to be risks and dangers all around them. When a workman comes to change the locks on their apartment door, the man begins to talk casually about his cousin who was raped, but Romeo stops him saying, 'No, no, no, my daughter was not raped she was assaulted.' The doctor tapes up the broken window with some brown paper and tape. He carefully peels Eliza an apple, cuts it into slices, and takes it into her bedroom. Her mother is showering her. He looks, and exchanges a look with his wife, but leaves the room. He asks Magda whether she knew Eliza was no longer a virgin, and the mother says she had an idea, because she's her mother. They discuss the motorcycle instructor who Eliza is seeing and disagree over his suitability as a boyfriend. Magda says that 'Nowadays you don't have to marry the first boy you hold hands with', and Romeo snipes, 'As if I was your first', to which Magda replies, 'Relax, I wasn't thinking about you. Not everything is about you.' This is a bitter exchange, but issued without temper. Magda is wan, stooped and seems exhausted. Romeo refers to the assault as an accident, as if he finds the sexual element of the assault difficult. His main concern, it seems, is that she should still sit her examinations, 'and that's final'. Magda says it is time to let Eliza decide. The family is reeling from this trauma, but its interrelationships are clearly fraught anyway. Romeo says he will try to get the exam postponed as he is not sure if she can write. That night, he hears Eliza crying in her room, and he goes in and holds her. There is clear tenderness and love between father and daughter, but the family is also in crisis.

In the morning the windscreen wipers have been pulled up on his windscreen. Taking Eliza to school again in his car, he hoots his horn at the same spot again, and a cut to Eliza's disapproving face shows that she suspects what is going on. At the school, the invigilators object to her wearing her wrist cast in case of fraud, but the father persuades the headmaster to let her in. Romeo visits his elderly sick mother, and reassures her about her medications. They discuss Eliza and she makes clear she does not want Eliza to leave to go to university but rather she wants her to stay in Cluj. She also wants him to clear grass from his father's grave and pour concrete to make a proper grave. He has said he will before, but he forgot. A picture is emerging of a professional man whose private life is a complicated entanglement of domestic relationships and obligations, most of which, it seems, he struggles to fulfil. His mistress Sandra, who is the English teacher at Eliza's school, offers support to Romeo over Eliza's attack, but also informs him that her period is six days late. Romeo responds calmly, but this is clearly a further complication in his private life. When Eliza is out of her examination she says that she did what she could but did not have time to finish.

As the risk to Eliza's examination success becomes clearer, Romeo decides he must take action. He goes to see the chief inspector, who calls Vice-Mayor Bulai, and says, 'My friend put in a good word about the transplant and we're hoping for a positive answer.' He asks Bulai to help the doctor, and, noting the doctor's hesitancy, says, 'Romeo it's for your child.' This is now a clear insight into the corruption and compromises in officialdom in this town. Romeo is getting pulled in by the chief inspector, as his needs in relation to his daughter become greater.

Romeo sits in the playground, deep in thought, then goes to see Bulai, and tells him the facts about the difficult liver transplant operation he needs. Bulai offers Romeo money, but he refuses. Bulai says, 'Come on doctor surely you don't live off your salary?' Then he says to Romeo, 'I hope you don't think you owe me for helping your daughter.' Bulai tells Romeo that he called the exam chief, and that he understands. Bulai helped the man once when his wife lost her job, and 'he's been grateful to me ever since'. He says, 'People should help each other.' This is seeming more and more like a corrupt system of quid pro quo, where officialdom runs on a system of mutual favours.

Romeo sees Sandra and asks if Eliza could have longer to write her answer in the next examination, but she says not really. Romeo sees her son, Matei, and it is now confirmed that Romeo was the doctor who operated on her after her accident. This is an ethically questionable basis for a relationship, and again contributes to the picture that is developing of a lifestyle and environment that is less than morally scrupulous. Romeo goes to see Eliza's examiner and discusses how the paper grading will work, and offers to pay if they will help Eliza. The examiner says nothing other than that, 'Mr Bulai helped me, I help you that's all.' But the deceit has to involve Eliza: she needs to identify her paper by making a mark on it, so they know it is hers: she has to cross out three words from the bottom line. Romeo clearly looks disturbed by this, and the teacher says that if the doctor has any doubts he should say so now – 'This can only work on trust.' Then Romeo looks at the examiner and says, 'I don't do such things', and the examiner says, neither does he, he does not doubt it. Romeo leaves, but stops to look for the body of the dog he thinks he hit with his car the other night. During his search, he is overcome with emotion, and bursts into tears.

Back at the flat, Romeo has raised the matter with Magda, who says, 'No – that's not the path I want Eliza to take in life' and she challenges Romeo, 'You know in your heart of hearts it isn't right.' They discuss the rights and wrongs of leaving Cluj, and cheating, and whether how you get away matters as well as where you go. Romeo is desperate for Eliza to leave Cluj and to go to Cambridge. It is increasingly consuming him, and he is convinced that it is best for her. So he has the conversation with her that he needs to. He tells Eliza that,

'In 1991 your mother and I decided to move back, we thought we'd change, we thought we'd move mountains; we didn't move anything.' He is revealing that his fears for her are based on their disappointments. He tells Eliza what he wants her to do, calling it 'a precaution for tomorrow's exam'. He says, 'Sometimes in life it's the result that counts. We raised you to always be honest: but this is the world we live in, and sometimes we need to fight using their weapons.' She turns away from him, her face wrought with disappointment. He confronts her with one of her deceits. He says to her, 'You can smoke – I know you have some there.'

The next morning, his car window is actually broken. So they drive to school with the window pushed out. As he beeps his horn as usual, for the first time Eliza asks him why he always beeps at a certain place, even when there are no cars. He lies to her. He says, 'Just to make sure' when it is plainly a signal to alert his girlfriend. The fact that Eliza asked him about this, suggesting she knows full well what is going on, follows directly from their conversation the night before. Now he has asked her to lie, she feels able to challenge him about his lies. Romeo asks her if she has water and snacks, she sighs no; it is he who is obsessed with this exam and her leaving Cluj. He tells her to eat because 'it helps the brain'. At the gate of the school, again he appears to be the only parent there. He says good luck and take care but she does not look back at him.

Romeo then goes to see the CCTV footage of the assault. In the 'law of the jungle' the policeman's brother is a funeral director who pays ambulance drivers to tip him off to fatal accidents. Bulai comes in to the hospital because he has to have another operation to remove polyps. He wants to pay Romeo with a pile of notes, but Romeo won't accept it. Bulai can see that Romeo is troubled by what he has arranged for Eliza, and says to him, 'But if you do something earnestly, with all your heart, you don't need to doubt it.' Romeo says, 'You think so?' As Romeo is waiting for Eliza after the exam, he sees Marius (Rares Andrici), the motorbike instructor and Eliza's boyfriend. They talk about how he cheated at the sports college in his finals, and Marius takes delight in his own dishonesty. Romeo asks Marius about the day of the attack, saying that somebody called the police on a pre-paid SIM card. Marius seems to know nothing. Eliza emerges, saying that the exam went well and she goes off with Marius on his motorbike. Romeo revisits the scene of the attack and compares it with photographs, then goes to his girlfriend's flat for dinner. Sandra asks him for help with finding a speech therapist for her son, Matei, and Romeo does not help her. He says he can help when the issues with Eliza are sorted out, but Sandra says it will be too late then. She is never a priority for him and needs to make some decisions because 'we can't keep up this uncertainty'. There is a ring at the door, and it is Eliza. She has come to get him because

Figure 4.3 Eliza (Maria Dragus) and Romeo (Adrian Titieni) have a frank conversation, in *Graduation* (2016), directed by Cristian Mungiu.

'grandma collapsed'. In a scene of high tension and activity, with a myriad of sounds, from the radio, ringing telephones, neighbours and mobile phones, everyone pulls together – Romeo, Marius, Eliza, a neighbour – and grandma comes round from her fainting spell. Eliza asks her father to talk to her mother. Clearly the request over the examination has pushed her beyond tolerating the impasse that her family has reached. Romeo asks, 'Can you imagine what we had to do so you could live like this?', but Eliza responds, 'You shouldn't have done it if it wasn't right.' And Eliza tells him, 'I don't want to go to the UK any more; I want to stay here with Marius.' Despite his determined efforts, she is rejecting his plan (Figure 4.3).

He goes home to Magda, and tells her about what happened tonight with his mother and Eliza. Then he tells her about his girlfriend, Sandra. Magda knows: but Romeo explains that he promised Eliza he would talk to her. Magda says, 'You shouldn't have influenced her grade; after that, what does all we taught her count for?' She says that she will follow Eliza wherever she goes, and tells him he has to move out: 'You stop sleeping here from tonight.'

The next morning, when he arrives at the hospital, there are prosecutors waiting for him, with a warrant for Bulai. The prosecutors are clearly suspicious of the doctor, and they say to him insinuating, entrapping homilies, such as 'You see a mote in your brother's eye but not the beam in your own.' They say, 'You have the reputation for being an honest doctor but everyone has a weak spot' and that 'He who persists in illegality will probably have to pay for it.' They say that things could be unpleasant for him and his daughter. Romeo refuses to let them speak to Bulai, and by now we are not sure if it is genuinely because of concern for his patient's health or because he is afraid for himself.

He goes to see the chief inspector, who tells him, 'You need your stories to match', but Romeo won't involve his daughter. The police want to find out something about the prosecutors to 'handle them'. So the mesh of corruption is within the criminal justice system as well.

Romeo is becoming increasingly nervous, and now thinks someone is following him. He confronts Marius about Eliza's assault, and accuses him of being there, watching and doing nothing. He says he has identified Marius from the screen grab and forbids him from seeing Eliza again. They fight and Romeo ends up on the floor. Back at the flat, Magda asks him to hand over his keys and to call first before he comes round. He asks his wife for forgiveness, and asks how they have become such enemies, but Magda only cries. So now, his daughter won't speak to him, his wife sends him away, his job is under threat and his girlfriend is possibly pregnant. He goes to see the examiner and tells him a prosecutor came. The examiner says he did not find Eliza's paper, so clearly she didn't mark it.

Romeo and Eliza go to the line-up at the police station, which is traumatic for Eliza and the language the suspects are asked to repeat is brutal. She says her attacker is not there. Afterwards, she and Romeo have a frank conversation. She asks him how he can have thought that Marius would not have defended her, and Romeo challenges her about not marking the paper. Eliza replies, 'You don't have to worry; I did what I thought was best.' Ultimately, Romeo is resigned, and confesses, 'I'm glad you used your own head to decide. Do what you think is best.'

By this stage, Romeo is like a wandering, raging and frustrated soul. His mobile phone rings all the time, and we do not know if it is work, Sandra, his mother, the prosecutors – it could be any of them, he has so many people drawing on his time. He sees a man from the line-up on the roadside and gets off the bus and follows him. Romeo looks for him but does not find him, and one wonders what he would have done if he had. He goes to Sandra's, to say that he has found Matei a speech therapist. In the park Matei throws stones at another child and is scolded. When he asks Romeo how he should have behaved, given the other child should have waited his turn, Romeo replies 'It's complicated – your mother will explain': Romeo is not in a position to tell the boy how to behave.

Romeo has to go to work and so takes Matei with him to the hospital and tells him to wait in his office. Monsieur Bulai has had a heart attack. His nurse assistant seems unable to look at him, her face displaying disgust or disappointment, presumably because of the persistent presence of the prosecutors or the neglect of Bulai. He speaks to Mr Bulai's wife, who gives him the wad of money that her husband wanted him to have. Also the prosecutors are there to speak to him. He says to them, 'Let's keep the kids out of it', and they reply, 'Sure, we'll see.' He collects Matei and they go to Eliza's school. There are images in murals on the school walls of healthy clever children at their books. The contrast with the grim reality of Eliza's life in Cluj is apparent. Matei sees an empty classroom, but then Sandra comes in and hugs him. From her countenance, it seems she may have had an abortion while Romeo looked after Matei.

Eliza tells Romeo that they let her write longer in the exam because she started crying, so she did not need to do anything else such as mark her paper. She joyfully joins her fellow students, and Romeo takes a graduation picture. Many questions are left unanswered, and so what do these loose ends mean? The fact that Eliza started crying may mean that she found her own way of getting more time in the exam without involving her father in any more dishonesty; whether or not the tears were genuine is impossible to know. However, isn't it fair in terms of natural justice that Eliza should have been given some advantage as a result of the assault on her so close to the exam?

Romeo thinks he is acting in his daughter's best interests, and is prepared to do so even if it involves compromises that affect his professional career and liability to prosecution. If we think about his preparedness for the choice he makes to engage in a moral and legal compromise it is possible to argue that his life is an array of compromises, from dishonesty to his wife, lack of commitment to his girlfriend, failure to honour his mother's wishes about his father's grave and failing to be honest with his daughter. He is a different example from Dr Cemal of Murdoch's proposal that 'by the time the moment of choice has arrived the quality of attention has probably determined the nature of the act' (OGG: 354). For Romeo, the background of his childhood, marriage, country and profession affect his values and his fears: he wants a better life for his daughter. We are given the opportunity across the film to see how Romeo's moral world is constructed, and the film enables us to understand his fear for Eliza, but perhaps we baulk at his insistence that she do so well in her examinations at all costs: particularly if it is not what she, her mother or her grandmother want for her. By contrast, we are given only a few moments of focus on Dr Cemal's inner life, and these are sufficient to convey that his action to conceal the truth is for the sake of the boy's future. He too has reflected on his life, but briefly; he has reflected more upon the price children pay for the sins of the adults. In terms of motivation, a Murdochian analysis would suggest that Romeo is motivated by his desire to achieve what he wants for his daughter, whereas Cemal is motivated by the particular circumstances of this boy to do what he considers to be the right thing, or something good. What Murdoch means by 'the Good', capital G, in relation to moral life and love, is what I will now move on to consider.

NOTES

1. For an examination of Murdoch's critique of consciousness in existentialism and linguistic behaviourism, see Maria Antonaccio's book *Picturing the Human* (2000), in particular Chapter 3.
2. Weil focuses on attention in *Gravity and Grace* (2002b). For a clear account of her thinking, see Mario Von Der Ruhr (2006).
3. The film is called *Das Wolkenphanomen von Maloja*, made by Arnold Fanck in 1924, and is available on YouTube: <https://www.youtube.com/watch?v=x51riLabuus> (last accessed 20 December 2018).

CHAPTER 5

Film, Love and Goodness

> How is one to connect the realism which must involve a clear-eyed contemplation of the misery and evil of the world with a sense of an uncorrupted good without the latter idea becoming the merest consolatory dream? (I think this puts a central problem in moral philosophy.) (OGG: 349)
>
> If one is going to speak of great art as 'evidence', is not ordinary human love an even more striking evidence of a transcendent principle of good? (OGG: 361)
>
> The sovereign Good is not an empty receptacle into which the arbitrary will places objects of its choice. It is something which we all experience as a creative force. This is metaphysics, which sets up a picture which it then offers as an appeal to us all to see if we cannot find just this in our deepest experience. (MGM: 507)
>
> God does not and cannot exist. But what led us to conceive of him does exist and is *constantly* experienced and pictured. That is, it is real as an Idea, and is *also* incarnate in knowledge and work and love. (MGM: 508)

In the previous chapters, I have explored some fundamental elements of the relationship between Murdoch's philosophy and cinema: film as 'the right type' of art; film as a moral fable; and film featuring Murdochian protagonists, with inner lives and states of moral vision. These chapters have all mentioned 'the good' and 'goodness', but I will now consider in more detail what Murdoch means by 'the Good', capital G. This is the concept from which our moral knowledge is derived, and which she suggests we are always already in relation with, whether we choose to acknowledge it or not. Murdoch speaks about it in terms of transcendence, but it is not religious: it is, however, similar to elements of religion, including prayer and meditation. In this chapter, I will set out what Murdoch means by the Good, both in form and content, and then examine how film can depict goodness in an oblique way so that we might come to realise what goodness looks like through the process of experiencing the film. This is not necessarily in a straightforward way where characters are clearly defined as right and wrong, good and bad, making choices and receiving consonant rewards, but rather perhaps when a film calls our assumptions into question. Through close analysis I will demonstrate how film calls our attention to form, mood, aesthetics and performance, and challenges our view of the actions of others, thereby changing our moral vision of goodness, love, the film and the world.

The film I will examine in most detail is *The Edge of Heaven* (Fatih Akin, 2007). In this film of multiple, connected narrative strands, matters of tolerance, generosity and hospitality are tested in the face of anger, politics, blind passion and cruel accident. People are shown to be complicated and changeable, but the reality of unexpected death is presented as a reason to choose outward-looking honesty and tolerance rather than isolation and lingering resentment. I will also look at two other films with Murdochian resonances. In *I've Loved You So Long* (Philippe Claudel, 2008), a family struggles to cope with the return of Juliette (Kristen Scott Thomas) after a lengthy absence which is incrementally explained. The complex way in which her experiences are revealed, both in the present and recalling the past, compel us to evaluate her as a person with an inner life, and not on the bare facts of her behaviour and melancholic comportment. And in *We Need to Talk about Kevin* (Lynne Ramsay, 2011), young Kevin is depicted as difficult and malevolent, and his mother Eva as both troubled personally and punished by her community. Eva's struggles as Kevin's mother, and Kevin's appalling behaviour, challenge the spectator to feel empathy with either of them, but the film's immersion into Eva's consciousness enables an identification with her that looks for the humanity in her situation and even enables a moment of sympathy with a frightened Kevin by the end of the film.

MURDOCH'S 'AUSTERE AND UNCONSOLED LOVE OF THE GOOD'

Paul S. Fiddes writes, 'Murdoch herself is on the quest for a Platonic coherence in the transcendent Good, but she believes it can only be reached through attending to the reality of others in the world' (2012: 96). This worldliness is vital for understanding goodness and love in Murdoch. Heather Widdows notes that 'the good, like all moral values, is discovered in everyday life, and its recognition is part and parcel of life' (2016: 71). This does not mean that it is easy to define – Murdoch does not define the concept, nor does she set out a clear, systematic way to understand what she means by it – that is not how she writes. For Murdoch, loving attention is the means by which to reach goodness:

> It is perfectly obvious that goodness *is* connected with knowledge: not with impersonal quasi-scientific knowledge of the ordinary world, whatever that may be, but with a refined and honest perception of what is really the case, a patient and just discernment and exploration of what confronts one, which is the result not simply of opening one's eyes but of a certainly perfectly familiar kind of moral discipline. (IP: 330)

This sentence contains the essence of Murdoch's thinking about goodness. Toril Moi stresses that this loving gaze is just, and as such is the essence of realism in Murdoch's thought: 'The same just, dispassionate, unselfish, and loving gaze, the same quality of attention, is required whether the object of our attention is nature, art, or life. To learn to love is to learn to see reality as it is' (Moi 2014: 194). This places Murdoch in conflict with those Oxford philosophers who argued that nothing is inherently good or bad, and that it was human activity to endow something with the value of goodness. This is where Murdoch sees metaphysics being stripped away from ethics, as good was no longer considered to be something transcendent. In 'Metaphysics and Ethics' she traces the line of this development through G. E. Moore, Charles Stevenson and Gilbert Ryle, and cites Hare in his *The Language of Morals* as saying that 'a man's morality is seen in his conduct and a moral statement is a prescription of a rule uttered to guide a choice' (M&E: 63). This 'current position' (in 1957) means that 'we are certainly now presented with a stripped and empty scene' (M&E: 63). For Murdoch, it is not at all a matter of human beings working out what they think is right and wrong and arguing why others should do as they say they should. Murdoch believes that as human beings we already know what the good is, we are oriented towards perfection even if we know we cannot achieve it, and so perfection exists as a transcendent aim for our journey as moral pilgrims.

> I have spoken of efforts of attention directed upon individuals and of obedience to reality as an exercise of love, and have suggested that 'reality' and 'individual' present themselves to us in moral contexts as ideal end-points or Ideas of Reason. This surely is the place where the concept of good lives. 'Good': 'Real': 'Love'. These words are closely

connected. And here we retrieve the deep sense of the indefinability of good, which has been given a trivial sense in recent philosophy. Good is indefinable not for the reasons offered by Moore's successors, but because of the infinite difficulty of the task of apprehending a magnetic but inexhaustible reality. . . . If apprehension of good is apprehension of the individual and the real, then good partakes of the infinite elusive character of reality. (IP: 333–4)

In this passage Murdoch makes clear that she sees goodness and love in everyday reality, but also that it is something magnetic and inexhaustible, conveying her perception of it as transcendent too. She argues for the ontological necessity of the Good in ways that are similar to the ontological argument for the existence of God, but for her there is no question of personification. Murdoch makes it clear that she believes 'we need a theology that can continue without God' (MGM: 511). Maria Antonaccio and William Schweiker explain this precisely and account for the significance of Murdoch' argument:

For her, the Good is a necessarily real, magnetic force which draws the self beyond itself in moral concern for concrete other individuals. In making this claim Murdoch not only reopens the question of the status of the Good within the moral life, but also reasserts the importance of the connection between morals and metaphysics. (1996: xiv)

This is a vision of a metaphysical Good, which is why Murdoch draws so heavily on Plato's image of the cave and the sun throughout her philosophical writings. The Good is like the sun, drawing us out of the cave and through stages of a spiritual journey with the aim of becoming morally better. Murdoch also recognises that images such as Plato's cave, and the pictures and metaphors that we use in our lives, help us to understand our moral journey. Heather Widdows goes so far as to say that Murdoch's philosophy is 'an exegesis of, or meditation on, Plato's Cave' (2016: 90). Widdows explains the importance for Murdoch of the concept of the individual and their inner life, and their inner activity, saying that 'it is upon this belief in the individual's consciousness and personal (moral) experience that Murdoch's moral philosophy is built' (2016: 21). As with the moral activity of M when she reflects upon and reconsiders D, it is moral change and inner, private activity which Murdoch is so concerned with.[1] And Murdoch believes this inner moral life is omnipresent, and that we are all capable of seeing 'a larger picture':

The felt need for this picture, or field of force, is answered by metaphysics and religion, and by general moral values, our sense of right and wrong. This is not a matter of specialised isolated moments of moral choice, appearing in a continuum of non-moral activity. These movements and responses are occurring all the time. The reality of the moral requirement is proved by the world. (MGM: 297)

To summarise, the Good, capital G, is a transcendent light, guiding our moral lives, but we are obscured from seeing it by our self-delusions and egoism. Through the cultivation of a just and loving gaze at a focus other than ourselves (art, nature, religion) we can increase our ability to perceive the Good and make ourselves morally better. Vitally, this improvement in the quality of our attention is with no eye on reward: 'In the case of art and nature such attention is immediately rewarded by the enjoyment of beauty. In the case of morality, although there are sometimes rewards, the idea of a reward is out of place' (OGG: 354). This is a major difference from Christianity and the hope of reward by a caring God, or salvation, or an afterlife. In fact, the search for reward detracts from the potential of prayer: 'Prayer is properly not petition, but simply an attention to God which is a form of love' (OGG: 344). The kind of objectual attention that prayer or meditation can be works for Murdoch's moral progress, but not if it is to a deity asking for a reward. Murdoch asserts 'This "Good" is not the old God in disguise, but rather what the old God symbolised' (MGM: 428). By this she means, that 'God was (or is) a *single perfect transcendent non-representable and necessarily real object of* attention ... moral philosophy should attempt to retain a central concept which has all these characteristics' (OGG: 344). This is what the Good is for Murdoch: 'Good represents the reality of which God is the dream' (MGM: 496).

WHAT DOES THE GOOD LOOK LIKE?

> The image of the Good as a transcendent magnetic centre seems to me the least corruptible and most realistic picture for us to use in our reflections upon the moral life. (OGG: 361)

Although this talk of goodness can sound idealistic, Murdoch is not saying that we are all innately good, rather that we are all innately selfish, and that 'it is surely in the tissue of life that the secrets of good and evil are to be found' (OGG: 343–4). There is nothing dreamy or deluded about being good: it is a form of realism.

> The idea of a really good man living in a private dream world seems unacceptable. Of course a good man may be infinitely eccentric, but he must know certain things about his surroundings, most obviously the

existence of other people and their claims. The chief enemy of excellence in morality (and also in art) is personal fantasy: the tissue of self-aggrandising and consoling wishes and dreams which prevents one from seeing what is there outside one. (OGG: 347–8)

The Good itself is not visible, but Murdoch says that 'beauty appears as the visible and accessible aspect of the Good', in art and nature (ibid.: 357). Good 'is a central point of reflection', 'the focus of attention when an intent to be virtuous co-exists (as perhaps it always does) with some unclarity of vision' (ibid.: 356). Although Plato wrote that the good man will eventually be able to look at the sun, it is not quite so for Murdoch. She believes that 'we can certainly know more or less where the sun is; it is not so easy to imagine what it would be like to look at it' (ibid.: 357). It seems that a good man may know what this looks like, but we need our egoistic vision to be unimpeded enough to be able to see it. Loving the particular is one way in which Murdoch envisions the practice, whether it is a carpenter dealing with his wood, tools and measurements, or a girl tending her potted plant or loving her cat who is 'a free being, a friend, a privilege to live with' (MGM: 497). These everyday instances of loving each other and cherishing other beings are full of imagination and art, and this makes them apprehensions of morality and goodness. This is something we are all able to do:

> On the road between illusion and reality there are many clues and signals and wayside shrines and sacraments and places of meditation and refreshment. The pilgrim just has to look about him with a lively eye. There are many kinds of images in the world, sources of energy, checks and reminders, pure things, inspiring things, innocent things, attracting love and veneration. We all have our own icons, untainted and vital, which we, perhaps secretly, store away in safety. (MGM: 496)

With these ideas of looking about with lively eyes, and storing our own secret icons, it is time to consider how these concepts can be seen in films. I will begin by examining how *The Edge of Heaven* interlinks many ideas about love and goodness, before looking at even more challenging scenarios of attending to goodness in *I've Loved You So Long* and *We Need to Talk about Kevin*.

THE DISCIPLINED OVERCOMING OF SELF:
THE EDGE OF HEAVEN

This film has been approached from many critical angles pursuing its themes of globalisation, the lives of Turkish-German guest workers, and transnational complexity including protest, activism and migration. But the film conveys these vast global issues through the particulars of the lives of a small group of connected individuals. The film begins with a young man, Nejat (Baki Davrak) stopping his car at a petrol station. In the shop, he hears music on the radio by a singer he doesn't recognise. The man in the shop tells him the singer is dead now, even though he's young, from radioactive poisoning from fallout from the Chernobyl disaster in 1986. Nejat takes notice but seems different from the men in the garage, perhaps a bit of an outsider or a different social class. We learn later that he has been living in Germany, which is the setting of the first of the film's three sections.

An intertitle appears, announcing that this coming section of the film is called 'Yeter's Death'. We go straight to a protest march in Bremen, Germany, and Ali (Tuncel Kurtiz), a Turkish man in his sixties or seventies, who is Nejat's father, smiles at the protesters benignly as he walks past on his way to find a prostitute. He walks along the street of the red-light district, surveying the sex workers, and selects a woman who tells him her name is 'Jessy' (Nursel Köse). He is soon ashamed, however, when he finds out her real name is Yeter, and that she is also Turkish. They speak in a matter-of-fact way about their transaction, she calls him 'grandad', performs fellatio and then they part. As Ali leaves, they speak in Turkish and she is overheard by two Turkish men passing by, who look threateningly at her, and she closes her blinds quickly.

We then see Nejat arrive at his father Ali's home, and Ali cooks him dinner. Nejat gives Ali a book, by Selim Ozdogan – *Demircinin Kizi* (*Daughter of a Blacksmith*, 2007) – about strained relations between a girl and her father. They drink raki, chat, discuss a racing tip and Ali puts on a bet. Even though it is an outsider, Ali wins! And at odds of 70/1, he has won 700 euros. They say goodbye at the station, and Nejat goes back to Hamburg. We next see Nejat at work, lecturing on Goethe at the university. He seems a lethargic and uninspired lecturer, speaking about German literature to a half-full lecture theatre. We then cut to a girl at the back of the room, with her head on her arms, fast asleep on the desk, which seems to confirm the suspicion that Nejat's lecture is not very dynamic.

Ali goes back to Yeter, and, after another sexual transaction, he asks her to move in with him, saying that he would pay her what she earns there at the brothel but she would sleep only with him. She asks for time to think about it. When she is travelling on the metro, the two threatening Turkish men come and intimidate her about her lifestyle. Their threats clearly influence her to accept Ali's proposal. When she meets Ali at the betting shop, she says she is left with 3,000 euros a month, and he says, 'All I want is for you to live with me and sleep with me.' Yeter agrees, and they go out for dinner happily.

Next we see that Yeter has moved in, and meets Nejat over dinner at Ali's house. We learn along with her that Nejat's mother died when he was six months old. Ali married a widow with a son but it didn't work out. Yeter discloses that her husband was shot in Maras in 1978, the occasion of a massacre by neo-fascists.[2] They have shared some of their backgrounds and losses, and are getting on well. The three of them argue over who goes up to the kitchen to get every course, in endearing attempts to be hospitable to each other. When Yeter is in the kitchen, Nejat tells Ali he is drinking too much, as he is becoming loud and a bit aggressive. Yeter and Nejat put a drunken Ali to bed, and have a chance to speak. Yeter tells Nejat she is a hooker, which takes Nejat aback, but he responds fairly calmly. Ali, meanwhile, has a serious heart attack and is rushed to hospital, where he has heart surgery. Yeter tells Nejat that she has a twenty-seven-year-old daughter who thinks she works in a shoe shop. Yeter says, 'I'd do anything for her, I don't want her to be uneducated. I wanted her to study and become like you.' A warm look between them conveys understanding and shared values. Ali is bad-tempered in hospital, saying that getting old is evil and there is nothing good about it. He instructs Yeter to water his tomatoes, and Yeter says they are ready to be plucked. Nejat says they should take Ali some of his beloved tomatoes. Nejat's love for his father makes Yeter start to cry. She confesses she misses her daughter and has not heard her voice for a long time, and that she cannot get hold of her for some reason. Nejat comforts her.

Ali comes home from hospital and is very difficult to live with. Yeter is sleeping in his bed and cooking for him, but he is constantly rude to her. He asks Nejat, 'Did you screw her?', and Nejat does not dignify it with an answer. Yeter has made borek for Ali, but he sends it away, shouting that the doctor said he is not to have pastry, but then he smokes, and Nejat points this out. He is nasty to Yeter, saying, 'I have my life and you have yours.' As she is saying goodbye to Nejat, she gives him the borek, and Ali shouts after her, 'Get me a raki girl.' Ali asks Yeter, 'Did you screw him?'; she says he is drunk. He gropes her, shouting 'I own you!'

He is disrespectful and obnoxious, and Yeter says she is leaving, saying to Ali, 'I've seen plenty like you.' She pushes him several times and he hits her once, hard. She falls and hits her head, and is killed. Ali cannot believe this and cries over her. The next we see is that Ali is put into prison, in a small cell with a toilet and a narrow bed. Yeter's body is flown back to Turkey. Nejat oversees this, and goes to the Turkish funeral, meeting Yeter's family. But her daughter Ayten is not there. Nejat says that he will stay in Istanbul until he finds Ayten. He goes to the police to ask about her, and a police officer asks him why he wants to find the girl, and he says he wants to finance her studies, 'because knowledge and education are human rights'. The police officer asks why he does not want to help a Kurdish orphan, and Nejat does not have an answer. This is not a selfless moral action, it is a personal matter of reparation in some way, because he knew how much Ayten's education meant to Yeter. Nejat puts up pictures of Yeter around town asking people to get in touch with him. He puts up a picture in a German bookshop and sees a sign that the shop is for sale. He speaks to the bookshop owner a short while, about Germans having a bookshop in Istanbul, and then he offers to buy it. The current owner finds it amusing that Nejat is a Turkish professor of German literature in Germany, buying a German bookshop in Turkey; but Nejat says that 'maybe teaching isn't my calling', and looks really happy in the shop. He also completely dissociates himself from Ali, saying to his cousin that 'a murderer is not my father'. In this way, Nejat is aligning himself more with Yeter's familial relationships, staying in Istanbul and searching for Ayten, and appears to have cut ties with Germany and his Turkish father in prison there.

This is the end of the film's first section, and it demonstrates several aspects that connect with Murdoch's thinking. Nejat is a scholar, but perhaps not suited to teaching. Ali killing Yeter, albeit unintentionally, has incidentally given Nejat purpose and enabled him to start again. He is freed from caring for his father, because he has effectively disowned him, and is instead committed to doing something that he is perhaps more able to do: take care of Ayten's education. However, this is also a fantastic journey, in that he does not know how to find Ayten, or whether she is interested in education at all. So, at this stage of the film, Nejat appears to be comforting himself with a somewhat deluded quest. He is pursuing what he believes to be the right thing to do, what Yeter said she wanted to happen, but he does not know whether this aim is realistic or fanciful, or even achievable. It is questionable, therefore, that his vision is clearly aiming for the Good, but rather is still self-focused and is somewhat consoling and delusional.

The film's next section is introduced with the intertitle 'Lotte's Death'. This section also begins with a protest, but a more ill-tempered one, in Istanbul, where a gun is used and then dropped. Another person picks it up, runs away and is pursued. They drop their phone, losing all their contact numbers, and they cannot get into where they want to go. They pull off their hood and show themselves to be a young woman to a resident in the apartment block who lets her through and up onto the roof, where she hides the gun. She catches the ferry from the European side of Istanbul to the Asian side, and when she arrives home she sees that police are raiding her hideout. As the police drag young women from the building they shout out their names, so that onlookers know who they are in case they cannot be found. The local people clap with approval, however, as they are taken away.

The woman flies to Hamburg and is met by a man who shows her where she can sleep, and gives her a hundred euros. She is then seen on the telephone, speaking in English, trying to find her mother. She gets an address, and looks up shoe shops, where she thinks her mother works, and we realise that this is Yeter's daughter, Ayten (Nurgül Yesilçay). She doesn't pay the man back his money, he gets angry and he throws her out. She sleeps in the university behind a vending machine, and then the next day we see her asleep at the back of Nejat's lecture. So the first connection in the film is made clear: she was the sleeping student we saw earlier, and now Nejat is in fact looking for her. Ayten washes in the university toilets, and then asks a tall blonde girl for money. The girl, Lotte (Patrycia Ziolkowska), says she can pay for her lunch and doesn't want the money back, saying, 'Next time we see each other you can invite me.' They get lunch in the university canteen and sit together. Ayten says she studies social science, Lotte studies English and Spanish. Ayten says she is from Istanbul, and then says to Lotte, 'Do you really want to know?' Lotte says yes, so Ayten tells Lotte the truth about her situation: but she says her name is Gul.

Lotte takes Ayten home to her mother's house, and introduces her. She says, 'This is the kitchen, you can take whatever you want, any time.' She says to her mother, 'This is Gül, she'll be staying with us for a while.' She shows Gül her room, then tells her she has been three months in India. Gül says she had to escape so all she has is these clothes that she is wearing. Lotte gives Gül clothes, some of which she rejects because of the American symbol on them. Lotte's mother Susanne (Hanna Schygulla) says Lotte is very generous, and Lotte says with conviction, 'We have to help her.' Susanne says that she doesn't even know her. They argue about asylum and harbouring illegal immigrants, but Lotte is unmoved, and says to her mother, 'Would you be kind enough to make her bed?' Lotte and Gül go out drinking beer and dancing; they smoke a joint, and then kiss; and they roll in drunk and giggling in the early hours, watched by Susanne from an upstairs window. They have a huge breakfast, using what looks like the entire contents of the fridge, and leave the mess to go off to the bedroom. Lotte strokes her lovingly, and Gül reveals her real name is Ayten.

Later that day, Ayten comes down to the kitchen where Susanne is shelling pecan nuts. Susanne asks her what she is escaping from. Ayten explains that she is 'a member of political resistance in Turkey; fighting for 100 per cent human rights, 100 per cent freedom of speech, 100 per cent social education'. Susanne suggests that things might be better for Turkey once they join the European Union, but Ayten says the EU is led by colonial countries and swears. Susanne says, 'I don't want you to talk like that in my house. You can talk like that in your house. OK?' Ayten is charmless and angry, and Susanne is offended and barely conceals her disapproval with her superior put-down.

Ayten sits on the steps of the house crying, and asks Lotte to help her find her mother. Lotte agrees, with eyes alight, and drives her off immediately to where Ayten believes the shoe shop is. They drive to Bremen, and as they drive along the road, the train alongside them has Nejat and Yeter on it in an agonisingly proximate coincidence. Lotte and Ayten get pulled over by the police because Ayten is not wearing her seat belt. As the police begin to check the car's credentials, Ayten leaps out of the car and runs away, but is caught by the officers, and shouts, 'Asylum!' She is put in an asylum centre, and they are told that Lotte can stay three nights a month. Lotte says it's not so bad, and people are nice, but Ayten asks Lotte to lock the door, and they sit opposite each other, as Ayten reaches out and they hold hands.

At Ayten's court hearing her appeal fails, as, although sympathetic to her plight, the tribunal cannot see why she would still be in danger if she returned to Turkey. Lotte is enraged and desperate to follow Ayten to Turkey. At home she rips out the contents of drawers and cupboards, and accuses her mother of hiding her passport when it is actually sitting on her desk. Her mother says, 'Look how blind you are', but Lotte will not be deterred. She goes off in a taxi, having hugged her mother, who says, 'Take care of yourself' and looks worried as she leaves. In Istanbul, Lotte urgently pursues Ayten's case. She is given the name of a pro bono lawyer, who says Ayten is considered part of an armed terrorist gang and she could get fifteen to twenty years in prison. When Lotte cries desperately, the lawyer says he could try to get her a permit to visit Ayten in prison, but it could take one to two months, and she must not mention Ayten's name to anyone. Back at the hotel, Lotte argues with her mother over the telephone about staying in Istanbul. Susanne asks, 'What about your studies?', but Lotte replies she has had enough. Lotte says, 'For the first time my life has a purpose. For the first time I'm needed. I've got to help Ayten.' Susanne challenges her, 'Do you know what your girlfriend has cost me? Did you ever ask yourself that? For a whole year I paid her solicitor's fees. And we lost.' Lotte asks her to ask her father, but Susanne will not do that. She implores Lotte, her voice softens, saying that she wants her to come back to Germany. But Lotte refuses, saying she can't. So, Susanne says angrily, 'Fine, then stay there. But see how you cope on your own. I won't help you. From now on you're finally on your own', and hangs up on her. Lotte shouts 'Mama!' down the telephone.

Lotte comes in to Nejat's bookshop looking for accommodation, and pins up her note next to photo of Yeter (Ayten's mother). She asks to look at a book on the Turkish legal system, and the shop assistant Cengiz (Emre Cosar) makes tea for them both. Nejat has a room for rent and he takes Lotte to see it. She wants the room, and tells Nejat about Gül, but doesn't use her real name: if she had, he would have known it was Yeter's daughter, who he's looking for. Ayten meanwhile is in prison, being spoken to by her comrades, who tell her they want the gun and threaten to kill her if she 'messes' with them. Lotte gets a fifteen-minute visit with Ayten, who tells her that most of the women are in there because they killed their husbands. Lotte says she wants to help her, and so Ayten asks her to get 'something' for her, namely the gun. Lotte goes and gets it, following the same trail as Ayten did, having to ask the women in the apartment to let her onto the roof. She takes the gun and puts it in her handbag. As she is walking back through the streets, some young boys grab her handbag. She runs after them, loses them, then comes across them rifling through the contents of her bag. One of the boys, aged no more than six or seven, says, 'What do you want sister?'; he points the gun at her and shoots her, fatally.

The police interview Ayten. They tell her Lotte has been shot dead, and they ask her to help them. Lotte's body is flown back to Germany, returning home, like Yeter's. The bodies of these two women, needlessly killed by casual male violence, are repatriated in opposite directions, never knowing they were connected by the love they share for Ayten. Lotte's love, however, might be considered by Murdoch to be 'a form of insanity whereby we lose the "open scene": *lose* our ability to scatter our loving interest through the world' (MGM: 346). Murdoch is writing about love that is self-centred, or unrealistic. From this, she argues, 'There can be a duty to fall out of love . . . Released, we return to our friends, our work, our ordinary pleasures!' (MGM: 346). She is capturing here the selfishness of the lover who zealously prioritises the beloved in the way Lotte does, abusing her mother's generosity and losing perspective on reality. Murdoch writes,

> Successful obsessive love may be accompanied by intense joy, but also by jealousy and fear of loss. There is a better sunnier happiness when together with the beloved we are able to be aware of other things, other people, other joys, illumined by secure mutual love, when we can stand together and look at something else. (MGM: 346)

This 'secure mutual love' is something that Lotte and Ayten are not able to achieve in the film, and it is perhaps difficult to understand why Lotte is so unquestioningly devoted to Ayten from their first meeting. The duty that Lotte feels that she – and Susanne – have to care for Ayten is perplexing, and there is something immature or naïve about her commitment to looking after her. Claudia Breger poses the question as to whether Lotte is exhibiting anything more than 'the proverbial gesture of the benign coloniser' (2014: 82). Breger suggests,

> We may in fact be inclined to keep distancing ourselves from Ayten's harshness or Lotte's naïveté. The latter in particular is explored more fully in the doublings and crossings of Lotte's relationship with her mother that emerge with the further unfolding of the film's narrative configuration. Not only is Lotte's generosity based on her privilege of maternal economic support; as it turns out, her simultaneous post-adolescent rebellion only repeats her mother's own story. (2014: 82)

In the telephone conversation with Susanne there are hints at a background of feeling unsure, from allusions to an absentee father, to having been in India for three months, or leaving her studies at the drop of her hat, as well as her saying that this is the first time she has been needed or had a purpose. This suggests that Ayten fulfilled a role for Lotte, and was a cause to support. In this way, Nejat and Lotte shared the idea that Ayten was someone they should help, but both thought about this in unrealistic ways.

The third section is titled 'The Edge of Heaven', which is the English title for the film, originally called 'Auf der anderen Seite', or 'On the Other Side'. This title suggests several possibilities for the boundaries and borders between the people in the film, including earthly life and the afterlife. Ali is now out of prison and is at the airport being deported from Germany. At the next ticket window is Susanne getting a plane ticket to Istanbul. She arrives at the same hotel where we saw Lotte making the telephone call to her, and she is shown to her room. Susanne does not speak to the porter, and seems to be moving, and looking at the world, through a fog of grief. We then see her pass the night and day in the room in the most evocative sequence of despair. She drinks from the minibar, rents the curtains, and herself and her clothes; she does not know what to do with herself, or how to be in her body, in this room. We view her from the top corner of the room, as if a security camera, spying on her grief. Cuts from one of her states to the next, wailing to immobility, show the changing light outside the window and the sounds of daytime traffic and night-time in the city. It is a realistic, honest depiction of the desperation of grief and the sheer incapacity and impotence in the face of the death of a loved one.

Susanne telephones Nejat, who comes to meet her at her hotel. As she wanders around the hotel lounge looking for him, he stands up and signals to her. She asks, 'How did you know it was me?' And he replies, 'You're the saddest person here.' This tender and honest moment shows Nejat's ability to see Susanne: to really see her inner state. It suggests his attention to her is sensitive and caring. It calls to mind Murdoch's observation that, 'The task of attention goes on all the time and at apparently empty and everyday moments we are "looking", making those little peering efforts of imagination which have such important cumulative results' (IP: 334). Nejat's observation captures his effort and his imagination, and his caring connection to Susanne does go on to have cumulative results. It is also clear how action is relevant to moral progress too, in that Nejat's open, welcoming, attitude to Susanne is what Murdoch would call, 'indispensable pivot and spur of the inner scene' (IP: 334). Susanne asks him how well he knew her daughter, and he replies, 'Well enough to like her.' Susanne asks to see Lotte's room, and Nejat takes her to his flat. Susanne tells him that she had been in Istanbul thirty years ago, and had gone hitchhiking to India, just as we know Lotte had done. Nejat shows her Lotte's room, and she asks to stay. She opens the boxes of Lotte's things, smelling her leather jacket, and finding her diary. She lies on the mattress and reads Lotte's diary, which we hear in Lotte's voice. Lotte says how she feels she was taking very similar steps to her Mama, and wonders 'perhaps she sees herself in me'. Susanne's eyelashes flutter, and she falls asleep, holding the diary to her heart. In the moments of her waking, as the camera pans across the room from a brightly lit window, she – and we – see Lotte. In this room full of light, there is a close-up on Lotte's smiling face (the front cover image), and then a shot of the room as we see Susanne reach for Lotte, in an image resembling a religious tableau. She looks so real, and so vital: but no, the next shot reveals she is not there. Lotte's face is even more remarkable than Murdoch's idea of the face showing 'spirit and matter . . . most intensely fused' (OTC: 98), as in this case there is no matter, only spirit. This beautiful but painful moment in the film drives home Murdoch's observation about the absence of the dead. Murdoch quotes Weil's *Notebooks*:

> To lose somebody: we suffer at the thought that the dead one, the absent one should have become something imaginary, something false. But the longing we have for him is not imaginary. We must go down into ourselves, where the desire which is not imaginary resides . . . The loss of contact with reality – there lies evil, there lies sorrow . . . The remedy is to use the loss itself as intermediary for attaining reality. The presence of the dead one is imaginary, but his absence is real, it is henceforth his manner of appearing (Weil 1956: 28). (MGM: 502)

Murdoch develops this idea of the absence of the dead one to argue that 'We must experience the reality of pain, and not fill the void with fantasy . . . We console ourselves with fantasies of "bouncing back"' (MGM: 502). The need, according to Murdoch, is to face the loss and the pain. She says,

> Here anything may help, any person, any pure or innocent thing which could attract love and revive hope . . . We have (gravity, necessity) a natural impulse to derealise our world and surround ourselves with fantasy. Simply stopping this, refraining from filling voids with lies and falsity, is progress. Equally in the more obscure labyrinths of personal relations it may be necessary to make the move which makes the void appear. (MGM: 503)

This bold and painful suggestion, that making the move within personal relations may draw attention to the very loss and pain that we wish to hide from ourselves, but that this may be effective, can be seen in Susanne's actions to go to see Ayten and decide to help her. As Breger points out, when Susanne 'steps into her daughter's shoes by identifying with Lotte's mission to help Ayten, Ayten helps herself' (2014: 85). We next see Ali sitting and reading under a tree. He is reading the book Nejat gave him, about a daughter and her father, and he is weeping. Nejat's cousin tells him that Ali is out of prison and has gone to Trabzon, and Nejat admits that nobody ever responded to Yeter's picture. In an uncharacteristic display of emotion, Nejat punches a pile of books onto the floor, and takes down Yeter's picture, leaving a gap on the noticeboard in the shop. He finds Susanne on the shop's doorstep. She asks to stay with him for a while, saying it did her good to sleep there. They go out to eat. When they toast, Susanne says they will drink 'to death'. This is a pivotal moment in the film. Susanne seems energised and also realistic about death. The next morning, as she leaves the flat and walks down the street, she says hello to the men playing backgammon in the café opposite, just as we saw Lotte do. This small gesture is indicative of looking outwards at others instead of staying trapped looking in. Susanne goes to see Ayten, who says sorry. Susanne says she wants to help her, because it's what Lotte wanted. Susanne studies Ayten's face: her remorse appears sincere. Ayten courageously chooses to use her 'right to remorse', which entails giving information to the authorities.

Susanne and Nejat stand in the window of his flat looking at the men going to mosque on the first day of Bayram, the festival of the sacrifice of Abraham's son, Isaac (Figure 5.1). Nejat tells Susanne that he was afraid of the story as a child. He asked his father what he would do, and his father said 'he would even make God his enemy in order to protect me'. Susanne looks at Nejat and asks whether his father is still alive. Nejat looks meaningfully at Susanne, as he realises the love that his father had for him, and what he himself must do now. He asks Susanne to look after his bookshop for a few days, and then we are back to the beginning of the film, as Nejat is on his journey to find his father. He drives through the forest roads to the coast to Filyos, then keeps on, to Trabzon, where his father is fishing. Nejat's decisions would seem to represent an adjustment in priorities that Murdoch envisaged as moral progress:

> A serious scholar has great merits. But a serious scholar who is also a good man knows not only his subject but the proper place of his subject in the whole of his life. The understanding which leads the scientist to the right decision about giving up a certain study, or leads the artist to the right decision about his family, is superior to the understanding of art and science as such. (SGC: 379)

It may have taken Nejat a while to feel able to see Ali again, but this would probably be seen to be 'the right decision' in Murdochian terms, in that he is seeing his father with love and compassion.

Figure 5.1 Susanne (Hanna Schygulla) helps Nejat (Baki Davrak) recall his father's love, in *The Edge of Heaven* (2007), directed by Fatih Akin.

As Ayten leaves prison, she is spat at by her fellow comrades for repenting. She goes to the bookshop, and Susanne offers her a room. Susanne wrongly pronounces the name of where Nejat's flat is; Ayten corrects her, and Susanne says it again. They embrace, and smile at each other. Humility on the part of Susanne, and Ayten, is facilitating their connection. As they leave the shop, the camera focuses on the space on the board where Yeter's picture was. If Nejat had not taken it down, Ayten would have seen the photograph of her mother, and discovered she is dead.

These bold steps that Nejat, Susanne and Ayten have taken are related to the difficult task of compassion and goodness. Murdoch writes,

> The self, the place where we live, is a place of illusion. Goodness is connected with the attempt to see the unself, to see and respond to the real world in the light of a virtuous consciousness. This is the non-metaphysical meaning of the idea of transcendence to which philosophers have so constantly resorted in their explanations of goodness. 'Good is a transcendent reality' means that virtue is the attempt to pierce the veil of selfish consciousness and join the world as it really is. It is an empirical fact about human nature that this attempt cannot be entirely successful.
>
> Of course we are dealing with a metaphor, but with a very important metaphor and one which is not just a property of philosophy and not just a model. (SGC: 376–7)

This work, of responding to and joining the real world, is difficult and does not guarantee a happy ending. In the village, Nejat sees an old lady working in the field, and she tells him that Ali has gone fishing. She says that the sea is getting choppy, and so he'll come in soon. Nejat moves to the shore, takes off his glasses, looks out to sea, sits and waits. This is how the film ends, without certainty that Ali will return or that they will reconcile, but with Nejat's decision to wait for him and to be open to seeing him. He has sought out his father. Since Yeter's death, the journey that Nejat has been on is one of growing clarity of vision, from realising he was not suited to his job, to accepting his failure to atone for his father's sins by finding and paying for Ayten's education, to deciding to open himself up to his father again. The role of Susanne facing Lotte's death and deciding to embrace it and confront the pain has inspired and enabled him in this vision. Their sharing of the story of a cruel and demanding God with Abraham and Isaac, and Nejat's memory of his father's devotion to him, has undermined the idea of God, and boosted the idea of the Good: this is what goodness looks like. It may look like Christian forgiveness, but it is brought about by the clear vision of his father's love, and the preciousness of that, and it is certainly compassion for one's family. In terms of Susanne's journey, she has determined to continue to do what Lotte would have wanted to do, and Ayten has risked her safety and betrayed her political comrades in order to enable that relationship to flourish. The film has been described as privileging 'humanist values over radical politics' (Mennel 2009), but in terms of Murdochian morality this is a story of particulars, and of individuals and their moral journeys.

I will now look at two films that also resonate with examples given by Murdoch in her writing about goodness, and which challenge conventional, simplistic images of right and wrong. The films thereby invite close attention in analysing issues of love and goodness and how they affect our vision and judgement.

LOVE AND DETACHMENT: *I'VE LOVED YOU SO LONG* (*IL Y A LONGTEMPS QUE JE T'AIME*)

Initially the most striking element of this film is the face of Juliette, played by Kristin Scott Thomas. This famously beautiful star face is grey, wan and impassive. She does not smile, and barely speaks, but simply smokes. She has been in prison, and is collected by her sister upon her release. Her sister, Léa (Elsa Zylberstein), has a busy, lively home, with a husband and two children, her father-in-law living in the house too, and a demanding job as an academic. She has to accommodate Juliette in her household, which includes assuaging the concerns of her husband Luc (Serge Hazanavicius), who has never met Juliette but of course knows all about her. Juliette is not that easy to have around: she is not used to speaking because she has been in prison for fifteen years for killing her young son. She moves slowly, as someone who is not used to having to get anywhere in a hurry, and she touches fabrics and stained glass in the house, as if re-familiarising herself with the different textures of luxury. It emerges that Léa never visited Juliette in prison. She says that she wrote at the start, but their parents told her she didn't exist. In this film, the sisters come to know and love each other afresh through a journey of getting reacquainted, and actually talking about the truth of what happened to Juliette's little boy. Juliette, a doctor, knew that her son was dying and would be in terrible pain, so she ended his suffering and was convicted of his murder. The reality of re-entering society with this history, but keeping the reason for her crime a secret, is made clear by matters such as how she accounts for her absence from Léa's life to her friends, to how she explains her conviction to a potential boss, and how Luc feels about leaving her with their children. The film progresses through Juliette gradually being able to demonstrate her normality and her humanity, whether it is playing piano with Léa and Luc's daughters, or treating Luc's dislocated shoulder by manipulating it back into place. Her sexuality is reawakened. She goes to meet her probation officer, and, as he speaks to her, she watches his mouth and his eyes. She has casual sex with a man she meets in a bar, and starts to build a friendship with Michel (Laurent Grévill) who is a colleague of her sister's. Her integration into social events is difficult, both physically, in relation to crowds and spaces, and also in terms of conversation and questions. It isn't until Léa realises the truth about Juliette's son's illness by discovering the results of medical tests, and that she keeps his photograph under her pillow, that she confronts Juliette about what happened and the truth comes out. The film ends with Léa's view of Juliette changed, by the revelation of the truth. So how might Murdoch's thinking relate to this scenario? Well, Murdoch would say that it is within the family that the moral work is done, and we have to do some too. This is a site of the frailties and difficulties of family life. Léa does not really know how to deal with the situation. Luc is uneasy around Juliette. Juliette is isolated from her family, and we are encouraged to have interest in her plight as she is clearly so damaged. We do not know 'the truth' about the death of her son until Léa does. The revelation that she killed her son as a mercy killing only confirms our tendency to view her with compassion and sympathy – if not empathy. Empathy arrives in the final scene of her disclosure where she breaks down and we become aware of the depth and magnitude of her torment. Her life has been characterised by isolation, intrusion and abandonment, by professionals, family and husband (who divorced her). The particularities of Juliette's situation include her medical knowledge and her capabilities as a doctor, as well as having an ill child. These all elicit more compassion from us and from her sister. It emerges that Juliette did not speak during her trial. She could probably have helped herself by revealing the explanation for her actions, but she tells Léa that she felt that she deserved the punishment for bringing him into the world, let alone for killing him. This film certainly presents a milieu of troubled motherhood: not one relationship is without difficulty, as Léa and Luc adopted children because Léa did not want to give birth, and Juliette's own mother effectively disowned her. Natalie Edwards develops the idea of the film's critique of the supposed joys of motherhood by arguing that the film shows 'that a murdering mother is not beyond our understanding or experience, but is beyond several illusory concepts that society would perhaps rather not question' (Edwards 2015). In this way, the film echoes Murdoch's proposals about family life, and where selflessness or goodness might be found. Murdoch believed that family is an important area of moral work, involving difficult adjustments and compromises. She writes,

> True conceptions combine just modes of judgement and ability to connect with an increased perception of detail. The case of the mother who has to consider each of her family carefully as she decides whether or not to throw auntie out. This double revelation of both random detail and intuited unity is what we receive in every sphere of life if we seek for what is best. (SGC: 379)

Léa constantly assesses how Juliette is fitting in, in the face of juggling the needs of each member of her family. When returning to the idea of what goodness looks like, Murdoch suggests it may be found in the family:

> The contingently existing saint who, if we were ever fortunate enough to *meet* him or her, might stand to us in the guise of a demonstration (to show it can be done), might be some quiet unpretentious worker, a schoolteacher or a mother, or better still an aunt. Mothers have many egoistic satisfactions and much power. The aunt may be the selfless unrewarded doer of good. I have known such aunts. (MGM: 429)

This reference to the egos and powers of mothers resonates with all three films in this chapter, and is a diversion of focus from the conventional image of motherhood as selflessness or unconditional love, to less obvious ones. Murdoch invites us to look beyond the conventional images, and to really look for the good:

> The possible saints, aunts, dissidents, social workers and so on, may or may not have any sort of religious vision. How can one know anyway? Some saintly figures are self-evidently 'religious', others may be invisible, buried deep in families or offices or silent religious houses . . . At the highest level this is practical mysticism, where the certainty and the absolute appear incarnate and immediate in the needs of others. (MGM: 430)

Figure 5.2 Juliette (Kristin Scott Thomas) and Léa (Elsa Zylberstein) learn to live together, in *I've Loved You So Long/ Il y a longtemps que je t'aime* (2008), directed by Philippe Claudel.

The loving aunt in this film, Juliette, is also a mother, but her role in this family household is to care as much as she is asked to, whether it is babysitting or cooking, and to be that special extra relative in the house, who can keep grandpa company or make playing the piano a treat (Figure 5.2).

There is an emphasis on women's stories in Murdoch's philosophical examples, which will be developed in detail in Chapter 7. She identifies women's lives as rich in moral activity, without explicitly claiming this as her aim. Simply by including examples from everyday life, such as family dynamics or housework, as well as female characters from novels, history and the Bible, Murdoch opens out the realm of moral philosophy genuinely to include all of us. And, importantly, the ordinary person can of course be exceptional, whether that individual is a mother, or a dictator, or good man in a concentration camp.[3] Perhaps we can see Juliette's love for her son as 'the highest love', in the following sense:

> One cannot but agree that in some sense this is the most important thing of all, and yet human love is normally too profoundly possessive and also too 'mechanical' to be a place of vision . . . That the highest love is in some sense impersonal is something which we can indeed see in art, but which I think we cannot see clearly, except in a very piecemeal manner, in the relationships of human beings. (OGG: 361)

Perhaps the idea of loving your child so selflessly that you are able to act ostensibly 'impersonally' and end his life is something that is very difficult for others to see clearly if at all. And the basis for our compassion should lie in the realm of experience, and what actually happens in people's lives, rather than assessments made in a vacuum or universal rules and principles. The guiding principle, as always for Murdoch, is the Good, as it is found in lives.

> The image of the Good as a transcendent magnetic centre seems to me the least corruptible and most realistic picture for us to use in our reflections upon the moral life. Here the philosophical 'proof', if there is one, is the same as the moral 'proof'. I would rely especially upon arguments from experience concerned with the realism which we perceive to be connected with goodness, and with the love and detachment which is exhibited in great art. (OGG: 361)

The last film we are going to look at in this chapter is one in which the matter of a mother's love is central, as is the question of loving the ostensibly unlovable.

THE REALISM OF COMPASSION: *WE NEED TO TALK ABOUT KEVIN*

In Lynne Ramsay's 2011 film adaptation of Lionel Shriver's best-selling novel, Eva Khatchadourian's (Tilda Swinton) motherhood is constantly under the spotlight. When Kevin is a baby, he is difficult to care for and to love, and, with her, never seems to stop crying. When he is a child he is combative and uncooperative, and as he gets older he is sadistic and manipulative to his younger sister, and bitter and hateful to his mother. The film shows Eva trying to carry on living after Kevin has committed a massacre at his high school, killing and wounding many of his fellow pupils with a bow and arrow, and has also killed his father and sister. For Eva, this entails holding down a job, cooking for herself and withstanding verbal and physical abuse, while consuming plenty of wine and pills, and scrubbing abusive graffiti off her house and car. Eva continues to visit Kevin in the juvenile detention centre, despite his insults and rejection. She looks at him with a mixture of disbelief and revulsion, and these visits prompt us to ask why she continues to go: is it loving attention, or looking for some glimpse of goodness in Kevin? Is it care for him? Fascination? Or is it simply out of duty?

At the final visit we see in the film, Kevin shows a glimpse of vulnerability as he is being readied for adult prison. But whether this is any kind of self-knowledge or repentance, or is simply self-centred fear of what lies ahead of him, is hard to decide. With a shaved head, and numerous scars, Kevin looks like he has already received some rough treatment during his time inside. The adult prison that awaits him, however, as he is about to turn eighteen, is clearly worrying him. On this, the second anniversary of his massacre, Eva looks at him as intently as ever, and says, 'I want you to tell me why.' Kevin seems to suggest he is beginning to get some insight, just by questioning, 'I used to think I knew, but now I'm not so sure.' A flicker of pleasant surprise can be detected on Eva's face, as a weakening appears on Kevin's. He looks like he wants to say more, but their time is up. Eva and Kevin hug, and this is significant because Kevin really grasps his mother as she cradles his head. This does appear to be a shift. Is this perhaps because Eva has made him realise he will leave prison at some point, and need to re-enter the world? Or is there perhaps something in her refusal to be sent away and her tenacity in visiting him that has, at long last, had an effect? In her chapter on love in Murdoch, Susan Wolf considers whether this idea of a loving gaze is simply 'the positive light conception', or rose-tinted spectacles (2014: 371–3). This is an important potential criticism of Murdoch's language and description: are we supposed to keep attending until we see every person as good? Wolf reminds us that the gaze Murdoch says we should cultivate is both loving and just, and that 'even if love can be imagined to paint its objects in a rosy light, justice cannot' (2014: 372). This loving vision must be free from fantasy, and any compassion must be real:

> One might at this point pause and consider the picture of human personality, or the soul, which has been emerging. It is in the capacity to love, that is to *see*, that the liberation of the soul from fantasy consists. The freedom which is a proper human goal is the freedom from fantasy, that is the realism of compassion. (OGG: 354)

Eva's attention to Kevin exemplifies this. I suggest that she continues to visit him to try to understand him, as well as out of a sense of duty, but also, frankly, because they only have each other now. She has certainly never been blind to Kevin's sadism and indeed has frequently been the only person who could see it. Her intelligence and strength are displayed through her persistence and ability to maintain a sufficient distance to observe her son without being clouded by emotion or judgement (Figure 5.3). In this way, Eva displays the ability that Murdoch describes here: 'The ability, for instance, to think justly about what is evil, or to love another person unselfishly, involves a discipline of intellect and emotion. Thought, goodness and reality are thus seen to be connected' (MGM: 399).

This film, and these ideas from Murdoch, challenge the basis on which we see and relate to our nearest and dearest. Are mothers driven by their egos, blind to their children's faults? Wolf suggests a mother like Eva might be, when she says: 'The loving gaze of, say, a murderer's mother, can hardly

Figure 5.3 Eva (Tilda Swinton) perseveres with realism and love, in *We Need to Talk About Kevin* (2011), directed by Lynne Ramsay.

be identified with a "just" gaze in virtue of its highlighting the good qualities in the murderer's character rather than the bad' (Wolf 2014: 380). Speaking in 1967, so using out-of-date terminology, Murdoch offers a more complex and nuanced understanding of family relations, however, when she observes,

> Our attachments tend to be selfish and strong, and the transformation of our loves from selfishness to unselfishness is sometimes hard even to conceive of. Yet is the situation really so different? Should a retarded child be kept at home or sent to an institution? Should an elderly relative who is a trouble-maker be cared for or asked to go away? Should an unhappy marriage be continued for the sake of the children? Should I leave my family in order to do political work? Should I neglect them in order to practise my art? The love which brings the right answer is an exercise of justice and realism and really *looking*. (SGC: 375)

Murdoch is saying that things are not so simple in families. The mother of a murderer may well be able to form a just and loving gaze upon her son, with work: 'the background condition . . . is a just mode of vision and a good quality of consciousness. It is a *task* to come to see the world as it is' (SGC: 375). Eva's work in visiting and studying her son, attempting to come to see him as he really is, and to try to understand him, is part and parcel of her slow, steady resilience, alongside her daily confronting of the reality of Kevin's murders and the loss of her husband and daughter. In this way, she exemplifies Murdoch's discussion of 'energy and discernment':

> We act rightly 'when the time comes' not out of strength of will but out of the quality of our usual attachments and with the kind of energy and discernment which we have available. And to this the whole activity of our consciousness is relevant. (SGC: 375)

The background to her relationship with Kevin is important here. Eva has never been blind to Kevin's faults. She recognises in him 'the real existence of evil: cynicism, cruelty, indifference to suffering' (SGC: 380), and she has also seen what is good, fun and interesting in the world, such as love for her husband, the innocence of her daughter, and the intoxication of travel and other countries. Like the other characters we have looked at in this chapter, she lives with the reality of death on a daily basis. And this, Murdoch argues, enables a clearer vision of virtue:

> A genuine sense of mortality enables us to see virtue as the only thing of worth; and it is impossible to limit and foresee the ways in which it will be required of us. (SGC: 381)

> Goodness is connected with the acceptance of real death and real chance and real transience and only against the background of this acceptance, which is psychologically so difficult, can we understand the full extent of what virtue is like. The acceptance of death is an acceptance of our own nothingness which is an automatic spur to our concern with what is not ourselves. (SGC: 385)

This is a concept that is both reassuring and terrifying: essentially we cannot know how we will need to be good, but all we can do is ready ourselves by aiming for goodness as our way of life. And this is how Murdoch thinks we can live our lives:

> There is a place both inside and outside of religion for a sort of contemplation of the Good, not just by dedicated experts but by ordinary people: an attention which is not just the planning of particular good actions but an attempt to look right away from self towards a distant transcendent perfection, a source of uncontaminated energy, a source of *new* and quite undreamt-of virtue. (SGC: 383)

This consideration of the contemplation of the Good by us all leads us to think about the role played by films such as the ones analysed in this book in the development of our inner lives and moral visions. I will now develop this by revisiting the idea of films as moral fables which we looked at in Chapter 3.

OUR OWN PATH TO THE GOOD

Make no mistake about it, Murdoch means us to be doing moral work in response to art and as part of our 'daily struggle with the world' (MGM: 427). After all, although the role of attending to art is a way of training our mode of attention, Murdoch's point is that 'Great art teaches a sense of reality, so does ordinary living and loving. We find out in the most minute details of our lives that the good is the real' (MGM: 430). The unique role of film in these respects is that it enables us to pay close attention to the lives of others on-screen, watching them learning from their journeys, and also we learn ourselves by close attention and perception. Film is able to show characters such as Nejat, Susanne, Juliette and Eva, in their 'daily struggle', and also to constitute this idea of contemplative perception for us:

> The best picture of most kinds of thinking is perception, and the best picture of serious contemplative thinking is serious contemplative perception; as when we *attend* to a human face, music, a flower, a visual work of art (etc. etc.). Such close mental attention involves the conception of 'presence'. (MGM: 424–5)

By choosing to pay contemplative attention to films such as *The Edge of Heaven*, *I've Loved You So Long* and *We Need to Talk about Kevin*, films with significant and deep moral thinking, we enable their complexity and power to affect us, and improve the clarity of our moral vision. For this to happen we need to accept that these films contain examples of thinking and relationships that are realistic and relevant, and then they can aid us in our overcoming of self. In a paragraph that connects remarkably closely with these films, Murdoch conveys the usefulness of thinking about Nejat, Susanne, Juliette and Eva:

> The energy of the attentive scholar or artist is spiritual energy. The energy of the bereaved person trying to survive in the best way, or of the mother thinking about her delinquent son (and so on and so on) is spiritual. One uses this word with a certain purpose, to set up certain pictures, to draw attention to similarities and to explain and clarify the obscure by the familiar. (MGM: 505)

Murdoch's discussion of the transcendent Good and its role in the everyday is a way to include spirituality and metaphysics in the discussion of the moral lives of individuals, as we struggle with work, families, love and death. This is the stuff of life, and Murdoch grounds us in the realism of morality and virtue. In the next chapter I will consider these concepts when viewed in more extreme forms in art as comedy and tragedy.

NOTES

1. See discussion of M and D in Chapter 3 at p. 62.
2. For further information about this massacre, this article is a useful starting point: <https://anfenglish.com/kurdistan/turkish-state-s-open-secret-maras-massacre-17610> (last accessed 15 August 2018).
3. Murdoch uses the example of the man in a concentration camp on several occasions. It is, for her, clearly an example of an extreme moral situation. For example, she describes 'the best kind of courage' as 'that which would make a man act unselfishly in a concentration camp' (OGG: 346). She also considers how 'merit in one area does not seem to guarantee merit in another', using as an example the idea that 'the concentration camp guard can be a kindly father' (SGC: 379).

CHAPTER 6

Film, Comedy and Tragedy

> Human life is chancy and incomplete. It is the role of tragedy, and also of comedy, and of painting to show us suffering without a thrill and death without a consolation. (SGC: 371)

> What is absurd is very often funny, though it can be appalling too. (MGM: 91)

> Truth and happiness are ideally frolicking together, so that it is a happy destiny when it's working well. Works of art make you happy. Even *King Lear* makes you happy, and yet it comes near to the edge of the impossible – that you could be made happy by a work of art which is about something terrible. (Interview in 1985, cited in Dooley 2003: 135)

In 'The Fire and the Sun' (F&S), Murdoch proposes that we should ask ourselves what we may properly laugh at, 'even in our private moments' (F&S: 398). This is not as pious as it may sound: many philosophers, from Plato, to Henri Bergson and Simon Critchley, as well as Murdoch, have been concerned with the mechanics of the joke and what makes us laugh, and the moral questions that this raises. This chapter will examine the basis of humour in *The Death of Stalin* (Armando Iannucci, 2017), the troubling treatment of rape in *Elle* (Paul Verhoeven, 2016) and the desperation of the void in *Manchester by the Sea* (Kenneth Lonergan, 2016), and consider the roles of comedy and tragedy in the films in Murdochian terms. We will assess the value of humour as a tool for dealing with difficult topics, the adequacy of tragic art for depicting suffering, and the moral questions involved in so doing.

MURDOCH ON COMEDY AND TRAGEDY

Murdoch was concerned with how the horrors of life appear to us in our contemplations, conversations and imaginations, and how they are treated by art. In her discussion of the 'tragic fragment', she conveys how we tend to extrapolate moments or elements from a terrible story. This reduction, or pocket-sized piece of information, Murdoch argues, is suitable for comedy, but less so for tragedy:

> A joke is a joke however often repeated, it is portable and has its conventional belongingness in life. But the 'tragic fragment' embarrasses and disturbs us or begins to sound suspiciously and inappropriately like art. There are stories which we hesitate to repeat lest we seem to be gloating over horrors or trying to gratify unworthy emotions in ourselves or our hearers. One might tell someone's dying words to his mother, but not repeat them at a dinner party. (MGM: 95)

This conveys the idea that by selecting and repeating fractions of a story about suffering, we not only diminish it, but disrespect those who it involves, and this reflects on us as tellers of the tale, both as to why we are repeating it and what we are getting out of it. In this way, Murdoch sees art as being the more honest and effective way of communicating tragedy, whereas conveying the terrible 'in real life' is inevitably a matter of only glimpsing the horror:

> Terrible events may be fiddled with by art, but as they appear in the stream of life, in conversation, newspapers, television, informal or formal books (and so on) these aesthetic 'limited wholes' tend to be unstable, so that we may see through the tale into the horror beyond. (MGM: 96)

For Murdoch, 'tragedy belongs to art, and only to great art', and it is here that the comic and the tragic may combine effectively: 'Shakespeare's tragic plays contain comic and irrelevant matter' (MGM: 94). *King Lear* is an example Murdoch returns to as epitomising tragedy, but also, as she expresses in the epigraph, a play which conveys pleasure and humour too. In further evidence that Murdoch recognises the possibilities that film could convey mental states and consciousness, she writes,

> Lear could be imagined living on as an image of death which would be more awful than the merciful end conventionally required. A clever cinema director could perhaps end a version of the play by continued shots of Lear, still alive, remembering, always growing older and older and always *thinking* those terrible torturing thoughts. (MGM: 121)

The film that Murdoch imagines is one we can all envisage. What is interesting here is the idea that Lear's thought could be shown, and we could share it: the medium of film, through its ability to compress time and convey silent contemplation, is uniquely able to express this painful process. It is similar to Dr Cemal's memory-jogging trip while looking at his photographs, or the shot of Jackie Kennedy's face caught in the car window as she looks at the crowds surveying her. These shots convey reverie, and through this the thoughts of the characters are shown to us, not simply told. These kinaesthetic and synaesthetic images and gestures work to hold us in the on-screen contemplations, which can impart or suggest insight and even revelation. Murdoch writes, 'We use our imagination not to escape the world but to join it, and this exhilarates us because of the distance between our ordinary dulled consciousness and an apprehension of the real' (SGC: 374).

Attending to these images on-screen attunes our imagination with the experience of the character, enabling it to affect our mental state, albeit not necessarily to share it: 'patient attention transforms accuracy without interval into just discernment' (SGC: 374). The suggestion here is that we may be changed or improved by the experience of sharing the thoughts and experiences of the characters and events on-screen, and that those changes may have a lasting effect beyond the end of the film. In other words, this is not just about how we experience the film at the time, but how our attending to the film might improve the quality of our understanding, compassion and discernment in everyday life. Murdoch sees this as a possibility engendered by all art:

> I should say at this point that I take my theory to apply to all the arts and not just the literary arts. The notion of a loving respect for a reality other than oneself is as relevant to making a vase as it is to writing a novel, nor does the theory only apply to arts which involve, in the obvious sense, imitation. The highest art is . . . tragedy, because its subject-matter is the most important and most individual that we know. ('The Sublime and the Good' (S&G): 218)

> What makes tragic art so disturbing is that self-contained form is combined with something, the individual being and destiny of human persons, which defies form. A great tragedy leaves us in eternal doubt. (S&G: 219)

These quotes encapsulate the excess spirit of a film, or the element that exceeds the story and the images on-screen. This picks up on the idea of 'the soul' that I looked at in Chapter 2, when discussing the evocations of which a film is capable, in that case *Under the Skin*. Murdoch here is describing the conceptual, philosophical angst that a film, such as *Margaret*, *Once Upon a Time in Anatolia* or *The Edge of Heaven*, can engender. These feelings are aroused by film form, as well as performance, sound, light, pace and space, and of course narrative. Being left in eternal doubt does not sound like the most pleasurable way to finish a film, but this is something of which a film is certainly capable. The way in which Murdoch describes tragedy as being about the individual being resonates with her concern that philosophy should be about particularity: individuals with specific lives, joys and problems, who are as singular as we all are, and yet also in relation to others, and societally and historically contextualised. Vitally, the tying up of narrative ends does not appease all of the realisations and challenges that the story has brought about, and in some ways the attempt to do so betrays the impossibility of so doing. In this way, 'tragedy in art is the attempt to overcome the defeat which human beings suffer in the practical world' (S&G: 220). The lack of consolation may make tragedy more realistic, but it also shows how art is not a 'safe' or reassuring place.

LOOKING FOR SAFETY IN IMAGES

Murdoch describes how we carry images or ideas with us which serve to reassure us. She writes,

> There are moral illuminations or pictures which remain vividly in the memory, playing a protective or guiding role: moral refuges, perpetual starting points . . . A Christian may think here of Christ upon the cross. But at a simpler level the story of his birth, complete with shepherds, kings, angels, the ox and the ass, may be a good thing to have in one's life. Buddhists speak of 'taking refuge'. Such points or places of spiritual power may be indicated by a tradition, suggested by work or subjects of study, emerge from personal crises or relationships, be gradually established or come suddenly: through familiarity with a good person or a sacred text, a sense of renewal in a particular place, a sudden vision in art or nature, joy experienced as pure, witnessing a virtuous action, a patient suffering, an absence of resentment, humble service, persistent heroism, innumerable things in family life and so on and so on. We are turning here to an inexhaustible and familiar field of human resources. Every individual has a collection of such things which might be indicated by various names and images. I have already used some: refuges, lights, visions, deep sources, pure sources, protections, strongholds,

> footholds, icons, starting points, sacraments, pearls of great price. Our moral consciousness is full of such imagery, kinaesthetic, visual, literary, traditional, verbal and non-verbal, and is full too of images of darkness, of stumbling, falling, sinking, drowning. (MGM: 335–6)

This lengthy quote describes how we have 'refuges' or comforting thoughts that we turn to for reassurance, and that these originate externally, from religions, or work, or personal experience. They might be a favourite passage from a novel, or a beach visited on holiday, or a scene from a film, that offers succour and reassurance. Perhaps the sight of Lotte's smiling face might be one of these; or a memory of a loved one, or a piece of family lore passed on through generations. This is a realm that film can nurture, with moments that enrich our thought and show instances of virtue or wisdom, and we each have our own 'collection'. This is a pleasing thought in itself: the recognition that we have something like a wardrobe of imagery that we can select from when needed, and that film – especially for the more cinephilic among us – forms a significant part of that wardrobe. This also shows how we can recall moments from films, as part of our own experience, in a similar way to how we recall experiences from real life. However, not all of this imagery is comforting, and we are also no doubt well aware of the darker, vulnerable imagery of which Murdoch speaks. These may also be fed by images from films that we wish we had never seen, or indeed from the television news. These images are not exceptional, but part of our everyday lives:

> What happens every day is important, images can affect the quality of our thoughts and wishes. The damage done to inner life, to aloneness and quietness, through the imposition of banal or pornographic or violent images by television, is a considerable wound. (MGM: 337)

Murdoch is not impressed by television, or the way it invades our minds and thoughts. Referring to it elsewhere as 'the dictator's best friend' she worries how it 'already erodes our ability to read' (MGM: 210). She perceives a need for quiet contemplation in order to cultivate imagination and respect for others, because 'a moral philosophy should be inhabited' (MGM: 337). She explains,

> Simply sitting quietly and calmly can be doing something good; subduing unkind or frenzied thoughts certainly is. Morality, as the ability or attempt to be good, rests upon deep areas of sensibility and creative imagination, upon removal from one state of mind to another, upon shift of attachments, upon love and respect for the contingent details of the world. (MGM: 337)

If we are to pay attention to the details of the world and their contingency, then we unavoidably have to deal with horror. And this is not the fantastic horror of science fiction or the monster movie, but rather the human elements of horror in their quotidian banality as well as their extremity, which shed light on the world we live in. Murdoch talks about Kafka's *Metamorphosis*, which is indeed fantastic, where the father kills his son, who has become a large beetle, and describes how we can 'see through it the real horrors which lurk in life' (ibid.: 340):

> art can deal with both the high and low experience, turning the latter into a kind of exhilarating though fearful surrealism: like the flying apples in Kafka's story. And in life too the absurd contingent, not the waterfall but the broken crockery, may produce a surge of cosmic misery and hatred, or may make us smile and turn the occasion into a sort of rueful aesthetic pleasure: as when we say, unseriously, this is too much, this really is *the end*! (MGM: 341)

Murdoch refers here to the way in which, in *Metamorphosis*, Gregor's father hurls apples to repulse him, which we can see as both a surreal nightmare and also as a painful rejection of the son by the father.[1] Murdoch also recalls the waterfall of the Kantian sublime, and stresses that it need not be something so majestic or vast in order to overwhelm us: 'a burnt saucepan or massive broken crockery accident' could do it, and that we see that there is some humour in this (MGM: 340). This is moral experience, not just emotional, in that we assess and react and learn from what we see and what we imagine. For Murdoch, 'our moral experience shares in the peculiar density of art, and in its imaginative cognitive activity' (MGM: 341). And, as I examined in Chapter 3, Murdoch proposes that we are doing this moral work all the time:

> The struggle against evil, the love of what is good, the inspired enjoyment of beauty, the discovery and perception of holiness, continues all the time in the privacy of human souls. This process is more like eating or breathing than a dramatic conflict with clashing swords and contradictions. The word 'tragic' is out of place. Of course there are dramatic moments and situations, but these are, if we look at the long threads of human lives, intermittent. 'Tragic' is another comfort word. We invoke the theatre of the tragic to help us to bear sufferings which it would be too painful to consider in all their detailed structures of accident and muddle. There is no deep analysis of terrible suffering. The horrors of the world recede into darkness. (MGM: 458)

Here, Murdoch examines the place of the tragic in our lives, and suggests that most of life is not in fact tragic, but, as set out in the epigraph to this chapter, 'chancy and incomplete'. This is a challenging proposition, and implies that we exaggerate the horror or tragedy of an event or a situation in order to avoid the more banal reality. This is resonant with Hannah Arendt's 1963 analysis of Adolf Eichmann as embodying the banality of evil, which attracted so much controversy upon its publication.[2] It is also consistent with the mindset of describing certain criminals as 'monsters', thereby denying their humanity and inevitable connection to the rest of us. These difficult issues are at the heart of the films in this chapter. They feature a range of individuals: from those we – and history – might consider to be monstrously evil, to archetypes of sexual violence and fatal negligence. How are we to experience these, particularly when we may be invited, or compelled, to laugh at them? Do these films function to challenge our preconceptions about the humanity, or lack of humanity, we expect to find in these characters? Murdoch argues that, 'If there is to be morality, there cannot altogether be an end to evil. Discord is essential to goodness. Moral evil exists only in moral experience and that experience is essentially inconsistent' (MGM: 488). This is a challenge to established boundaries of good and evil, asserting that these matters are perhaps not as fixed as we would find comfortable, and yet Murdoch does not wish us to be too serious about it, which is why we must also consider the role of humour: 'Not all metaphysicians have a sense of humour. Does metaphysics founder on the funny? Not necessarily – a little light and air often improves the scene . . . Funniness mocks totality' (MGM: 491).

This is precisely what *The Death of Stalin* aims to do: to mock the totalitarian regime in Stalin's USSR and those who were in control. This is an interesting film to consider in relation to Murdoch's thinking as she famously began her political outlook as a communist but migrated further and further to the right as she became increasingly disenchanted with the Soviet communist experiment (Browning 2018: 23; 'A House of Theory' (HT): 173). What I will consider here, however, is the role of comedy in this film about the brutal, murderous regime and the individuals who sat at Stalin's high table. The film questions the morality of laughing at these caricatured individuals, when they committed acts of such cruelty.

MOCKING TOTALITY: *THE DEATH OF STALIN*

The film begins at a piano concert in 1953. An intertitle announces that 'For 20 years Stalin's NKVD security forces have imposed the great terror', and that 'Those on Stalin's list of "enemy" names are arrested, exiled or shot'. The scenario of the piano concert is designed to show the grip of terror that the ordinary people are held in: when Stalin telephones the director of the concert to ask for a recording, and the director realises the concert is not being recorded, absolute terror strikes. The director has to get people off the streets to come back in to the hall so the concert can be repeated and a fake audience can applaud. There is an uneasy mixture of the comic and the horrific. The director says, with faux reassurance, 'Sit down, don't worry nobody's going to get killed', conveying how likely it actually is that people in this society would get killed for minor infractions. This unease is bolstered by an old-fashioned sexist joke. When the director Andreyev (Paddy Considine) tells his staff to get more people in off the street for the audience, he says they should get fat ones 'so we need fewer', and the conductor says 'I could get my wife – she'd deaden the acoustic.' This is an old 'my wife's so fat' joke, which sets an off-kilter and uncomfortable tone for the humour.

The pianist, Maria (Olga Kurylenko), refuses to re-play the concert, saying that Stalin killed her father and brother. She says she won't do it, 'as God is my witness I will not do it'; but Andreyev bargains with her, and she agrees to do it for 20,000 roubles. The recording is made, and Maria slips a written note in the record sleeve before it is taken to Stalin. We see Stalin (Adrian McLoughlin) in his study going down his list of people to be executed. Stalin has a little high cockney voice, and his Central Committee members appear as boorish buffoons, with Georgy Malenkov (Jeffrey Tambor), Nikita Khruschev (Steve Buscemi) and Vyacheslav Molotov (Michael Palin) telling a story about throwing grenades to keep warm, the actors performing in their familiar comedic styles. Head of security, Lavrenti Beria (Simon Russell Beale) goes to action Stalin's list, saying to the soldier he has tasked to do the killing, 'Shoot her before him but make sure he sees it', and 'Kill him, take him to his church and dump him in the pulpit.' These instructions convey the callous attitude to killing and the express purpose of making an exhibition of the murderous acts. The soldiers drag people screaming from their homes; these scenes are more familiar from war films where homes are raided and families torn apart, as a son identifies his father to the soldiers. By now we have a complex and contradictory picture: there is cruelty and terror, fear and death, along with gags and slapstick. Some lines of dialogue are cruel and horrific, others are light and silly.

The committee members are hanging out with Stalin. They joke and leap around, chest bumping in slow motion for maximum ludicrousness. Stalin says it's time for a cowboy movie, and asks, 'Who's in my posse?' They all sit around watching a western and then the cronies leave, drunk, cheering 'Long live the Communist Party of Lenin and Stalin; long live John Wayne and John Ford!' It transpires that one of them, Molotov, has been put 'on the list'. Khruschev advises Malenkov to make a note when he gets home of everything he thinks he said tonight, then he can go over it in the morning. So even after this night of social drinking, movie watching and fooling around, their lives and liberties hang in the balance.

Stalin, now alone in his room, gets the recording of the concert and puts it on the record player, and he finds Maria's note. It says 'Josef Vissarionovich Stalin, you have betrayed our nation and destroyed its people. I pray for your end and ask the Lord to forgive you. Tyrant.' He laughs, derisively, but collapses, and appears to die on the floor of his study. In the morning, Stalin's breakfast is brought to him, and we next see a message being delivered to Beria saying that Comrade Stalin is very ill. Beria is busy torturing someone for names; as he walks down the corridor he gives instructions about someone else, saying, 'Have his wife moved into the next cell and start working on her until he talks; make it noisy.' He adds, 'Some women will do anything to get their husbands released.' This exploitative, disrespectful attitude towards women's bodies runs throughout the film.

Beria takes charge of the scene in Stalin's room, sending the housekeeper away. Stalin has urinated on the note from the pianist, but Beria removes it and keeps it. Malenkov arrives and is upset, knowing he must take Stalin's place. When they discuss calling a doctor for Stalin, Beria reminds them that all the doctors have been put away for treason. Khruschev arrives and says he feels sick; they cry and hug ostentatiously, with Stalin on the ground, 'lying in a puddle of indignity'. Others arrive, and they all try to avoid kneeling in the urine. They lift him up, taking him first one way, then the other, in a style reminiscent of classic slapstick, before getting him onto his bed. Since 'all the best doctors are in the gulag or dead', they plan to call on a woman, Comrade Timashuk (Cara Horgan), who has 'a proven desire to survive and is good at fellatio'.

Khruschev and Kaganovich (Dermot Crowley) discuss the future of the union, possible reforms and factionalism, as Beria and Malenkov discuss this elsewhere in the same woods, observing each other from a distance, and they all run to meet Stalin's daughter Svetlana (Andrea Riseborough) when she arrives, and try to curry favour with her. She is like an English 'jolly hockey sticks' stereotype, who asks for tea and buns to mop up her brother Vasily's (Rupert Friend) vodka. Svetlana wants a second opinion on her father's death, but all the doctors left are there in the room. There is a farcical denial of Stalin's death, and then he seems to be alive, but then dead again, playing with the reactions of the committee, who do not know whether to cheer or curse.

Beria changes the names on Stalin's 'list', and says it is time to 'reset your watches' as he is going to do things differently. A soldier goes straight into a cell and shoots someone. Beria releases Molotov's wife, Polina Molotova (Diana Quick), who was imprisoned by Stalin. Khruschev goes to see Molotov and tells him Beria and Stalin put him on a list. Molotov thinks Beria had his wife killed, and he says in front of Beria that she was a parasite, but in fact Polina is back and walks into the room with Beria, who announces, 'I kept her safe.'

In this farcical scene, Molotov then embraces his wife and welcomes her back. This conveys the idea that their emotions are mixed up and related to loyalties outside family, but that they are all at the mercy of the state's operations.

Malenkov is having formal photos taken, and Beria teases him because he is wearing a girdle, which he says is for his bad back. However, Malenkov has turned tough, and says to him 'Don't you ever humiliate me again.' Of the girdle, he says, 'Let's make this a test of your discretion': he has already assumed the egotism of the leader and is commanding loyalty. At the committee meeting, Malenkov is voted in as General Secretary, Khruschev is appointed as an unwilling funeral organiser, and Beria announces he is halting some deportations and pausing arrests and executions. Malenkov's measures are carried unanimously, despite people not actually agreeing, giving the lie to the proposed 'collective leadership'. We then see executions stopped halfway down a firing line: one man is shot, the next now released. When the people come back home having been released, the magnitude of feeling is on display, from the wife's joy to the discomfort with the son who betrayed him.

An extravagant funeral and laying in state is organised. The decorated war hero Field Marshall Zhukov (Jason Isaacs) arrives, and is portrayed as a tough guy with a Yorkshire accent and no-nonsense attitude. When Vasily shouts obscenities, Zhukov kicks him. When he shouts, 'I want to make a speech at my father's funeral', Zhukov says, 'I want to fuck Grace Kelly.' This is all played for laughs, as the characters become pure caricature. As mourners arrive, Khruschev curses, 'Jesus Christ it's the bishops! I thought we'd banned those freaks. Sneeze on the bastards as they go past' (Figure 6.1).

Figure 6.1 Khrushchev (Steve Buscemi) and Malenkov (Jeffrey Tambor) argue over who invited the bishops, in *The Death of Stalin* (2017), directed by Armando Iannucci.

Beria speaks to the pianist Maria and lets her know he has her note to Stalin. He has learned that Khruschev is associated with Maria, through her teaching his niece piano, and confronts them both with the note. Beria says allegiance to the party line was demanded, and that defiance of the party line would make you a traitor. He says it is a new reality, but Khruschev objects, saying, 'So you're the good guy now? You locked up half the nation, you raped them, you killed them?' And Beria responds, 'And now I'm releasing them.' He is buying popular support by appearing to soften and release prisoners. Khruschev orders the trains into Moscow be reopened; the people come back in, and are massacred by the NKVD. The committee members then start to fight over the people they've killed.

As they carry Stalin in his coffin, the committee are planning to overthrow Beria, and Khruschev lies about Malentov being on board with the plan. Zhukov bursts into the committee room as they are meeting and says they are staging a coup and that the army is taking over. They lock up Beria in the toilet, and Khruschev proclaims that the only choice they have is between Beria's death and his revenge. Malenkov, weakly, says, 'I want it on record that this was not my first course of action.' Beria is accused of rapes and perversion, in a hastily assembled court, and he is found guilty and sentenced to be shot. He is dragged out and shot, and his body is burned. Khruschev says over his burning remains, 'I will bury you in history.' This is a shocking and bleak sequence, where the gags have been toned down, and the callousness of the removal and execution of Beria is merciless. Now they talk about Malenkov, and ask if they can trust him. To which Khruschev says, 'Can you ever trust a weak man?' Khrushchev is now at the heart of the state and in control. The film ends with the pianist playing at a concert, and the intertitle announcing,

> After Beria's execution in 1953, the central committee took control of the Soviet Union.
>
> In 1956 Khrushchev moved to demote other members of the party, including Molotov and Malenkov.
>
> At long last he became head of Soviet Government and Commander in Chief,
>
> Until his removal in 1964 by Leonid Brezhnev.

Brezhnev (Gerald Lepkowski) is sitting behind him at the concert, looking at the back of Krushchev's head, confirming the idea that there is always somebody plotting to take the leader down. The film's closing credits are photographs of ordinary people, and cast members, with individuals being rubbed out or cut out from the image. This is a fittingly cold-blooded ending to a film that has pitched the horrors of the Stalinist regime as something between satire and black comedy.

The questions this film raises include whether the horrors of Stalinism are a suitable subject for such comic treatment, what the purpose is of presenting them this way, and, further, what our response to the film should be, and what our actual response tells us about ourselves. Thinking about it in Murdochian terms, one of the first questions we can ask is the purpose of the film. Is it malicious, or is it in fact designed to ridicule but also demonstrate the brutality of these people? Murdoch writes,

> Of course any religious or moral view will be rightly critical of the kind of humour which is fundamentally malicious. But on the whole we in the west attach value, prudentially and morally, to the possession of a sense of humour. It is an important fact, often neglected at a theoretical level by philosophers and theologians, that the funny is everywhere to be found. (MGM: 92)

The funny may be found everywhere, but the context and the tone is important to think about:

> 'A sense of humour', often treated as an identifiable faculty all on its own, needs to be looked at critically, even with suspicion. There is a perfectly familiar distinction between amiable joking and malicious or corrupt mockery. We must shun spiteful wit, yet not forget the social uses of satire. (MGM: 325)

The Death of Stalin is certainly satire, in that it mocks and lampoons these men in order to reveal the personal power games that lie behind the machinations of state. It undermines their credibility and in fact their competence and historical reputations, and it does so not only by suggesting their cruelty, but also their weaknesses, and their disregard for human life, and women in particular. Their attitudes towards women, especially Beria's, offers a particular challenge as the 'humour' is focused on how they see women only in terms of using them for sex. This line of jokes weights the film more heavily towards something that is not easy to laugh at. Particular performances, and lines of dialogue, are very funny, but reflecting upon what we laugh at when we watch the film is philosophically intriguing. Henri Bergson described the 'spark of spitefulness' that nature has implanted 'even in the best of men' (Bergson 2008: 93). This spark enables us to laugh at things that are neither just nor kind-hearted. But perhaps laughing at such reprehensible politicians serves a function for us in dealing with the politicians we see leading countries today. Anja Steinbauer argues that,

> Jokes about politicians and others in positions of power and influence abound, possibly a token of trying to alleviate our sense of powerlessness. Though jokes and satires can be tools of protest, they are often ways of coming to terms with existing power structures and even oppression. They can be symptomatic of resentment. (2015: 3)

Steinbauer repeats some sexist jokes, and says they clearly are not funny, but asks where does the fun end? As she says, the ethics of humour are extremely complex, and a lot depends on who is telling the joke. Murdoch suggests that,

> There is a bad absurd (degrading, hurtful), but is there not also a good absurd? Loss of dignity need not be loss of moral stature, can be surrender of vanity, discovery of humility; and a sense of the ludicrous is a defence against pretensions, not least in art. (F&S: 450)

This suggests that laughing at those in power might not necessarily be as destructive as it seems. Although Murdoch also concedes that 'there is something anti-authoritarian about violent laughter . . . The frightened or guilty mind will always wonder: what are they laughing at?' (F&S: 450). Simon Critchley writes that 'the fact remains that humour is a nicely impossible object for a philosopher. But herein lies its irresistible attraction' (Critchley 2002: 2). By this he means, partly, that there are many theories about why we laugh, from Hobbesian superiority, to Freudian relief theory, and the incongruity theory that Critchley sees in Kant, Schopenhauer and Kierkegaard.[3] A discussion of all these different approaches is beyond the scope of this chapter, but Murdoch certainly engages with some classical philosophical approaches to humour and the comic.

In 'The Fire and the Sun', Murdoch analyses Plato's mistrust of the comic. She describes how, according to Plato,

> Images of wickedness and excess may lead even good people to indulge secretly through art feelings which they would be ashamed to entertain in real life. We enjoy cruel jokes and bad taste in the theatre, then behave boorishly at home. Art both expresses and gratifies the lowest part of the soul, and feeds and enlivens base emotions which ought to be left to wither. (F&S: 391)

This sounds judgemental and puritanical, but, as Murdoch points out, Plato's comments about the results of the consumption of art are expressed in moral and political terms. This is less a criticism of the art itself but more of the effects on the consumers. And Murdoch agrees that Plato is right to talk about the 'cheapening and brutalising effect of an atmosphere where everything can be ridiculed' (F&S: 398). This is what leads Murdoch to suggest that we should ask the question, 'What may I properly laugh at, even in my private thoughts?' (ibid.). Although Murdoch finds that Plato's view of art as illusion is 'positive and complex', she argues that images, as 'valuable aids to thought . . . must be kept within a fruitful hierarchy of spiritual endeavour' (ibid.: 421). In other words, we must work to consider the value and virtue of images, and in this way, 'Good art . . . provides work for the spirit' (MGM: 453). Murdoch believes that 'what we look at profoundly affects what we do', and that 'art remains available and vivid as an experience of how egoism can be purified by intelligent imagination' (MGM: 453). But the dangers of art are real unless we realise its role. Again drawing on Plato, and his highly cinematic parable of the cave, Murdoch argues that the flickering light of the fire 'suggests the disturbed and semi-enlightened ego which is pleased and consoled by its discoveries, but still essentially self-absorbed, not realising that the real world is still somewhere else' (F&S: 423). But these cave images are not the same as film images in any direct allegory of the cave; the cinema is less a display of unreal shadows than a hall of reflection where 'work for the spirit' can be undertaken. Murdoch sees that Plato's objection to art is partly founded on the fact that 'art is playful in a sinister sense . . . a spiteful amused acceptance of evil, and through buffoonery and mockery weakens moral discrimination' (F&S: 443). If art is over-imbued with philosophical completeness, there is a danger it may 'become a magical substitute for philosophy, an impure mediator professing to classify and explain reality' (F&S: 444). This is a vital step in Murdochian film philosophy: the film may indeed be important, revealing art, but it is our reflection upon it that makes such art philosophically valuable to us. We need to put that effort in to attending and seeing the nature of morality as it is shown to us in art. If we do, then Murdoch sees nothing wrong with challenging, absurd, comic art:

> The absurdity of art, its funniness, its simplicity, its lucidity connects it with ordinary life and is inimical to authoritarian mystification . . . The absurd is the comic, as well as what defeats or teases the intellect. (MGM: 90–1)

> Comic art can be revolutionary and dangerous as well as carrying the tender and the sentimental as far as they can be carried in good literature (Dickens). (MGM: 91)

The Death of Stalin stages a jarring clash between cruelty and comedy, and is thereby what Murdoch might consider to be 'a juxtaposition, almost an identification, of pointlessness and value' (SGC: 372). In the face of this, our task is to cultivate 'the ability to see it all clearly and respond to it justly' (ibid.). Murdoch wonders whether 'one of the greatest achievements of all is to join this sense of absolute mortality not to the tragic but to the comic' (ibid.).

This is all very well, but this talk of cultivating just and clear attention might be an outmoded or self-centred approach:

> So it may be felt that not only 'personal spirituality', but also moral philosophy and traditional theology are out of place in a world tormented by poverty, misery and cruelty: that old-fashioned theoretical generalisations, or calm reflections upon inwardness, are too abstract and dreamy and indeed selfish to be *true* for a post-Hitler post-Stalin over populated nuclear planet. (MGM: 362)

After all, 'History is indeed a slaughterhouse and this is in numerous ways an inhospitable planet' (MGM: 365). However, Murdoch believes that, 'A good (decent) state, full of active citizens with a vast variety of views and interests, must *preserve* a central arena of discussion and reflection wherein differences and individuality are taken for granted' (MGM: 366).

Murdoch is concerned that we should reflect upon social lying, and that it might lead to a more general indifference to truth. She asks us to keep in mind what 'malicious mockery' looks like, remembering Plato's warning that 'malicious merriment, apparently harmless, can foster more general and sinister spiritual ills: cynicism, cruelty, hatred' (MGM: 380–1). These considerations are part of what Murdoch considers to be our process of moral discipline, which is slow and steady, and therefore less likely to be a reaction to a gag in the film, but more likely to be developed in our private thinking about the film and our responses. Part of this learning is to distinguish 'a tender smile from a mocking smile' (MGM: 385), and other terms and concepts that form 'the very texture of being and consciousness woven and working from moment to moment in language' (MGM: 385–6). This next film certainly requires us to enter an arena of differences and individuality, and assess the nature of the smiles of ourselves and those on-screen.

TEASING THE INTELLECT: *ELLE*

The film begins with sounds of panting, shouting, the crashing of china or glass, and then the sound of a slap or hit. The first shot is of a grey cat's impassive face. We hear a man orgasm, and the cat walks away derisively: the spectacle is over. Then we see the scene that the cat has been watching: a rapist in cat burglar gear, including balaclava, wiping up his semen as a woman lies beneath him on the floor. He stands, pulls up his trousers, throws the semen covered tissue on the floor, and leaves through the window. She gets herself up slowly and looks around, with no emotion. She sweeps up the breakages while still in her dress and shoes, with blood on her thigh. Then we see her put her dress in the bin, and look in the mirror – she has grazes on her cheek. She lies in the bath and a spot of blood from between her legs spreads into a patch. She disperses it.

Next, she is ordering sushi on the phone, in her dressing gown, stroking her cat, and checking what a 'holiday roll' is. This is perplexing, as she seems to be genuinely alright. Her son arrives and asks if she is OK. She says that the graze on her face is because she fell off her bike. They quarrel over the son's pregnant girlfriend and she says she will give the son three months' rent but wants to see their new flat first. She sees him off and looks around a little nervously. She gets a hammer and checks the windows, and then she sleeps holding the hammer. Next morning, she instructs all the locks be changed.

What are we to make of this extraordinary opening sequence? This well-off, middle-aged woman has been subject to a violent attack, which left her with injuries, and she seems to be able to carry on without being affected in any serious or emotional way. She does not call the police, or tell her son, but, more than this, she is able to order takeaway food, and discuss financial arrangements with her son in a level-headed manner. The only impact on the evening appears to be that she ordered food to be delivered rather than cook for them. It is certainly a disorienting and unnerving opening to the film.

The cut is to a violent video game, showing footage of a beast raping and killing a princess. The woman we have seen being raped, Michèle (Isabelle Huppert), adjudges that 'the orgasmic convulsions are far too timid'; and the other woman in the room, her friend Anna (Anna Consigny), says it is 'as if they're scared of sex'. A young man, Kurt (Lucas Prisor) challenges her, saying, 'Your background in publishing and literature is completely inappropriate for assessing playability.' Michèle replies, 'The fact is the boss here is me and we're six months behind.' Referring to the content of the game, she says the orc needs to feel thick warm blood. Another young man, Kevin (Arthur Mazet) says to her, in smiling infatuation, 'I love you.' Michèle is tough, fearless at dealing with all these young men, and in charge of a company. She is also sensible. She goes for a blood test and to get checked for sexually transmitted disease. The doctor says he could prescribe a PEP (a post-exposure HIV drug) but she says no, because there are too many side effects. She explains that she has done her research on the drug, and she can't miss any work. She concludes, with a smile, 'I guess we just roll the dice.' This shows that she is not in denial about the rape, and is aware of possible risks to her health, but does not appear to be traumatised or distressed by it.

She goes to a coffee shop, where she receives a telephone call from her lover, wanting to meet. She tries to put him off, saying, 'I have my period, I'm not well', but he persists, saying he'll wear a condom, and that 'a little blood doesn't turn me off'. But she stays resolute and says she can't meet. At that point, a woman, who we have seen looking at Michèle, passes by and pours her tray rubbish all over her, saying, 'Scum! You and your father!' Michèle gasps, but takes it without objection, as if accustomed to such public abuse. This is baffling, but adds to the picture of Michèle that we are building: she is resilient, calm and composed, even in the face of assault, abuse and attack. The mention of her father is intriguing, and we will discover more about this in due course. In the meantime we meet her mother, who is entertaining her young lover in her apartment. Michèle and she discuss the fact that her mother pays for her sex life, and her plastic surgery. As the lover leaves, Michèle says to him, 'She's HIV positive'; but her mother says, 'I told him you'd try that one.' Then, she has a sip of her coffee, and says it's very good. Her mother asks what she would say if she remarried. Michèle replies, 'It's simple, I'd kill you.' Her mother says, 'You're so selfish it's frightening'; to which she agrees, 'It's true.' This scene is comedic, but also chilling. The brutality of the verbal exchanges between mother and daughter is quite extreme, with cracks about HIV and murder, then praise for the coffee, but also the mother's behaviour is unusual and provocative. It seems that Michèle's father is in prison, and she won't go to visit him. Her mother tells her that he has a parole hearing coming up.

When Michèle arrives home, she meets her neighbours, an attractive young couple, Rebecca (Virgine Efira) and Patrick (Laurent Lafitte). She shares a smile with Patrick, who looks back at her as he walks away. The next morning, the rapist comes back. She fights more this time, shouting loudly, but he hits her, and hurts her, ripping her clothes and exposing her body. Again, the cat watches. When the man has left, Michèle turns to the cat and says, 'You didn't have to claw his eyes out but scratch him at least, I'm just saying.' Michèle gets a text message saying, 'You were very tight for a woman your age.' She considers the message impassively. She remains practical, and goes to a store to buy pepper spray and an axe. She then goes to meet her ex-husband Richard (Charles Berling) for dinner and deliberately reverses into his car while she is parking, as if just for mildly hostile fun. She asks him if he would say she is 'tight for a woman of her age', and, unsurprisingly, he looks stunned. This shows that she is dwelling on the content of the text message, rather than the fact of it or any added level of threat its arrival on her telephone might mean. Their friends arrive, Anna and her husband Robert (Christian Berkel). Once they are all seated, Michèle says she has something to tell them, and says, 'I was assaulted at home. I guess I was raped.' As the shock registers on Richard and Anna's faces, the champagne arrives, and Robert says, 'Ah very good', then looks around at the others and realises he is being inappropriate, and tells the waiter to wait a few minutes before popping it. Anna asks if she is alright, and Michèle says yes, and she's seen a doctor, but that she didn't report it. She says she avoids the police 'because I won't ever deal with the police again', again insinuating that she has a troubled background in relation to the law. Richard wants her opinion on his computer game idea, and when she points out that somebody trashed his fender, he says 'Somebody?' He knows it's her, and she just smiles and says bye.

At their office the next day, Anna's husband Robert has arrived but Anna's not there, and he knows it. He's come to see Michèle, as he is her lover. He closes all the blinds in her office. She says to him, you know I went through a traumatic experience recently, but he says, 'You acted as if you were soldiering on like nothing happened. I'm sorry if I'm insensitive, that's just me, right?' He starts to undo his belt and drops his pants. He says, sarcastically, 'I know you're a wilting flower but surely you can touch it.' Michèle gets the wastepaper bin and masturbates him – so is prepared to please him, to accede to his demands, even though she is not particularly in the mood. At 1.24am, when she is still at the office, she receives another text from the rapist, saying, 'I like the blouse you're wearing today. The cream colour. My sperm won't leave a stain.' This is plainly a threat of a third rape, and she looks around anxiously. Kurt, the young man she belittled earlier, is working late too, and she appears to wonder if perhaps he is the assailant.

As Michèle has lunch with her mother she asks if she has experienced any incidents, and her mother replies that a man threw a pizza at her. Michèle wonders if it is 'a new cycle starting'. So we are becoming aware that there is a reason why members of the public might assault her and her mother, and perhaps Michèle is considering whether the rapes are part of this. Her mother says that a film about her father, called *The Accused Will Rise*, aired on television last week, because of his imminent parole hearing, and that this 'refreshes people's memories'. Michèle's mother wants her to see him, but she says she would rather gouge her eyes out, and that she'll never see him again. She shows Michèle a picture of him; he looks like a very ordinary old man. Michèle looks at it but says put it away, and her mother looks regretful, and says that he's just a man. Michèle adds, 'Who also happens to be a monster.' So although Michèle and her mother speak quite calmly together today, it is clear that they have been through something terrible with the father.

We see the second rape again, but this time Michèle gets hold of a heavy ashtray and smashes it over his head. A cut to her sitting at her desk, smiling, reveals that she was reliving the rape but imagining her response to have been violent, and this pleases her. At this, a bird flies into her window, and, as it is dying, the cat gets hold of it. Michèle is appalled by the cat and manages to rescue the bird. She telephones the vet, as she carries the bird around on a pillow. There is a contrast between the human world, where she wishes to cave in her attacker's head with an ashtray, and this other world where she wants desperately to save the life of this little creature. As she is walking around the flat, she sees that the film about her father is on the television, and we learn more about what happened. Footage of a quiet residential street is accompanied by a solemn voiceover saying that it 'bears no trace of the atrocities that happened here thrity-nine years ago'. It goes on to say that the name of her father, George Leblanc, is a name associated with a horror story: 'an urban folktale from another era'. The voiceover asks, 'What drove George Leblanc, a practising Catholic, loving husband and father, to commit such monstrous and senseless acts? And what role exactly was played by his daughter Michèle?' She is faced with footage of herself as a ten-year-old girl, in her underwear, in front of a fire. The voiceover says that after thirty years of psychiatric evaluations, the questions remain, 'as banal and chilling as ever – why?'

She puts the now-dead bird in a box and then in the bin; her neighbour says I hope it's recyclable, as Michèle watches a car pass her, go to the end of the road, turn round and come back with its lights off. She goes into her flat, and sees the car is still there, so she picks up the axe and pepper spray, runs around the block, axes the car window and sprays the driver, who turns out to be Richard, her ex-husband, worried about her. Back in her kitchen, this is played for laughs, as Richard is moaning about the pepper spray and Michèle is splashing his face with water.

At work, somebody has inserted her face on the rape victim in the computer game and it is sent round the whole office. She tells Anna that other things have been sent too, and Anna tells her to call the police, saying that 'It's different this time; you're the victim.' Michèle says, 'I was the victim then', but no, she doesn't want police involved. At the hospital, her son's girlfriend is in labour, and when the baby is born, it is clearly mixed race and not her son's child. The girlfriend, Josie (Alice Isaaz) looks defiantly at Michèle as she breast feeds, revealing her tattoo of the name Eric: Michèle's son is called Vincent (Jonas Bloquet). Michèle tells the nurse how she and Anna both gave birth here the same night. Anna's baby was stillborn and she asked to breastfeed Michèle's baby. Michèle said fine, and Anna and Vincent have always been very close. Michèle says she looks at Vincent and doesn't know him. We gather from this that Michèle did not have the strongest maternal feelings for Vincent when he was born, and does not feel that close to him.

As the film progresses, a number of men continue to circle around Michèle, creating an array of possible suspects. The handsome neighbour, Patrick, has fought with a prowler near her flat, and sees her in safely, becoming flirtatious.

Kurt at work is often staring at her. She asks Kevin to teach her to shoot. Christmas is approaching, and Michèle watches her neighbours assemble nativity figures in the garden. Michèle masturbates as she watches Patrick, then goes and asks them to a party at her apartment. Anna helps Michèle with preparation for the party, and Michèle says they should put a toothpick in her ex-husband Richard's girlfriend's food. Anna jokes that they should just poison her, and they laugh. However, during the meal, the girlfriend does indeed remove a toothpick from her mouth, suggesting Michèle acted on her malicious impulse! The meal is a tumultuous affair, with a sulky Josie, religious Rebecca saying grace, and Michèle caressing Patrick's crotch under the table with her foot. Michèle's mother announces that she and her young lover are engaged to be married, and everyone claps but Michèle, who bursts out laughing riotously. Rebecca wants to put the midnight mass on television; Robert is jealous of Patrick; Richard and his girlfriend leave. With the mass on the television, Michèle says, 'Damn him, close the book, ring the bell, blow out the candle': an incantation of excommunication. She explains to Patrick that her father made the cross on her and local children until other parents asked him to stop. Her father was offended, and went into every house on the street, killing them all: 'twenty-seven human victims, six dogs, a couple of cats, he spared a hamster – you couldn't make it up'. She then explains her role in it all. 'I was doing my homework when he arrived home, blood all over him.' Patrick says that they don't have to go over it, but she says it does her good to talk. She recounts how her father decided to burn everything in the house, and she helped to feed the fire:

> We gutted the place, curtains, carpets, tables, chairs, all in the fire. It was exciting, you get caught up in it. We were about to burn our clothes when the police arrived.
>
> Someone snapped a photo, bizarrely it's that photo that stuck in people's minds. Me, half-naked, smeared with ash. The photo of a little girl as psychopath, next to her father, the psychopath. My empty stare in the photo is terrifying. Not bad, uh? Cognac?

She slaps him on the thigh. She has enjoyed shocking him, as if it is part of her flirtation with him (Figure 6.2). Meanwhile, her mother challenges her about how rude she was, says she's cruel, and then collapses. In the ambulance she asks Michèle to go and see her father. She's had a stroke. Michèle seems unmoved by this, and asks the doctor if she could be making it up, faking it. The doctor is surprised by the question, and says there is a strong possibility she might not wake up, but is stable for now. Michèle says to her unconscious mother that she won't visit her father, and that she doesn't care for deathbed requests, calling this stroke an abject stunt. She says to her mother that she has

Figure 6.2 Michèle (Isabelle Huppert) offers a cognac, in *Elle* (2016), directed by Paul Verhoeven.

given up on morality, and is acting like a teenager. She adds, 'This aneurysm thing is just treachery. Disgusting.' As she changes the television channel in the hospital room she fails to notice that her mother is in cardiac arrest, from which she does not recover.

Walking through a park with her family, looking for a spot to dispose of her mother's ashes, she has a showdown with Josie and Vincent over the paternity of the baby, and just throws the ashes over the wall with no ceremony or emotion. The identity of her rapist is still a mystery, but the relationships with the various men in her life continue to develop. One windy night, while she is working, Patrick comes over to help her to close her window shutters. They touch in front of the window and embrace; he seems quite tender and hesitant, but their relationship is certainly becoming sexual. At work, she checks Kevin's computer and finds out that he created the video game with her face on it. She instructs him to drop his trousers, saying, 'Show me your dick and I might not fire you.' She looks at his penis and says, 'The guy I'm looking for is circumcised.' Later that day, the rapist breaks into her house again. He comes from behind the curtain, and she fights him and stabs him through the hand. She pulls off his mask – it's Patrick – and she throws him out. The next morning, as she collects her post she sees him going to work with a bandaged hand. So now she knows her attacker is her neighbour. She sees on the television news that her father has been refused parole. She curses him on the television, but then goes to prison to see him, only to discover that he hanged himself in his cell the night before, in the knowledge she was coming. She stands over his dead body in the morgue and says to him, with grim satisfaction, 'I killed you by coming here.'

As she is driving home, a stag leaps out in front of her car. She swerves and crashes, shouting again, with raw, unfettered expression, like she shouted when raped. Michele has been injured. Her leg is bleeding and she is not able to get herself out of the car. She calls Anna and Richard, but they are both on answerphone, so, surprisingly, she calls Patrick, who comes to help her. He pulls her out of the car and helps her home, where he disinfects the wound and bandages her leg. She studies him, closely, while he does it. She says, referring to his rapes of her, 'How was it? Was it good? Answer me, did you enjoy it? Why did you do it?' He seems embarrassed, and grumbles that 'It was necessary'.

In the supermarket, Michèle and her son, who has been thrown out by Josie, come across Patrick. He invites them for dinner that night as Rebecca and her parents have gone to see the Pope. There is of course a pointed irony in the fact that such a religious woman is married to this sex offender. It is yet another element of this film, along with the paternity of Josie's baby, and the juvenile inadequacies of the men at Michèle's workplace, as well as Richard and Robert, that the film world is bizarrely blind to, replete as it is with abundant self-centred delusions.

At Patrick's that night, Vincent has too much to drink and passes out. Michèle flatters Patrick about the work he has done on his boiler and effectively seduces him into showing it off to her, in the basement. They go down the stairs to the basement, Michèle with her walking stick, and they have a rough sexual encounter. He threateningly declares that all the noise down there is muffled by the door, then he hits her, throws her against the wall, and goes to hit her again. She says, 'Do it', but he halts, saying it doesn't work like that for him. So she hits him too, and he violently penetrates her, as she shouts and shouts. She shouts a lot after the sex too, and Patrick looks at her oddly, not understanding her response.

The video game is finally complete and the team applaud Kurt. Anna tells Michèle she knows Robert is having an affair. They have a launch party for the game, and have put Vincent in charge of it. Patrick comes, Robert, Richard, all the men in Michèle's life. Michèle tells Anna it was her sleeping with Robert. Michèle decides to leave the party, and Patrick drives her home. In the car she says to him, 'You don't expect to get away with what you did to me? I'll do what I should have done. It's about your wife, and others. I'll go to the police.' Back in her flat, he comes over again with a mask on. She hits him over the head, he rips her blouse and throws her around, hitting her. Vincent arrives and hits Patrick over the head, splitting his head open. Patrick staggers up to his feet and pulls off his mask, and Michèle smiles at him. He asks, 'Why', and dies. Vincent cries. Michèle says, 'It's over.' Police come, and ask questions, and say, 'Who could imagine such a thing?' The men in this film world seem to have no idea about themselves or the world they live in.

Rebecca is moving out of her apartment, and Michèle goes over to her to say she's very sorry for all she has been through. Rebecca says, 'I have faith . . . what's it for if not to get through the tough times. Patrick was a good man, but with a tortured soul. I'm sincerely glad you could give him what he needed, for a time at least.' This exchange reveals that Rebecca knew that Patrick was a rapist but that she turned a blind eye to it. The mismatch between the religious sentiments and the brutality of the rapist's actions is extreme, and the fact that the two women can talk is surprising.

Michèle repaints a room in her flat yellow. Vincent and Josie arrive in a convertible, with Josie saying of Vincent, 'He deserves it.' The car seems to be a reward for killing the rapist. As they head away from the car they realise that they have forgotten the baby and go back for it. Their self-absorption continues unabated. Michèle goes to the grave of her mother and lays flowers; her father's next to it has 'monster' scrawled on it in graffiti. Anna comes up behind her, and they walk along through the cemetery together. Anna says she has kicked Robert out, and apparently 'he's hit the bottle'. Anna asks Michèle, 'What did you see in him?' And Michèle replies, 'It was just one of those things, an opportunity, I wanted to get laid.' Anna says, 'That's no excuse, it was shabby', to which Michèle replies, 'Worse than that even.' They have this honest exchange about what happened, and are able to forgive and move on. Anna announces that she's going to sell her house and move in with Michèle for a while. The film ends with the two friends laughing as they walk through the graveyard.

Unsurprisingly, reception of this peculiar film was mixed. Nick James considered it to be 'a serious revision, or subversion even, of the cinema of sexual violence' (James 2017: 28). This is true in some ways, but director Paul Verhoeven says to James, 'She starts an affair with the rapist, and accepts, in some way, a sadomasochistic relationship with him' (James 2017: 31). It does not seem accurate to describe the peculiar campaign of investigation and destruction that Michèle conducts against Patrick to be an affair. *Sight and Sound* staged a debate between Erika Balsom and Ginette Vincendeau, with Balsom describing how the film shows that 'sexist aggression, in varieties more and less brutal, is an everyday experience' (Balsom and Vincendeau 2017: 33) and Vincendeau arguing that 'the film and its reception are a demonstration of how deeply internalized misogyny is, including by women' (ibid.). While Balsom sees the men in the film as 'pathetic, all of them', Vincendeau considers that Huppert embodies the violent fantasies of two men (Verhoeven and Philippe Dijan, who wrote the novel on which it is based) and the culture at large, and that she 'lends cultural legitimacy to a trashy movie masquerading as "postfeminist" intervention' (ibid.). For Molly Haskell the film 'staggers – albeit mesmerizingly – from one gratuitous moment of erotic-comic grotesque to another' (2016: 40). Haskell develops her analysis into an appreciation of this 'cascade of mischief and evil', and highlights an element of the film that strikes at the heart of attempts to swathe it in ironic comment. Haskell writes, 'Movies are visceral and rape is rape; the sight of a masked intruder brutally violating a woman has a tendency to short-circuit the more contemplative parts of the brain' (ibid.).

Haskell's analysis extends to the director and the star, Paul Verhoeven and Isabelle Huppert, and she proposes that 'you may see it as two people exploiting their own dark talents to the point of self parody' (ibid.). In other words, this film, according to Haskell, is like the zenith of their career images, in that Verhoeven's 'weaponised femmes fatales are extended sick jokes about women's empowerment' (ibid.: 41), and Huppert has specialised in playing women with dangerous erotic fantasies. Haskell refers to Huppert's 'sphinx half-smile' (ibid.) which is in evidence particularly in the scene where she tells Patrick about her father's crimes, shedding doubt upon the veracity of her tale and questioning her reasons for telling it. There is certainly an amoral alliance between Michèle's day job and her personal life. By this I mean that the young men in her company are indulging their fantasies, including her in them, and producing sexually violent material. Similarly, Patrick and Robert both live out their sexual fantasies by using Michèle, and she seems inured to all of them. Huppert's performance imbues her character with a disinterest in the little things. As Margaret Barton-Fumo observes, 'The intricacies of her movements betray, fabulously, a woman who cannot be bothered with life's inconveniences: she may head a video-game company, but she repeatedly looks down her nose at her cellphone, pointer finger raised, like a bored technological novice' (2017: 46). This is an accurate description of Michèle's attitude to the minutiae of life, but it is her response to the bigger events that attracts the most attention. Her response to being raped is without emotional distress. She is far from quiet during the assaults, and in fact yells loudly, with a deep-throated shout, rather than a scream or cry. Each rape has a different dynamic between Patrick and Michèle, and, as the other elements of the film develop, it becomes what Dennis Lim describes as 'a wry, almost-screwball comedy of manners about one woman's rather unusual response to a rape' (2016: 66). Her response, so unsettling, is hard to fathom, and her inscrutability, in relation to this and other matters, makes it difficult to decide whether she is traumatised, in denial, unperturbed, or something else.

As with *The Death of Stalin*, this film begs the question of whether these matters are suited to the way they are presented. Whilst the rape scenes are not played for laughs, there is humour in Michele's odd reactions and her exchanges with other characters. Lara Cox writes that a rape joke 'will pose a disempowering affront to the women in the audience in a way that men are unlikely to experience' (2015: 10). This is not what happens in *Elle* beyond the opening rape scene, because Michele is not the focus of the joke for being raped; rather it is her brutality that elicits humour. What is required on our part, to withstand the sight of repeated rapes, and the humour surrounding the death of her mother and father, is a more prolonged version of what Bergson called, 'a momentary anaesthesia of the heart', which he said was demanded by comedy (2008: 11). This is an evocative concept that conveys what is required by some of the humour in *Stalin* and *Elle*, but Haskell's observation accurately conveys how difficult this is when the scene is one of such violent sexual attack. Our experience of what we see in a film is not momentary, even if it is moments we remember. Watching a film is more immersive than that. As Murdoch says, 'aesthetic enjoyment is not a momentary quasi-perceptual state of mind. That is, the art object is not just "given", it is also *thought*' (S&G: 210). To borrow part of Murdoch's analogy, we might receive a picture of a rose with a single, momentary reaction, but not the whole of a film, which has a mood and a journey of thought and emotion. That is the sustained engagement of a film, which enables the attentiveness to art that Murdoch calls for: 'It is the apprehension of something else, something particular, as existing outside us' (S&G: 216). And attending to the individual is the particular task, which, if we are enclosed in our own fantasy world, means we are 'not grasping their reality and independence' (S&G: 216). *Elle* challenges us to believe in Michèle as a very particular individual. Understanding her as a character requires us to look beyond ourselves, and conventional expectations, and think about her as a woman with a history and personality. If we can look at her with a gaze that is a just and discerning one, then we can see what Murdoch means when she talks about love which is art being 'something deeper than our conscious and more simply social morality, and to be sometimes destructive of it' (S&G: 218). The rape scenes are shocking, they are 'intrusions', and as such fit Murdoch's description of how 'the outer world often enters the inward eye with an intensity of significance which punctuates a reflective reverie which does not initially concern it' (MGM: 266). Murdoch says that these are not necessarily unusual experiences, but that 'marvels are happening all the time' (MGM: 266). Well, the rape scenes may not be marvels, but they are profoundly intense scenes that viscerally strike the viewer and compel us to assess their impact. The film requires us to 'switch' from what Murdoch describes as 'ordinary awareness to aesthetic contemplation' (MGM: 312). In other words, we need to think outside our own reaction to such a scene and assess how it is working in this film. This enables us to understand the uniqueness of this character and her milieu. As the child of a mass murderer, who joined in with her father's post-killing clean-up, she has had a lifetime of abuse, rejection and reflection. Rather than suggest that women in general can choose to not be upset by rape, the film shows how this particular woman, with the experience and genes of a killer, can view her rapist with interest and toy with him forensically, like her cat with a dying bird, and see events through to his destruction, understanding that it is because of his weaknesses. Her indifference to the suffering and death of her mother and her father demonstrates her heartlessness to humans, and the specificity of her father's crimes and her involvement in them makes Michèle unique. In terms of morality this is a peculiar film world, but a Murdochian analysis enables us to assess Michèle's story without revulsion at the film's contents, or its treatment of them. It is a provocative idea about what a person needs to be in order to withstand such horror. A more realistic picture of survival post-catastrophe is portrayed in the next film.

THE EXTREME HORRORS OF REAL LIFE: *MANCHESTER BY THE SEA*

The film opens with establishing shots of a picturesque fishing village, and then the Chandler brothers on a fishing boat, the *Claudia Marie*, playing with the son of one of them. There is clearly a lot of love between them as they are mucking about together. We next see one of the brothers, Lee Chandler (Casey Affleck), at work, clearing snow, being a janitor at a block of flats, fixing plumbing, mending a fan, clearing a drain. As he cleans his hands, he hears one of the women saying she's in love with him. Then another woman is really rude to him about her repairs, and he says, 'I don't give a fuck', and she throws him out. He is hauled in front of the boss but will not apologise. He goes out and gets drunk. He is not interested in attention from a woman who spills beer on him, but rather he checks out a couple of men who are wearing ties, and goes and starts a fight with them.

The next day, as he's clearing snow, he receives a telephone call to say that his brother Joe is in hospital, and he says that he'll be there in an hour and a half. By the time he arrives, his brother has passed away from a cardiac arrest about an hour before. Joe's friend, George (C. J. Wilson) was with him at the time, at the boat, and is very upset. Lee asks questions, but then switches into coping gear: call their uncle, call his wife (then corrects himself, 'ex-wife, Randi, sorry'). He seems quite dazed. We then see a flashback to Dr Bethany (Ruibo Qian) telling Joe (Kyle Chandler) and the family about his congestive heart failure, and that most people with this condition have a life expectancy of five to ten years. His wife Elise (Gretchen Moll) responds to their stressful family discussions with a bad temper and storms out.

The next scene is in the morgue where Lee sees his brother's body. Lee's body language is tense with repressed sadness, as he looks at the doctor out of the corner of his eye, then looks with scared eyes at his brother as the sheet is pulled back. Lee touches him, hugs him, puts his head next to his, kisses his cheek, and cries; then wipes his face and pulls himself together. He is practical, asking about procedure, and telling George they need to talk about the boat and the website. He knows he has to go and tell Joe's son, so signs for Joe's belongings, and then we see Lee remembering the boy in another flashback to the brothers teasing the kid about there being sharks in the water, and the boy catching a fish.

Lee drives through Manchester, which looks picturesque, sleepy and innocent, with pretty houses, a church and a bell tower. Another flashback to his earlier family life: his wife is in bed with a cold, a vaporiser filling the room with steam. Lee comes home having been drinking, and shows how he really loves his children, playing with them all and cuddling them. He talks about his nephew Patrick's face when he caught the fish being like when they took the girls on the merry go round: 'pure joy'. Now he has to go to see Patrick at hockey practice to tell him his father's died, while all the hockey team are watching and waiting. One of them says, 'So that's *the* Lee Chandler.'

Patrick's (Ben O'Brien) friends hug him, and he leaves with Lee to go and see his father's body. Lee tells him that 'he looks dead. He doesn't look asleep or anything, but he doesn't look gross either.' They have a few miscommunications and are quite bad tempered with each other, but then apologise. Patrick asks his friends over, and asks for pizza, because 'there's nothing to eat here'. He and his friends chat about his dad, and about memories of going out on the boat, and about *Star Trek*. It is all quite sensitive and mature, and then Patrick asks Lee if Silvie (Kara Hayward) can stay over. Lee says yes, and also agrees to say that she stays downstairs if he speaks to her parents. Lee says to him, 'Am I supposed to tell you to use a condom?' And Patrick replies, 'It's OK, we've had the discussion – just let me know if we're making too much noise.' Lee looks a bit perplexed by the confident teenage attitudes, but Patrick still calls upon him for advice, asking whether he should call his mother Elise. Lee replies that nobody knows where she is, and then they hug. Lee then has a flashback to them all coming in to the house and finding her passed out on sofa, drunk and naked. We then see Patrick in his room composing an email to his mother, so clearly he is in contact with her privately.

In the morning, as Lee is talking to the morgue on the telephone about 'the next steps' for his brother, Silvie and Patrick get themselves breakfast very noisily: rattling cereal boxes, metallic scrunching of tin foil, dishes being put down on the table with no attempt to be quiet. Then Silvie says, 'I don't think Lee needs to be here for this', so Lee gets up and leaves the room. There is a generation clash here, between Patrick and his friends' cool confidence and self-centredness, and Lee's role of having to handle practicalities and also seemingly to serve Patrick with transport, food, money and social indulgences. Patrick is clearly not fully processing the death of his father. He tells his ice hockey coach not to take him off the ice because he could really use the distraction, but the coach says the ice is not a distraction, and offers him support, which Patrick plainly does not want. In the car, Patrick wants to put music on, and when Lee says they have to go to the solicitor, Patrick is not at all interested. At the solicitor's, Joe's will is read, and it says that Lee will be Patrick's guardian, which Lee cannot cope with at all. We then see into the heart of the film, and Lee's background, which explains why Lee is living the life he does and recoils at being made responsible for Patrick.

Lee looks out of the window and recalls a night when he was drunk and playing pool in his basement with his friends. Randi (Michelle Williams) comes down and gives them a piece of her mind, saying it is 2am, and she has children sleeping. She is tough talking and they apologise and leave. In the present, Lee is overwhelmed with memories. He then recalls going out once his friends have left, very drunk, to buy more booze from the mini-market. As he stumbles back to his house, he sees that the house is on fire. He looks, with onlookers, astounded: his house ruined. He then sees Randi, screaming, as they try to get her into an ambulance, struggling with her and with the stretcher mechanism. Lee is left, crying, his brother holding his arm. The firemen bring out the little bodies of his children wrapped in sheets, as his brother holds him. The soundtrack is the most melodramatically mournful music,[4] as the horror of these few moments is conveyed without words, but with images and incremental realisations.

We see Lee telling the police that he and his friends had had beer, a joint and some cocaine. He says he was cold and built a fire to warm up the house while he went to the mini-market. He says that about halfway there he realises he can't remember if he put a screen on the fireplace, but he figures it's OK, so he just keeps going to the store, and that's it: a log must have rolled out of the fire. The fireman say they pulled Randi out as she had passed out downstairs, then the fires broke and they couldn't go back in again. The officer says, 'Look Lee, you made a horrible mistake, like a million other people did last night. We're not going to crucify you. It's not a crime to forget to put the screen on the fireplace.' Lee cannot believe he can just leave in light of what he has caused. He grabs an officer's gun from his belt and tries to shoot himself but it jams. Officers and others grab him and get the gun. As Lee emerges from this memory, Patrick's state of mind is entirely different as he's playing on his phone. They exchange angry words about the boat, and a passer-by (played by director Kenneth Lonergan) says 'great parenting', leading to Lee shouting and swearing at him. Patrick and Lee argue about Patrick seeing his mother, and going to the funeral parlour, and are generally snarky with each other. It transpires that the morticians have to keep Joe's body in a freezer until spring because the ground is too hard to bury him. Patrick is unhappy about this, they both are, and they argue more: they can't find the car, Patrick expects to be driven around town, and doesn't say thank you. He has a different girlfriend too, Sandy (Anna Baryshnikov), who he says he is 'working on'; in other words, he's trying to have sex with both girls. Lee and Patrick are operating in different zones of concern, with Lee fully facing the realities of his brother's death, and Patrick doing his best to keep everything the same. Lee sits in the car outside Patrick's friend's house while they have band practice. The mum Jill (Heather Burns) comes and asks him in for a beer, but Lee doesn't want to go. Randi calls him to say she's sorry about Joe, and that she's pregnant: Lee doesn't know what to do with himself, and says he's got to go.

Joe's funeral in shown in slow motion. Patrick hugs his friends, and Randi arrives. She looks smart, her husband looks preppy, and Lee stares at him. Randi hugs Lee, and he looks away. Randi turns back crying, comforted by her new partner. In the service, Patrick's mobile telephone goes off. It is just indicative of his teenage life, but Lee's face registers disbelief. Back at the house Patrick is hugging everybody, and people look at Lee, as if assessing how he's coping or just what he is like these days. After the funeral, Patrick wants to ask his girlfriend over, but Lee doesn't want her to come.

Patrick argues his case for staying in Manchester, and we see a flashback to when Lee moved away. Joe calls little Patrick to say goodbye to his uncle Lee, and they have a hug. In the present, in the kitchen, Patrick opens the freezer door, and food falls out, which he tries to push back into the freezer. He bends down to pick things up, and then hits his head on the door, and has a breakdown, crying floods of tears. Lee is shocked by Patrick's tears, and flails around trying to do the right thing: 'Do you want me to get rid of the food? Take you to hospital? Call your friends?' Patrick locks himself in his bedroom and Lee breaks it down. He asks Patrick if he is having a breakdown, and says, 'I can't let you have a breakdown with the door closed.' Lee says, 'And if you are going to freak out every time you see a frozen chicken I think we should go to the hospital – I don't know anything about this.' It becomes clear, when Patrick says, 'I just don't like him being in the freezer', that wrestling with the freezer made him think of his father and overwhelmed him. Lee says he will stay with him until he calms down, and Patrick says, 'OK I'm calmer now can you please just go away', and Lee says, 'No.' This refusal to do what Patrick wants reminds Lee of when Joe and Patrick visited his new room after he moved away. Joe says, 'OK let's go get some furniture', and Lee says, 'Get off my back.' But Joe makes Lee go, and we see from Lee's room later that they did get furniture.

Lee tells him they are moving but not yet, and Patrick is not happy about it. Lee goes back to his flat to get some of his things, including photos of his children, which he wraps carefully in blankets. He looks out of the window in his brother's house at the view of the town and punches the glass, cutting himself quite badly. Patrick's mother calls and Lee hangs up on her. Patrick challenges him about this, and tells him that she's nearby in Essex, and wants him to come and have lunch and meet her fiancé. Lee admits that he hung up on her because he didn't know what to say to her, and he didn't tell Patrick because he didn't know what to say to him. We see what Lee's life is like in Manchester. He goes looking for work from an old contact: the man is friendly, but his wife says, 'I don't wanna see him in here again.' He sits in the lounge with Sandy's mother Jill while Patrick and Sandy try to have sex upstairs, but he quite clearly just cannot make small talk.

Lee takes Patrick to his mother's house for lunch. Trying to find the house they argue with each other, but he says, 'Text me if anything gets weird.' Lee goes to the door and meets Elise and her fiancé, Jeffrey (Matthew Broderick), but doesn't stay. Jeffrey is stiff and authoritarian, and insists on saying grace. Elise is very nervous, and says, 'I know I'm gonna be a shock to you in lots of ways, everything's great. This is your home too, I want it to be.' Her nerves are so bad, however, that she leaves the table and goes into the kitchen and Jeffrey goes to see what she's doing in there, presumably worried she'll be drinking or crying. After the visit, Patrick describes them to Lee, by saying, 'She was very nervous and he was very Christian.' When Lee reminds Patrick that they too are a Catholic family, Patrick takes it to mean that Lee is still trying to get rid of him. Jeffrey emails Patrick and says, 'I'm going to ask you to write to me in future to arrange any further visits.' So living with his mother is clearly not going to be an option.

Patrick and Lee watch television. Patrick is being quiet, still thinking that Lee is trying to get rid of him. They go into Joe's gun room, and Patrick asks, 'Who are you gonna shoot, you or me?' But Lee has an idea that they can sell the guns and buy a motor for the boat, which they do. They go out on the boat, with Sandy. She takes the wheel, the boat goes wild, and Patrick straightens it up and teaches her. Lee really smiles to himself – a big toothy smile – and swings his leg in a joyful kick. Chirpier music accompanies their outing: 'I'm beginning to see the light', by The Ink Spots and Ella Fitzgerald. Later on we see that Patrick and Sandy have had sex, and Patrick kisses her head lovingly, suggesting this might actually be the beginning of something meaningful.

Lee meets Randi with her new baby by chance as they are both in town. Randi's friend leaves them to talk, and she introduces her baby as Dylan. She asks to talk, even though she says she doesn't have anything big to say, but then wonders if they could have lunch. She says that she said a lot of terrible things to him, but that 'My heart was broken and it's always gonna be broken and I know yours is too.' Lee shakes his head, unable to handle the conversation, but Randi continues, saying, 'I should fuckin' burn in hell for the things I said to you . . . I love you.' Lee really cannot respond with a full sentence: he mutters, 'I'm sorry I've gotta go', 'there's nothing there', 'I gotta go', even as Randi says to him that he can't just die. He is completely unable to cope with this confrontation of his past. So, he goes to a pub, and gets into a fight, and even though George rescues him, Lee keeps fighting until he gets knocked out. When he comes round at George's house, the first thing he says is 'Where's Patrick?', and he finally breaks down and cries to George's wife. For the first time, Patrick actually thinks of Lee; he sees the photos of his kids, and asks, 'Can I get you anything Uncle Lee?'

Lee dreams that his little girls are sitting on the sofa next to him (Figure 6.3). One of them says, 'Can't you see I'm burning?', and he says to her 'No honey, you're not burning', but then he is woken up by a smoke alarm. He's burnt the sauce and the house is full of smoke. Nothing dramatic happens. Patrick says, 'Uncle Lee what's that smell?' He says, 'It's OK I just burnt the sauce, everything's OK.' But it shows how tortured his mind is by the death of his children, and the constant reminders that he has. He tells Patrick that arrangements have been made. He's got a job in Boston, starting in July, and Patrick is going to live with George: 'Everything is staying the same except you don't have to move.' Patrick says but why can't you stay, and Lee has to concede, 'I can't beat it, I'm sorry.' Patrick cries and he holds him.

Figure 6.3 Lee Chandler (Casey Affleck) dreams of his children, in *Manchester by the Sea* (2016), directed by Kenneth Lonergan.

At Joe's burial, Randi's baby is crying, so she passes it to her husband who takes it away. Lee sees the grave with his parents' and Joe's names on it. Patrick asks for money for ice cream and Lee tells him that he's getting a flat with a second bedroom, so that he can come and visit sometimes. As they walk home, they bounce a ball between them, still with their slightly grumpy banter: Patrick sarcastically says Lee's throw is great. Lee says let the ball go, Patrick doesn't, they just trundle along. The final shot is of the two of them fishing off the boat.

This film is an exploration of living in the void, or what Murdoch calls 'real ordinary familiar despair' (MGM: 504). Murdoch describes this as 'An opposing companion to happiness', and 'something extreme: the pain, and the evil, which occasion conditions of desolation such as many or most human beings have met with' (MGM: 498). Lee is existing in a state of desolation. He would probably have felt better had he been sent to prison and punished like Juliette in *I've Loved You So Long*, and of course he did try to end his life, but in fact he has had to settle into living a life of sorts. Murdoch writes,

> It is not easy to discuss such a matter or to take it as a single subject. Those who have experienced such black misery and recovered may prefer to forget. Art, which consoles and to which we also return for wisdom, tends to, or may seem to, romanticise despair. Innumerable poems, stories, pictures, portray it in ways we are easily able to tolerate and enjoy. Christ on the cross is an image so familiar and beautified that we have difficulty in connecting it with real awful human suffering. (MGM: 499)

Thinking about tragedy in art in this way does pose the question of how it is connected to such painful suffering in real life, and how we might relate to the deadening daily half-life that Lee lives, which is a far more realistic depiction of life after such horrors than high-pitched emotion. Life continues, and then another sad event comes along, the death of his brother, and this still has to be dealt with, despite Lee's personal trauma. In this way the film is more of an investigation of how to behave appropriately in relation to others, than it is a story about a death or a tragic event. Murdoch believes that 'really great art gives us a mixed and sombre delight which is akin to our recognition of morality' (S&G: 219). This seems to be an appropriate description of this moving film, which is so tenderly insightful about the relationship between uncle and nephew, and so unflinching in its confrontation of the practicalities of death and bereavement. There are some genuinely funny moments in this film, such as the sight of Patrick's band practising wearing their hoodies and taking things very seriously, and when Lee confronts Patrick about the frozen chicken. As we have seen from Murdoch's thinking about tragedy in life, it is simply part of every day, and might be over-egged in order to make it seem more exceptional. Like the broken crockery that Murdoch speaks of, the frozen chicken and the burnt sauce are as likely to cause a breakdown as the sight of Joe's body in the morgue.

Murdoch describes how,

> The comic is often paired as an opposite with the tragic but the two concepts are asymmetrical and different in kind. It is not that the comic is unserious and the tragic serious. The comic is capable of the highest seriousness, in life and in art; whereas the attempted tragic or bad tragic may be pretentious lying nonsense not capable of seriousness at all. Indeed, fortunately for the human race, the comic is everywhere, it is in the air which, as being every one of us an artist, we breathe. The tragic is not the same as sorrow – sorrow, grief, of course is also in the air we breathe. Tragedy belongs only to art, where it occupies a very small area. One might even be puzzled by the high prestige which the form enjoys, as if we needed for psychological reasons to inflate the idea. There are extremely few good tragedies and, one may say, bad tragedies are not tragedies. (MGM: 92–3)

In saying this, Murdoch sheds light on the role of Lee's flashbacks of the fire that he caused and that killed his children. It is a segment of memory, featuring sights that struck him at the time – his wife being sedated, his children's bodies, his house destroyed – accompanied by an overwhelming soundtrack that conveys the bleak horror of it all. It is a 'tragic fragment'. Murdoch stresses the artistry of such glimpses:

> Real life is not tragic. In saying this one means that the extreme horrors of real life cannot be expressed in art . . . We become accustomed, in the technically perfect 'art work' of television, to structured glimpses, real and fictional, of human misery. (MGM: 93)

This seems to describe the house fire scene perfectly. It is the 'structured glimpse' that fuels the rest of the film, explaining why Lee has the temperament that he does, and also showing how he cannot stay in Manchester in his brother's house to care for Patrick. That is the subject of the film: the effects of the circumstances of the death of his children, and not the ins and outs of the circumstances themselves. In more exploitative works, perhaps 'disaster movies', the minutiae of the disaster is the focus, as Murdoch observes: 'Catastrophes are of course constantly made the subject of bad art, such as we continually see on television or in the cinema' (MGM: 94).

Murdoch discusses the perceived value of tragedy as an art form. She writes,

> We tend to feel that tragedy is connected with high morality and is good for us ... For this we should *not* simply see the virtuous man overthrown or the bad man successful or the total villain destroyed, *but rather* the not especially good man brought down, not by evil or wickedness, but by some fault, frailty, or weakness of character. (MGM: 99)

Well this would seem to be a precise description of what happens with Lee: we see his life destroyed by a fleeting lapse of care. And that this fault results in death is essential for the tragic to do what Murdoch says it must, which causes us distress:

> Its subject matter is contingency and death, the profound difference between suffering and death, the connection of truth and justice with the apprehension of death, the elevation of morality to the religious level ... In tragedy the compulsory nature of death is an image of its place in life. Such are the solemn thoughts which a contemplation of this great concept may inspire in us. (MGM: 117)

Murdoch talks specifically about the void which results from bereavement, which I will quote here at some length:

> There is ... a guiltless remorse when some innocent action has produced an unforeseeable catastrophe. A common cause of void is bereavement, which may be accompanied by guilt feelings, or may be productive of a 'clean' pain. In such cases there is a sense of emptiness, a loss of personality, a loss of energy and motivation, a sense of being stripped, the world is utterly charmless and without attraction. Guiltless bereavement can occasion most intense pain, but is often followed by recovery, when, it is said, 'nature' reasserts itself. Duties perceived in this emptiness may be a source of healing. There is no one there, but the pain is there and the tasks. In time the annihilated personality reappears, the victim returns from the strange absolute country of death which he has visited, and resumes his ordinary interests, which in his grief he found senseless. He is made by merciful nature to forget what it was like ... Even extreme guilt may be clouded over as ubiquitous nature prompts the conclusion 'Why bother' ... But, it may be said, surely in many cases something good can be retained or learnt from the experience of emptiness and non-being? ... There is nothing that cannot be broken or taken from us. Ultimately we are nothing. A

reminder of our mortality, a recognition of contingency, must at least make us humble. Are we not then closer to the deep mystery of being human? When we find our ordinary pursuits trivial and senseless are we not right to do so? (MGM: 500–1)

This description of the deadened, numb indifference to daily tasks is an apt description of how Lee is when we meet him, and yet Murdoch speaks here of guiltless remorse, when Lee is in fact overburdened with guilt. And the fact that he has a reputation in town, and difficulties finding work, shows how it is a public belief, not just a personal one. Lee faces rejection and isolation as well as his own torment. He may have reached the 'why bother' stage, but he certainly rises to meet his duties in relation to Joe and Patrick as far as he can. The lesson that Murdoch writes about, that recognition of contingency with which she is so concerned, is a difficult and challenging lesson to learn, and this film shows us that pain in fact does not go away; but also it does not stop you from being a decent person, and that people will still love you even if you make terrible mistakes and feel lost. This calls upon us to embrace what Murdoch calls 'the sublime', which is 'the proud energetic fear with which the rational being faces the contingent dreadfulness of the world' (MGM: 100): 'Art can rarely, but with authority, show how we learn from pain, swept by the violence of divine grace toward an unwilling wisdom' (F&S: 458).

When discussing art, Murdoch says that it is 'a special discerning exercise of intelligence in relation to the real'. She goes on, 'In the shock of joy in response to good art, an essential ingredient is a sense of the revelation of reality, of the really real . . . the world as we were never able so clearly to see it before' (F&S: 454). This shock of joy is something that we recognise from realising the significance or insight of a film, and I suggest we feel it even in relation to a film as moving as *Manchester by the Sea*. It would be sentimental and unrealistic were Lee to be able to move back to Manchester, where Randi has a new life, and to settle back in to the town where such horrors happened. There is comfort in the fact that Lee dedicated himself to doing the best he could for Patrick, and that he will keep him in his life, with their fun and frank relationship, but that he also has faced his past and knows that he is too damaged to live in its footsteps again. To revisit what Murdoch writes,

> We have (gravity, necessity) a natural impulse to derealise our world and surround ourselves with fantasy. Simply stopping this, refraining from filling voids with lies and falsity, is progress. Equally in the more obscure labyrinths of personal relations it may be necessary to make the move which makes the void appear. (MGM: 503)

As with many of the characters in the films in this book who face up to their losses, we see here that Lee faces up to his, making the void appear, but it can be seen to be progress. He has a new job, a bigger flat and visits from Patrick to look forward to. There are moments which convey the bleak stasis of Lee's world, such as when he puts his hand through the window, when he cannot speak to Sandy's mother, or his emotional reactions in the hospital. These moments, captured and supplemented by the level of bodily and mental pain that Affleck conveys through his performance, enable us, if we watch carefully, to see more than we are told, and perhaps we can think of these moments in Murdochian terms, as being where the frame does not fully meet:

> I spoke earlier of situations where what is wholly transcendent and invisible becomes partially, perhaps surprisingly, visible at points where the 'frame' does not quite 'meet'. This image describes certain kinds of experience where it is as if, to use another image, the curtain blows in the wind (of spirit maybe), and we see more than we are supposed to. (MGM: 505)

This is of course a beautifully cinematic turn of phrase, but it is also useful conceptually for thinking about the notion of excess of meaning, or feeling, or thought. When we discern moral, philosophical notions in a film, they may be glaring, but they may also need to be spotted, where the frame doesn't quite meet.

This chapter has looked at how films can deal with extreme suffering. The films I have chosen are, in turn, satirical, fanciful and brutally honest. As Murdoch says, 'human beings are remarkably good at surviving and people make jokes in dark situations which would appal the outsider' (MGM: 502). Some may think my Murdochian analysis using the language of 'lessons' and 'wisdom' is overstated or stretched. Murdoch addresses the potential irritation of this attitude:

> Someone may say, if you are always noticing images of God or Good or seeing spiritual ladders, or being some sort of artist, you are very lucky. Your view of spiritual refreshment as everywhere available is ridiculously optimistic, even sentimental. It seems to neglect how miserable we are, and also how wicked we are. (MGM: 498)

There can be no doubt about the misery of human life, and of the wickedness and misery of the characters in the films in this chapter. And, as Murdoch says,

> Extreme suffering, from one cause or another, is likely to be the lot of everyone at some time in life; and innumerable lives are hideously darkened throughout by hunger, poverty and persecution, or by remorse or guilt or abandoned loneliness and lack of love. (MGM: 504)

Murdoch's non-theological take on suffering is both mystical and realistic. She contemplates the metaphysics of the void, but also the fact that comedy is everywhere: 'Theological truth is abstract. Out on the battle-front of human suffering people will use such devices as they have for survival' (MGM: 504).

Murdoch's analysis of the image of tragedy shows us both the inadequacy of art for capturing the full reality of life's horrors, and also the role that 'structured glimpses' can play for us when we view them with just discernment, attention and thought.

NOTES

1. For a discussion of the oedipal significance of the relationship, see Meg Harris Williams (2017).
2. See Arendt (2006: 250); and the introduction to the volume by Amos Elon.
3. Simon Critchley's book *On Humour* contains discussions of a range of approaches to the topic, and Noel Carroll's *Humour: A Very Short Introduction* (2014) is an excellent overview.
4. *Adagio Per Archi E Organo In Sol Minore* by the London Philharmonic Orchestra.

CHAPTER 7

Film and Women's Stories

The point of liberation is not, and this is to differ with certain views of women's lib, to say we're better, or we're special, or we're wonderful, but just to be equal, to be ordinary, to join the human race, to be people, just people like everybody else. (Interview in 1978, cited in Dooley 2003: 83)

Murdoch's relationship with feminism is not straightforward, and needs some clarification and explanation. Her philosophical thinking, however, is of great value in understanding how film can involve us in women's stories. In this chapter, I am going to set out some ideas about Murdoch, gender and philosophy, before going on to examine three films in detail as stories about women that benefit from thinking about them in terms of individuality, honesty, compassion and morality. The films are *Certain Women* (Kelly Reichardt, 2016), *The Unknown Girl/La fille inconnue* (Jean-Pierre Dardenne and Luc Dardenne, 2016) and *Girlhood* (Céline Sciamma, 2014).

Iris Murdoch was born in 1919, the year after the publication of Marie Stopes's book *Married Love*, which challenged perceptions about women's sexual pleasure and equality between the sexes in marriage (Stopes 1919). This was a highpoint of feminism's first wave in the United Kingdom, but that period would not be known as such until the 1960s, after the onset of second-wave feminism arising in North America with works such as Betty Friedan's *The Feminine Mystique* (1997), first published in 1963. Iris Murdoch's education was during the period between suffrage and the second wave, and so, when we think of her in light of today's discourses of feminism, third-wave, post- or intersectional, we do have to keep in mind that, in Nora Hämäläinen's words, Murdoch's 'concerns were elsewhere, and her scene was different' (2015: 753). As Marije Altorf observes, 'with the exception of de Beauvoir's *The Second Sex*, it is doubtful whether Murdoch was familiar with existing feminist literature' (2007: 177). Murdoch said in 1976 that '*The Second Sex* is a very good book and makes me like her as a *person*, although I've never met her' (Dooley 2003: 32).

Murdoch is committed to gender equality, but is not convinced by siphoning off interests or studies as 'women's interests' or 'women's studies'. She sees this as a mistake. Her reasoning is that women's stories are human stories and women's studies are – studies. Murdoch consistently expresses passionate belief in the importance of women's education. In conversation with Michael O. Bellamy in 1976, she said,

> I'm not interested in women's problems as such, though I'm a great supporter of women's liberation – particularly education for women – but in aid of getting women to join the human race, not in aid of making any kind of feminine contribution to the world. I think there's a kind of human contribution, but I don't think there's a feminine contribution. (Dooley 2003: 48)

This neatly summarises Murdoch's thoughts on women's lib. She was forthright about her support for women's education but less supportive of other aspects of the women's movement. These views were mainly expressed in interview, and so not part of her philosophical writing per se. In conversation with Jack I. Biles in 1977 she said,

> I'm not interested in the 'woman's world' or the assertion of a 'female viewpoint'. This is often rather an artificial idea and can in fact injure the promotion of equal rights. We want to join the human race, not invent a new separatism. (Dooley 2003: 62)

She was very concerned not to separate people or groups into ghettos based on any aspects of their identity, but was focused on the significance of individuals. Harold Hobson, theatre critic of *The Times*, got into a sticky situation with Murdoch over the fact that women were not admitted to the Athenaeum Club which is where they met for their interview in 1962. Challenging Murdoch on her assertion that men try to suppress women, she responded by taking him up on the way he had 'thanked heaven because women were kept out of the Athenaeum'. She states,

> Clubs are a special case. I suppose men can have the Athenaeum if they want to. But the notion that women are inferior is deep, very deep, even in our fairly sensible society, and it does nobody any good. Men and women are still thought of as having stereotyped parts to play, regardless

of their temperament. But any individual is a mixture of masculine and feminine and would be best employed just being himself and treating people as individuals, too. (Dooley 2003: 5)

This focus on the individual, in their fullest selfhood, is what Murdoch is interested in. But she is also perfectly aware of her privileged position, saying to Sheila Hale in 1976,

Women who think of themselves as something separate are joining a kind of inferiority movement, like women's clubs. I realize I am lucky. I have never felt picked out in an intellectual sense because I am a woman; these distinctions are not made at Oxford. (Dooley 2003: 32)

Murdoch is also committed to equality for homosexuals and her novels are notable for their inclusion of characters who are gay or sexually ambiguous.[1] She said to Jeffrey Meyers in interview in 1988,

I'm very much in favour of gay lib, and I feel very strongly that there shouldn't be any sort of prejudice against homosexuals, or suggestions that homosexual love is unnatural or bad. I hope such views are tending to disappear from society. (Dooley 2003: 233)

For a writer and thinker who was open-minded about gender and sexuality, it is ironic that her gender has affected her reputation as a cultural figure, especially in the way that her private life has been the focus of attention over the years (Bolton 2015b).[2] A number of clips of Murdoch can be found online: in discussion with Bryan Magee in 1977 about literature and philosophy (as the only woman in a series called 'Men of Ideas'); in conversation with Frank Kermode in a programme for Sixth Forms, discussing her novel *An Unofficial Rose* (1962); in a discussion about determinism with David Pears, in 1972; being interviewed by James Atlas for *92Y/The Paris Review Interview Series* in 1990; and interviewing Jiddu Krishnamurti in 1984. What these clips show is the philosopher at work. She is a public intellectual, known for her work as a novelist and a philosopher, not her private life, or her later illness. What is usually discussed in these clips is the unique relationship she has to the disciplines of literature and philosophy: she talks about art, the type of thinking that art requires as opposed to science, and the metaphysical nature of the relationship to art, involving love and choice, and change. These appearances show her engaged in philosophical discourse, responding to, and asking, questions. They enable the viewer to have a – limited – encounter with her as a thinker. When we watch, and listen to her speak, we can hear her voice, see her facial expressions, and notice what makes her laugh. Watched and studied alongside the written words of Murdoch's philosophy, these videos are a valuable contribution to furthering understanding of her moral thinking, and a record of her working that is suited to the discursive discipline of philosophy. These issues pertain to the image of Murdoch as a philosopher, and to her presence in contemporary culture; but what of the role of gender in the philosophical work she produced?

THE ROLE OF GENDER IN MURDOCH'S PHILOSOPHY

This is an area that is open to contestation, and is well aerated by Sabina Lovibond in her book *Iris Murdoch, Gender and Philosophy* (2011). On the M and D parable, Lovibond writes that

> the conclusion to be drawn is that some of our most valuable moral accomplishments leave no trace in the public realm, and that an ethical theory which does not know how to interest itself in anything outside that realm will fail to honour such accomplishments. (2011: 24)

This is significant because of the 'gendered' character of the public–private opposition, so Lovibond explains how

> this vindication of the private is another feature of Murdoch's moral philosophy which has proved attractive to feminist readers, and the intimate, domestic nature of the M & D story suggests that for Murdoch, too, the blind spots of existentialist–behaviourist ethics may have something to do with its masculine origins. (2011: 24)

One problem with this, however, for Lovibond, is that 'much of the critical force of feminism has been directed, precisely, against the excessive "obedience" or compliance hitherto demanded of women' (2011: 32). In other words, is unselfing not precisely the act that women have always done far too much, and should they not be thinking more about how to put themselves first? Lovibond assesses that, 'There is . . . some difficulty in combining the event of *claiming what is due to you* with that of the *extinction of self-will*' (2011: 94).

Nora Hämäläinen considers that Lovibond argues 'that Iris Murdoch's philosophical and literary work is covertly dedicated to an ideology of female subordination' (2015: 743). Hämäläinen does not agree with Lovibond, and cites Altorf's reconstruction of Murdoch as a 'woman philosopher', focusing on both her intellectual integrity as a philosopher and the intellectual benefits of being an outsider (2015: 744). Hämäläinen argues that Murdoch was unhappy with the freely choosing agent of modern philosophy, believing it to produce an overly narrow view of morality compared to the complexity of our actual moral lives: 'she wanted to supplant this thin understanding of the moral agent with a richer idea of the moral person as a complex human being with an inner life and morally significant movements of consciousness' (2015: 744) (see MGM: 171–2). The type of individual that Murdoch believes we should all be aiming to become is perhaps associated with some qualities traditionally seen as belonging to women, as Hämäläinen notes: 'The inward, soulful, multifaceted perspective on moral consciousness and her persistent emphasis on the good person as "loving" and moral perception as "a loving gaze", could perhaps be seen as providing an ethics that is culturally coded as feminine' (2015: 745). Murdoch herself, however, does not attribute gender to any of these qualities. Lovibond is not right, according to Hämäläinen, to argue that rehabilitating Weil's idea of attention is indicative of an attachment to female submissiveness (ibid.: 746). As I have explored in earlier chapters, here Hämäläinen makes clear how the figure of the good person that Murdoch evokes is 'far from that of the submissive mother, wife, or muse – it is the religious subject struggling with suffering and opening up for grace. It thus occupies a space that is genderless and always adversarial to habitual relations of power' (ibid.). Christ is one of Murdoch's favourite models, and even when she strips him of deity 'the notions of attention and obedience preserve this radical aspect' (ibid.). Whereas Lovibond sees Murdoch's adoption of Weil's unselfing as an action that shows a lack of interest in 'outer, judicial, social, structural consequences of this kind of ethic', Hämäläinen corrects this. She explains that,

> The 'self' that is exorcised in Murdoch's act of attention is a very specific entity: it is 'the fat relentless ego', which interferes with our capacity to see things and people as they really are. Anxieties, desires, wishful thoughts, hopes, fears, pride, and vanity are among the aspects of our ego that blind us from reality, and in order to see more accurately, we need to let these go. Unselfing is thus not to be understood as a wholesale self-denigration but rather a kind of deliberate purification of the self that we undergo in order to see more clearly. (Ibid.: 747)

Hämäläinen explains that Murdoch is not proposing we subjugate ourselves in order to surrender to another, but rather that we work to let go of our own ego so that we might see reality more clearly. In fact, Murdoch shows her awareness of the type of asceticism and suffering of which Weil approves, and does not go along with this herself. She believes, as Hämäläinen notes, that 'extreme demands on oneself (even demands of self-effacement) can coexist, in a life, with a thorough understanding of the mutuality and complexity of moral and political life with others' (ibid.: 748). The Murdochian individual is a social, historical and encultured being, and this is how Murdoch's contribution to moral philosophy can be identified: 'Through a creative secularization of some of Weil's core ideas, Murdoch achieves a perspective on the dynamics of moral personhood that is unique in her own context of Anglophone twentieth-century moral philosophy' (ibid.). We can see more clearly, therefore, how Murdoch is acutely aware of differences between people, who see different worlds, which, as Hämäläinen points out, is similar to contemporary feminist and postcolonial thinkers: 'Our very conceptual frameworks, our patterns of attention, our capacities for understanding are formed by both cultural and individual biases and limitations' (ibid. 752).

This is similar to the concept of the lived bodies of feminist phenomenology, described by Iris Marion Young as 'always encultured' (2005: 17), and Murdoch refers to our conceptual vision as well as our physicality. As Megan Laverty writes, '"unselfing" involves an acceptance of one's own perspective as inherently limited – embraced as personal, historical, provisional and incomplete . . . if anything is abandoned, it is an illusion of the self as inviolably important and master of everything that it surveys' (Laverty 2007: 93). As Hämäläinen explains, Murdoch's unselfing is 'a kind of work that the individual person does in order to see what is in front of him (people, art, nature) in a more truthful light' (2015: 753):

> Unselfing, in this sense, essentially involves the recognition of structural bias, of privilege, of inequality as well as the recognition of personal fault. Developing the structural criticism latent in the notion of unselfing requires only a tiny step forward: that of paying attention to the social/structural roots of some of our biases. For us who are marinated in post-structuralist feminism, this is an easy, obvious, and indeed necessary step to take, but we must keep in mind that Murdoch's concerns were elsewhere, and her scene was different. (Ibid.)

Now Hämäläinen's observation about Murdoch's 'scene' becomes clearer, and how we can think about her ideas in our current 'scene' becomes more accessible:

> Turning attention away from the self is not submissiveness in a sociopolitical sense. It is not a matter of choosing an inferior position in search of some obscure spiritual goal, but rather of overcoming both the 'fat, relentless ego' and the shackles of convention that bind us to given, biased, and potentially oppressive manners of looking. A substantial conception of the human being but not an inflated notion of 'self'; self-scrutiny without self-preoccupation; self-forgetfulness without self-denigration – these are elements of a complex economy of the self in relation to goodness and to our surrounding reality. (Ibid.)

Thanks to Hämäläinen's argument, we can see how 'both the inner world of the individual and the collective world of society and politics are spaces for moral/epistemic transformations' (ibid.: 754). Although Murdoch was critical of Derrida's structuralism (MGM: 197–202), seeing this as another totalising, domineering mode of thought which attempted to explain away individuality and morality, it does not mean that she was not both aware, and critical, of social structures and conventions which imprison us and proscribe our behaviour. For Hämäläinen then, Murdoch's critique of convention is a structural and historical critique 'on a par with the feminist interrogation of patriarchy, although its focus is on discernment and complexity lost rather than on substance and complexity gained' (2015: 754). Her analysis sheds light on structural inequality and oppression, and conventions that restrict our moral world views, and Altorf helps us to understand how Murdoch not only critiques this state of affairs but offers alternatives and possibilities for thinking about things differently.

Altorf agrees that Murdoch 'demonstrates a keen awareness of sexual inequality, yet this is something she never addresses in her essays' (2007: 175). For example, in conversation with Barbara Stevens Heusel in 1987, she says,

> People sometimes ask, 'Why don't you write about women's problems?' Women's problems are problems among other problems, and I write about them also. I just don't write only or mainly about them. Unfortunately, it's still a man's world. A man doesn't have to explain what it's like to be a man, but a woman has to explain what it's like to be a woman. (Dooley 2003: 207)

Murdoch's inclusion of women in her philosophical examples, arguments and parables, however, makes it clear just how much she does 'write about them also', and highlights how women's lives are missing from philosophical discourse generally. This is one of the most refreshing and enjoyable aspects of reading Murdoch's philosophy: her equitable consideration of lives, female, male, animal and vegetal. From Isabella in *Measure for Measure* (MGM: 379), to Maggie and her pagoda in Henry James's *The Golden Bowl* (MGM: 306), and to wondering who led the better New Testament life, Mary or Martha (MGM: 332), Murdoch includes women as the objects of her attention and the subjects of stories and images. Altorf draws on the notion of the philosophical imaginary from Michele Le Dœuff to account for Murdoch's imagery in a way that demonstrates her potential contribution to philosophical thinking:

> The philosophical imaginary expresses her engagement with imagery, metaphors and myth, and in particular her research into the part a specific image, or imaginative idea, can play in a philosophical argument.

> Philosophical imagery, Le Dœuff maintains, has arisen from the interplay between cultural, social elements and the constraints of philosophical writing. An image may appear once in a text, but it can also reappear throughout an author's oeuvre. (Altorf 2007: 183)

This describes how a philosopher has a range of images, metaphors and myths that they like and find useful, and return to as tools for explaining their thought and building their arguments. Murdoch undoubtedly has an array of these, and they are indeed unique to her. The idea of the philosophical imaginary highlights how, in her 'philosophical struggle', Murdoch is concerned with the position of people who are outside philosophy. Altorf observes,

> While Le Dœuff is mainly concerned with the exclusion of women, Murdoch is more generally concerned with those outside philosophy; they seem to have stepped out of the nineteenth-century novels she favours so much: virtuous peasants, or 'some quiet unpretentious worker, a schoolteacher or a mother, better still an aunt' (EM: 244) [*sic* MGM: 429]. The virtuous peasant may be slightly problematic because of a similarity to, for instance, the noble savage. Yet Murdoch recognises that not all philosophy is universal when it does not allow space for such mothers or aunts or for the supposition that 'an unexamined life can be virtuous' (IP: 299). (Altorf 2007: 184)

The point about the virtuous peasant is also picked up by Lovibond, who accuses Murdoch of having a 'sentimental cult of the "ordinary"' (2011: 42). She is referring to Murdoch's Weilian celebration of 'the inarticulate but devoted carer for others' (ibid.) and the suggestion that such people might need no improvement. Murdoch is not including the possibility, as Lovibond argues, that the aunt might be a shop steward or a sociologist (ibid.). Murdoch's work is, however, as Altorf writes, 'saturated with imagery' (2007: 184), and I have drawn out many of these so far in this book, such as caring for a plant or a cat, families facing decisions, and, of course, M and D. And this book argues that we can increase our understanding of the relevance of Murdoch's philosophical thinking by seeing how the principles are at work in film through other images, and in the world around us. This is not a matter of illustrating Murdoch's philosophy, but of understanding it in action, in our lives, all the time. For Le Dœuff, images don't just illustrate but 'they simultaneously counter a quite different argument, thus adding voices to the dialogue' (Altorf 2007: 184). Murdoch's voice has a lot to add to the film philosophy dialogue!

Altorf concludes that assumptions about philosophy and feminism may have deterred assessment of Murdoch's philosophy from a feminist perspective. She argues,

Feminism should not be thought of as more partisan than philosophy; it is not necessarily the secluded thinking Murdoch takes it to be, any more than philosophy is the universal quest for truth . . . her philosophical writing shares important concerns with those of feminists like Alcoff and Le Dœuff, more so than perhaps she herself may have allowed for. (Ibid.: 185)

Altorf's work is central to understanding how Murdoch's philosophy can relate to women in film philosophy. Through appreciating Murdoch's philosophical imaginary, which features women as so many examples, from real-life scenarios, literature and the Bible, we can open out our thinking to understanding her concepts of just, discerning vision in many contexts. Alongside this is her lack of deference to any male philosopher or academic, such as Ryle, Hampshire, Sartre, Derrida or Freud, as she demonstrates how she is not in thrall to any other thinker except perhaps Weil. Even Plato is rigorously examined.

In 'The Idea of Perfection', Murdoch states that she is interested in 'the fact that an unexamined life can be virtuous and the fact that love is a central concept in morals' (IP: 299). She explores this open and inclusive aspect to moral philosophy, and goodness, through the parable of M and D. The aim of the parable is to show that M 'observes D or at least reflects deliberately about D, until gradually her vision of D alters' (IP: 313).[3] This alteration could, Murdoch explains, 'be described in terms of M's visual imagery', so how M sees D herself or D's qualities (ibid.). This activity is happening in M's mind and is changing how she sees the world. It is not about M trying to be a better person for the sake of a metaphysical witness. What Murdoch is doing here is liberating morality and philosophy 'from the domination of science: or rather from the domination of inexact ideas of science which haunt philosophers and other thinkers' (IP: 320). Existentialism tries to solve this, she argues, by 'attributing to the individual an empty lonely freedom . . . to "fly in the face of facts"', and we have already seen what Murdoch makes of that (IP: 321). Psychoanalysis, she claims, is a 'muddled embryonic science' that we need not be overwhelmed by: 'even if M were given a full psychoanalytical explanation of her conduct towards D she need not be confined by such an explanation' (IP: 321). Murdoch rejects these attempts and instead tells us to learn from lives, not words:

Words may mislead us here since words are often stable while concepts alter; we have a different image of courage at forty from that which we had at twenty. A deepening process, at any rate an altering and complicating process, takes place . . . Knowledge of a value concept is something to be understood, as it were, in depth, and not in terms of switching on to some given impersonal network. (IP: 322)

As she mentions in 'Vision and Choice in Morality', a new type of language is called for to understand how moral vision in the lives of individuals evolves and develops (or doesn't). As Murdoch explains,

> As moral agents we have to try to see justly, to overcome prejudice, to avoid temptation, to control and curb imagination, to direct reflection. Man is not a combination of an impersonal rational thinker and a personal will. He is a unified being who sees, and who desires in accordance with what he sees, and who has some continual slight control over the direction and focus of his vision. (IP: 332)

Despite Murdoch's occasional use of the image of the uneducated or inarticulate person, her main concern is with 'the ordinary person' – all of us – as differentiated from the professional philosopher. This is, as Murdoch explains, a 'general metaphysical background to morals', and as such is not 'a formula which can be illuminatingly introduced into any and every moral act' (IP: 334). It is a stance that is not only oppositional, but also inclusive and egalitarian. It is a philosophy of morals founded on love, and that is open to all: 'It is in the capacity to love, that is to *see*, that the liberation of the soul from fantasy consists. The freedom which is a proper human goal is the freedom from fantasy, that is the realism of compassion' (OGG: 354).

Murdoch accepts that human beings are naturally selfish and that 'we are anxiety-ridden animals' (SGC: 369). In art, we can see an image of human beings that we can steadily contemplate, and this might be the only place where we can see such an image.

> Art transcends selfish and obsessive limitations of personality and can enlarge the sensibility of its consumer. It is a kind of goodness by proxy. Most of all it exhibits to us the connection, in *human* beings, of clear realistic vision with compassion. The realism of a great artist is not a photographic realism, it is essentially both pity and justice. (SGC: 371)

This is an interesting concept in relation to film. Richard Rushton argues that 'films help us to shape what we call "reality"' (2011: 2). Rushton stresses how films create, rather than simply re-present, reality to us. This approach enables us to conceive of how many of the examples Murdoch gives can be envisaged as scenes or moments in films, and that perhaps we even know them already from the films we have seen and/or the lives we have lived/known. Her call to really look at real people enables the role of women's lives to come to the fore. Murdoch says we must reject 'the dry symbol, the bogus individual, the false whole' and move towards 'the real impenetrable human person. That this person is substantial, impenetrable, individual, indefinable and valuable is after all the fundamental tenet of Liberalism' (AD: 294).[4]

Certain Women, *The Unknown Girl* and *Girlhood* are all stories about girls and women, their lives, and things that they do. Each film holds our attention on these women as individuals, who we attend to through the particulars of their carefully wrought circumstances on-screen. They also convey the women as contemplative people, attending to others, reflecting on their lives, which include aspects of their femininity as elements of their lived bodies and societal lives. These provocative, affective and intelligent films merit close analysis of the form and content of the visions they present: not consoling, but challenging; not overly dramatic, but asking questions that are moral, political and psychological.

CONTEMPLATIVE OBSERVATIONS: *CERTAIN WOMEN*

This film features a certain point in four women's lives, and their gender is not foregrounded other than to show that it impacts upon their lives. These are simply what Murdoch would call human stories, but they are stories about women's lives in a short period of time, in intense detail. The women are not superheroes, nor are they experiencing extreme marvels or tragedies. The allusive, incomplete tales offer glimpses behind the curtain of the lives of these women. They are more than snapshots in a conventional portmanteau movie. These vignettes look backwards and forwards around the screen time each woman occupies, indicating the past experiences that have shaped them (legal practice, marriage, manual work), and the acquired behaviours and practices that inform their daily lives (frustration, imagination, loneliness).

The film begins with the authorial stamp – a film by Kelly Reichardt – and a train crosses the Montana landscape, with a huge flat mountain backdrop. Morning is breaking. In a screen split by a dividing wall between two rooms, indicative of post-coital separation, half a naked man, Ryan Lewis (James LeGros), is glimpsed on the right, pulling on his pants, and half a naked woman, Laura Wells (Laura Dern), is glimpsed on the left, in bed, pulling on her socks. The woman reclines, wearing her bra, and smiles with an inquisitive, appraising, but loving, expression at the man as he finishes dressing. It emerges that it is a lunchtime assignation, and the light outside seems oddly dark and gloomy. She has to get back to work, but one of her clients has just turned up wanting to see her. He wants to progress his case, but she needs to take him to another personal injury lawyer for a second opinion since he does not accept her advice that they have reached the end of the line. The client, Will Fuller

(Jared Harris), wants to talk and strategise, but she has to go to court so she manages to get him to leave. She cleans her skirt with a lint roller, and rips off the used sticky paper, like we all do, as she watches Fuller through the window. He seems to have nowhere to go, and just stands by a lamppost.

The second-opinion lawyer is an older, white, bearded man. He explains the legal situation in relation to Fuller's claim: that the contractor was clearly negligent but Fuller's previous settlement precludes a tort claim now. Fuller accepted what they offered and that cleared them of any further penalty, so he can't sue again. Fuller accepts this completely, with no discussion. Laura looks at him incredulously. As she says on the telephone to Ryan, she has been explaining this for eight months: 'It would be so lovely to think that if I were a man, I could explain the law and people would listen and say OK; it would be so restful.' They then begin a conversation about their relationship, with Ryan referring to 'his situation' as a reason why they need to cool things, but Laura has to go because Fuller has just got back in her car and does not want to leave. He starts saying hateful things about his wife, wishing she would 'lay down on the highway', and saying he is going to get a machine gun and kill everyone. She tells him to get out of the car, but he promises to stop. Laura puts music on the radio and he starts crying; she's exasperated but doesn't say anything. She is having to deal with all the emotional fallout from his situation, and it is very unlikely that the other lawyer would have to do this. Laura is seen as far more approachable, and, in fact, she does not reject him.

At home, we see Laura lying on her sofa with a beautiful, large sleeping dog, stroking it with her feet. She appears to be single, as she is spending the evening at home with just the dog, and sleeps alone. Her telephone rings in the middle of night because Fuller has started a siege at the court building. At the scene, they fit her with a microphone (she remembers the cop from a custody case) and they send her in to find Fuller. They say to her, 'Keep him engaged, like he's been hurt, blame the system, make her feel like you're on his side.' As they send her in, they say, 'You'll be great, atta girl.' There is a decided lack of care for Laura as they seem to just want her to solve the situation. She goes into the building and finds Fuller, chatting away to him as she looks for his court files. They have a normal conversation with the security guard that Fuller is holding hostage, teasing him and saying, 'Big Man is a member of the Samoan Royal Family.' Fuller asks Laura to read his court letters. He's very angry and on the edge: her telephone rings and he brusquely tells her to leave it. When she has finished his letters, Big Man says to him, 'You got screwed', and Fuller thanks him for the acknowledgement. He is clearly desperate, asking what he can do now. Laura says he should get physical therapy, and be nice to his wife. He lets Big Man go, saying that he should tell the police that, 'If they try anything I'll kill the woman: she's my lawyer – I've got reason to kill her.' He gives instructions to Laura to walk ahead of him, and she does what he says although she keeps trying to get him to turn himself in. He wants her to pretend he has the gun on her, but in fact he has headed out of the back of the building, telling her to wait before she goes out of the front. She does, and when she goes out she says he is unarmed, but he has been picked up by the police around the back of the building. Nobody pays any attention to her, and Fuller is driven off in a police car.

The power of this episode lies in the lack of drama. There are no moments of extreme horror or terrible cruelty, just a level of sadness and unremitting harshness. For Laura, this is manifest in Fuller's lack of respect for her professional opinion and his reliance upon her as a confidante. He is happy to threaten her, however, when looking for someone to blame. As far as the police are concerned, she is a handy conduit to Fuller, and they cheer her on with vacuous sexist support, but they seem have no care for her. And her lover is unavailable because of 'his situation', which we guess is a marriage, and we soon find out we have guessed correctly.

The next story begins with Gina Lewis (Michelle Williams) walking through the forest. She is very slim, wearing smart running gear: she looks very 'city' and professional. She stops to look at a plot of land where she wants to build a house. She listens to the peace and the beauty of running water. As she heads back towards the family campsite, she hears her husband and daughter laughing. Her husband is Laura's lover. She notices him texting somebody, and she asks what they were laughing about. Ryan starts showing a silly skit that he was doing, and she looks away, unamused. This is an awkward scenario, with Gina plainly distanced from her husband and daughter emotionally.

In the car, Gina asks her daughter Guthrie (Sara Rodier) if she brushed her teeth. Guthrie says yes but Gina doesn't believe her and Guthrie snaps, 'Why do you bother asking me if you don't believe me anyway?' When it is just the two of them, Ryan says to Guthrie, 'Let's be nice to your mum today, cut her some slack.' Guthrie says, 'Why, is she sick or something?' He says, 'She works really hard, she does a lot for us. Neither of us would do very well without her.' Guthrie says, 'You're building her a house, how much better can you be?' Gina's daughter clearly has hostile feelings towards her and is much more relaxed with her father, who is having an affair.

Gina asks Ryan to speak to the man whose sandstone she wants to buy, saying that they trust him. Guthrie is angry that this is going to take longer as she wants to go home, saying that Gina lied about how long they would be. Ryan tries to cajole her, and Gina says, 'I don't know why you indulge her.' Ryan answers, 'Well you did say it wouldn't take all day' and Gina says, 'You really can't help it, making me the bad guy, always.' Gina does not seem to like Guthrie very much, or respect Ryan, and her role in the family is that of the bad guy breadwinner.

They go to speak to the local man, Albert (Rene Auberjonois) who has a pile of sandstone on his property that Gina wants for her house. Gina tries to be kind to Albert, asking if he needs anything, then she asks him if he wants to sell the sandstone in the garden and he ignores her completely. He will talk to Ryan, who says the same things to Albert that Gina says, and says he will give them the sandstone. Gina says she wants to pay him for it, but he just doesn't engage with her. Albert looks at Gina with suspicion and a lack of connection. His look seems to say, 'What kind of woman are you?' They have a moment where they bond slightly when they hear the call of the quails. Albert says it sounds like they are saying, 'How are you?', and Gina, who smiles and looks the most relaxed she has so far, repeats the intonation of the call saying, 'I'm just fine.' She looks happy, and Albert looks at her with a softened expression. This leads him to say to Ryan, 'Your wife works for you?', to which Ryan laughs and says, 'Ha that's funny no she's the boss actually.' Albert remains perplexed.

As the family pulls away in the car, Guthrie disgruntled and surly, Gina criticises Ryan for not helping with the negotiations with Albert, while Ryan says he was giving Albert 'wriggle room'. We then see them loading up the stone on a lorry. She waves at Albert, but he doesn't wave back. This melancholy segment conveys Gina's strained isolation within the family unit, and also suggests that she is a strong-minded individual with plans that she needs to fulfil. She craves the peace and beauty of this landscape, looking most relaxed when listening to the sounds of nature. There is tension between the needs of the woman who works hard and has her own dreams, and her ability to also have fulfilling loving relationships within her family. She is critical of her husband and daughter. The picture is of a life that is torn, uneasily, between work and leisure, individuality and family.

The final story begins in stables, early in the morning, with the horses being released, fed and cleaned out by someone dressed up against the bitter cold in thick layers and boots. The working boots belong to the rancher (Lily Gladstone), who has a little dog companion. She makes her food, eats it and watches television, all on her own, and then drives into town. At the wheel of her car, her beautiful face is serene and open. We have not seen her speak to another person yet. She turns into the car park of the college, and sits and waits in the car. Then she goes into the building, and into a classroom where there are three others, who look at her and each other in silent comment and judgement. The rancher looks around and settles in to a desk.

The young teacher, Elizabeth Travis (Kristen Stewart) arrives, slightly flustered, saying she has never taught a class before. She asks them all to introduce each other, and a woman says, 'We all know each other', but of course they don't know the rancher, and she doesn't know them. In fact, nobody ever asks her name, so we don't know it. They say that they don't know anything about the law, and interrupt her with self-serving questions about their pensions and employment rights. The class stops at nine o'clock, and the rancher speaks to Elizabeth. She isn't registered for the class, and admits she just followed some people in. We haven't seen her read any documents, she simply sits at her desk and watches. Elizabeth tells her that she has to drive back to Livingstone tonight, which is a long way – four hours. The rancher shows Elizabeth where the diner is and they go together. Elizabeth eats, but the rancher doesn't. She stares at Elizabeth, bashful, entranced, as she hears how Elizabeth took this job before she finished law school, but she is still having to do it even though she now has a full-time job in Livingstone. Elizabeth asks if she made a fool of herself in class, and the rancher says no, that it was interesting, and that she never knew a student had any rights. She explains that she cares for the horses, and says it's just a winter job, but we can't be sure that it is. She offers to show Elizabeth the ranch and the horses, but Elizabeth has to get back. She stands and watches Elizabeth drive away, with a slight smile creeping across her lips. She then buys a microwaved burger from the garage and eats it with relief: so she was either too self-conscious to eat in front of Elizabeth, or the food in the diner was too expensive for her.

The next morning, the rancher follows the same routine with the horses and the dog. She talks to the horses, they come to her, and she walks them gently, feeding them and caring for them. The animals are confident, they trust her and rely on her. The little dog chases her on the tractor. The sun comes up, and the landscape and the animals look beautiful. The only sounds we can hear are horses whinnying and the clip-clop of their hooves, the tractor engine and the busy little dog barking. We see the rancher lying in her bed looking at the plaster lines on the ceiling: another day, another routine. We see the thick coats on these horses, and the furry dog amuses itself by playing and diving on something. The week passes and class comes around again. Elizabeth starts, and passes out handouts. The rancher beams at her, and looks at the handout, but doesn't read it. Again the other students ask questions about themselves, their pay and their parking spaces. After the class, they go to the diner again, and Elizabeth shows she is clearly keen to not have to teach this class, asking the rancher if she knows anyone who could teach it. The rancher says no, and that she 'don't know anyone at all'. She begins to open up, and tells Elizabeth that she broke her wrist breaking in a horse, and tells stories about growing up with her brothers. Elizabeth also confides that she was afraid she would go to law school and end up selling shoes. They seem fairly easy together, but their interest in each other does not seem equivalent: Elizabeth is hungry, and tired, and wants to leave town, but the rancher never eats, even when offered some of Elizabeth's food, and just watches Elizabeth lovingly (Figure 7.1).

Figure 7.1 The rancher (Lily Gladstone) lovingly looks at Elizabeth (Kristen Stewart), in *Certain Women* (2016), directed by Kelly Reichardt.

A close-up shot of a horse being groomed shows again the denseness of their coat and the repetitive, attentive work that the rancher does for these animals. Then she cleans her teeth, straightens her hair parting and brushes her hair into a ponytail. The next shot is of her riding her horse into town, at a gentle, steady pace. The rancher seems to be in symbiosis with the horses, as if they understand they are safe with each other. After class again, it becomes clear that the rancher has brought the horse to give Elizabeth a ride to the diner. Elizabeth is surprised, and says it's been a while since she has been on a horse, but the rancher tells her not to think about it. Elizabeth mounts too, and they ride off to the diner, slowly at a steady pace, with the moonlight catching the hair on all three of them. This has a dreamlike quality, and conveys the feeling that the rancher is truly happy. She is showing what she can do, and sharing this most precious skill and relationship with Elizabeth, without words.

At the diner, the rancher returns to their conversation from the week before, showing she has been thinking about it, and asks Elizabeth why she was afraid that she would end up selling shoes. Elizabeth says that it is the nicest job a girl from her family would ever have had. But, she explains, she is now a lawyer, and she goes through her working routine, which certainly sounds exacting. Clearly the drive to teach this class is too much for her. She says to the rancher, 'It's nice of you to bring the horse. Will you take me back to my car?' The rancher's face is smiling and peaceful as Elizabeth holds onto her on the horse. Back at the car, Elizabeth says thanks, to the rancher and the horse, and the rancher watches her drive away.

Another morning routine with horses, hay, stables and dog. She goes to the laundry. She gets through the week until class again only to find it is a different teacher: a man, who announces he is recently divorced, and who practises law in town. The rancher walks out and drives straight to Livingstone. She finds some law offices, and sleeps in her truck. In the morning, she asks a grumpy man if this is the right office, but it isn't. The secretary helps her track down Elizabeth, as Laura Wells walks in with her dog. The rancher drives to Elizabeth's office and goes up to her in the car park, saying she drove over to find her, that she's sorry she stopped taking the class as she looked forward to it. Elizabeth says she asked for a replacement because the drive was too much. The rancher says, 'I just knew if I didn't start driving I wasn't going to see you again. I didn't want that.' This is a declaration of her love for Elizabeth and yet it elicits no reply at all. After a pause, the rancher says, 'OK – well I have to go feed now. Animals be wondering where I'm at.' Elizabeth says nothing.

They part, and the rancher looks back at the building, sighting Elizabeth briefly in the lobby, who does not look back. As she drives away, the rancher's eyes widen in tears. The everyday noises of driving the truck, and the lack of soundtrack music, strip away any sentimentality or melodrama from this moment and emphasise the inescapabilty of her pain. There is no comfort. As she drives, her head starts to nod, and she falls asleep. Her foot slips off the pedal and she drives off the road into a field, travels for a few metres and then comes to a halt. Nothing dramatic happens; there is no crash, and no explosion. The car just stops, and silence reigns.

The two women in this segment have shared an incomplete interlude, where not everything has been spoken between them. The character of Elizabeth is fairly straightforward: a young woman who is achieving more than anyone in her family before her, working hard, over-committed, but assertive enough to get herself out of this job situation that is too much for her. It is not clear, however, whether she feels any attraction to the rancher, or even anything like burgeoning friendship. It is not suggested that she stopped coming to class because of the rancher. She made it clear from the first week that this was too much for her and she wanted to stop it. However, she is clearly not pleased to see the rancher in the car park of her offices, and gives no response at all to her efforts. This is ambiguous, and consistent with the circumstances. The rancher appears to have developed a crush on Elizabeth, and this also is unsurprising given that she has no human company at the ranch, let alone female company of her own age. She has been brought up with boys, and is skilled with horses, and does not have many accoutrements of conventional femininity. Her individuality is conveyed through her work, her placid, loving personality, and her warm gesture in thinking of, and sharing, the horse ride. Elizabeth's silent rejection of her gentle overtures is painful and moving, especially because of the journey she has made to open out to her and our knowledge of her isolation back at the ranch.

The film ends with a brief revisit to all three women. Laura visits Fuller in prison, bringing him a choice of milkshakes, which is greatly appreciated. She asks him how he is getting on in there, and he says it is noisy, lonely and he has no privacy. Also, that his wife has left him and gone to live with another man who was in prison when they met, on a farm with forty cats and says she has never been so happy. He fails to understand the appeal, and says, 'I'm a guy in prison, what's wrong with me?' He's upset that Laura did not write back to his letter, and she says that she didn't know what to say. He tells her, 'You could talk about anything, talk about your day, just so you put it in an envelope and put it in the mail', as mail is so precious in prison. Again, the kindness of the visit and the milkshakes is not enough. Laura is expected to be devoted and caring too, and to send letters to ex-clients in prison.

Gina's house is being built, and the whole family is there to help as she is cooking food on a barbecue. Her daughter doesn't say thank you for the food or the napkin, and Gina doesn't take any notice. Ryan tells her to stop working, then asks her to get him a beer too, but then says he was just kidding. She wanders off on her own to the car, lights a cigarette, has a sip of wine and looks at her plot. Her demeanour is quietly excited as she confidently looks to the future.

The last shots are of the stables, as the routine goes on today as every day, clearing out the hay and caring for the horses. As the film ends, the dedication comes onto the screen, 'FOR LUCY', which was the name of Reichardt's beloved dog, who played 'Lucy' in her earlier film collaboration with Michelle Williams, *Wendy and Lucy* (2008). Murdoch would certainly have approved of this, as she loved dogs and wrote about many dog characters in her novels, who she considered to be 'virtuous dogs' (Brans 1985: 43).

This film is an insight into the lives of four particular, 'certain', women, which is both subtle and razor-sharp. Wendy Ide called it 'an unassuming masterpiece', describing how the film conveys 'an ache of longing or a small stab of triumph' (2017). It could be said that not much happens in the film, except the particularities of everyday life. One of the things that marks the film out is the fact that all the women are working: as an established lawyer, a businesswoman, a junior lawyer, and a rancher. Michelle Orange describes how isolated the women are, and also how the film breaks familiar moulds of women characters by refusing archetype and insisting on the individual: 'that these are working women, negotiating vast and often hostile territory, is at once incidental and the film's strongest undercurrent' (Orange 2017: 178). Murdoch considers work to be an important part of facing life and being truthful. When asked about the question of levels of sophistication in life, and how this might affect goodness, Murdoch says that 'a simple person can be either good or bad, and obviously a sophisticated person could be either good or bad' (Brans 1985: 46). For Murdoch,

> goodness at every level of sophistication demands the ability to face life and be truthful, and the ability to be honest and faithful and loving, and the ability to give help. Facing life honestly is important at every level of sophistication. (Ibid.: 46)

This addresses Lovibond's allegation that Murdoch sentimentalises the virtuous peasant: in fact she applies the same standards to all. And part of this 'facing life honestly' is good work: 'I think getting hold of work, which is good, which you want to do, which you think you can do well, and which you feel does something for yourself and perhaps for other people is important' (ibid.: 47). Although Murdoch knows that many people are not able to find work, and she considers this to be tragic, she sees work as including all learning, whether it is of a language or a craft, so her main concern is with education. Work, she considers, is good: 'And if you can find a work which connects you with the world and allows you to use your talents, I think this is quite a large part of the good life' (ibid.: 47).

Laura, Gina, Elizabeth and the rancher are all working women, and the only one we do not see at work is Gina, who appears to be needing a return to nature for some honesty and succour. The role of work in the other women's lives is as varied as they are: we see Laura being challenged because she can no longer help Fuller to get money for his injury at work, but he wants her to help him through friendship and communication. Elizabeth is keen to carve a path for herself in the law, so there is pressure and pride in what she is doing. For the rancher, her work is solitary in terms of human contact, and demanding in terms of responsibility and care for the animals. Of all the women, perhaps it is the rancher who falls into a spell of delusion, seeing Elizabeth as something she is not, but has to come back to reality when her fantasy is shattered. In this film, it is the person with the least sophisticated lifestyle who has to learn to face reality, and the contrast between one week's experience when they share the horse ride, and the next, makes the realisation all the more painful.

These portrayals of individual women, who incidentally brush up against each other (through Laura's affair with Ryan, and the rancher going to Laura's office), are specific and particular, filled with the minutiae of their lives. The fact that they overlap, and are unremarkable in some ways, means that this level of detailed attention could be paid to any one woman, anywhere. This film just happens to be about these four certain women. We are not involved in detailed ways with their thoughts and feelings, rather we are shown what their lives are like, and invited to pay attention to what they do, how they respond to others and where they might be going. Murdoch talks about the information we gather to see what a person's vision is like:

> The data in questions are all 'events' and 'activities' which are either overt (conversation, story-telling) or if introspectible are identifiable and in principle exposable (private stories, images, inner monologue). Now activities of this kind certainly constitute an important part of what, in the ordinary sense, a person 'is like'. When we apprehend and assess other people we do not consider only their solutions to specifiable practical problems, we consider something more elusive which may be called their total vision of life, as shown in their mode of speech or silence, their choice of words, their assessment of others, their conception of their own lives, what they think attractive or praiseworthy, what they think funny: in short the configurations of their thought which show continually in their reactions and conversation. (VCM: 80–1)

We study the configurations of the thoughts of Laura, Gina, Elizabeth and the rancher, looking for 'data' to see what they're really like. We see how they conduct themselves, solve problems, and what they say and do not say. We also see how they treat and are treated by others. Through this intimate, attentive film, we observe these individual women who are not dramatically changing, but who are all, internally, doing moral work. The way in which Gina craves and appreciates nature is a sign of her individual journey towards a more honest life, albeit that her family relationships are damaged in several ways. The rancher's care for the animals is, in Murdochian terms, a sign of virtue, albeit that it does not seem to be leading to happiness for her at the moment. That all the women are on journeys is an important element of the film's contemplative strength, and the incompleteness makes it good art in Murdochian terms: 'There are times when it is proper to stress, not the comprehensibility of the world but its incomprehensibility' (VCM: 90).

The stories of Laura and the siege, Gina and Albert, and Elizabeth and the rancher, are not all clear in moral terms. They are ambiguous, allusive and perhaps, in Murdoch's words, 'they incarnate a moral truth which is paradoxical, infinitely suggestive and open to continual reinterpretation' (VCM: 91). The examples Murdoch gives of such stories are from the New Testament: 'the woman who broke the alabaster box of very precious ointment, or the parable of the prodigal son' (VCM: 91). Murdoch describes how the fact that these stories are both concrete and ambiguous means they provide 'sources of moral inspiration which highly specific rules could not give' (VCM: 91). The stories in *Certain Women* critique the social conventions that slight the women due to their gender, and their race, in the rancher's case as a Native American (seen mainly in the attitudes of the other students at the first class). They are stories about women, and they compel our attention through the intense significance of the smallest moments of their individualities. The film does not offer complete answers, but in this way it answers Murdoch's call for a 'fresh vision':

> There are . . . moments when situations are unclear and what is needed is not a renewed attempt to specify the facts, but a fresh vision which may be derived from a 'story' or from some sustaining concept which is able to deal with what is obstinately obscure, and represents 'a mode of understanding' of an alternative type. (VCM: 91)

Such concepts might be 'hope' and 'love' (VCM: 91) and *Certain Women* shows us fresh visions of both of these, and invites us to respond in kind. We see each woman as an individual moral agent, wrestling and deciding, and moving forwards. As such, the film accords with Murdoch's thoughts on incompleteness in novels, pictures or music: 'This too is art, an intimation of our mortality and our limitation, a reminder of contingency, presented to us as a source of energy and understanding and joy' (MGM: 87–8).

WITHIN A WORLD WE CAN SEE: *THE UNKNOWN GIRL/ LA FILLE INCONNUE*

The Unknown Girl is a more fully explored but equally nuanced depiction of a stage in a woman's journey. The film begins with a young doctor, Jenny Davin (Adèle Haenel), listening to a middle-aged man's lungs with her stethoscope. She says 'listen' to a young man in a white coat, Julien (Olivier Bonnaud), her student. She tests him on the differential diagnoses. She's efficient, diligent and knows her work. A buzzer rings and she admits a caller: her workplace system is established, and she is in control. She confirms the diagnoses of bronchitis, and arranges an X-ray using the university hospital.

There is then an emergency situation. A child is having a seizure. She tells Julien to get a cushion for the child, but Julien stands rooted to the spot, staring at the child fitting on the floor. The boy's mother wipes his mouth and, Jenny having soothed him and eased his way through the seizure, he finally responds to his name. Jenny is cross with Julien. She says to him sternly that she wants him to learn one thing: to make a good diagnosis. She says, 'If a patient's suffering moves you, you make a bad diagnosis; a good doctor has to control his emotions.' He says, shamefacedly, that he couldn't help it. She takes a call on her mobile phone. The surgery door buzzer goes, and Julien gets up to answer it. She instructs him to 'Leave it, we've already overrun by an hour.' She adds, 'Someone who comes this late doesn't care how tired we are.' Julien worries that it might be urgent, but she says that if it was they would have rung twice. Then she tells him, 'You mustn't let patients tire you out, or you won't make a proper diagnosis.' She is still angry with him and he walks out. She follows him as he leaves, getting on his bicycle. She challenges him to explain himself, but he just looks at her angrily.

We next see Jenny in a different office as she is introduced to a new team. She is taking over from someone who is leaving this practice. She is welcomed warmly, and shown her name on the door of her new office. Her mobile phone goes, and she ignores it. She says she's very happy to join the team, and they all toast with a glass of champagne. Her phone goes again and she answers the call from a patient who wants to see her. She goes to his home straight away. The patient is a boy who has written a song to thank her and say goodbye. The words are sweet and moving, thanking 'Dr Jenny'. She says that it is a lovely song, 'bravo', and that since she is here she will examine him. Although moved, she is still professional. And then she says that she will still be his doctor if he wants her to be. We have been introduced to Dr Jenny Davin in quite a detailed way: we have seen her diligence and professionalism, and that she can be angry and caring. We have also seen how highly she is regarded by her seniors, and that she is on the cusp of a new stage in her career.

Next day, police detectives stop her outside her surgery, and tell her that a woman was found dead nearby on a building site. The police ask to see the footage from the surgery surveillance camera, in case it shows anything of the woman. Julien has not shown up to work, and Jenny calls and leaves a message apologising for last night. She takes her coat off; she is wearing a plain jumper in the same style as the day before, she puts her hair in a ponytail, has a quick cigarette and gets down to work. She sees a patient who drinks too much and needs antidepressants, and a man with a burned leg, whose interpreter tells her that he hasn't been to hospital because they will ask for a passport. She is firm and kind with these patients, not flinching from telling them what they must do.

The police return, having watched the security video. The dead girl is the person who rang the surgery buzzer. Jenny is understandably upset, and her face registers shock and disbelief. The police are not critical, and say it is normal not to open that late. Jenny watches the video, and the girl's face on the doorstep is plain to see. She was found with no identification, no mobile phone, nothing to identify her. Jenny asks how she died, and is told it was an open skull fracture: she either fell on the concrete bank or someone pushed her. Jenny asks if there were any signs of violence, but apparently the external autopsy did not reveal any. Jenny watches the video again. The young black girl, her hair in bunches, appears agitated. She rings the buzzer, knocks on the door, looks around her and then runs on. She is clearly running away from someone. Jenny says, 'She's young.' The police ask what could have made her come to ring the bell, and Jenny says maybe the light from the waiting room. They thought she

Figure 7.2 Ange-Déborah Goulehi as 'the unknown girl', the girl who rang, in *The Unknown Girl/ La Fille Inconnue* (2016), directed by Jean-Pierre Dardenne and Luc Dardenne.

might have come to the surgery before. Jenny suggests they see Dr Habran, who she replaced three months ago. They get her to watch the video again, and they pause and zoom in on the girl. This forces Jenny, and us, to see her more clearly: a young woman, with furrowed brow and pleading posture, in a metallic padded jacket and short skirt (Figure 7.2).

As Jenny is driving along in her car she takes a call on her mobile. It is good results from a scan on a patient, revealing there is no brain tumour and no epilepsy. Jenny smiles at the news, and calls the family to tell them. She goes to the building site to see where the girl died. The crane operator describes where he found her, with her head on a block of concrete. She looks down at the precise spot. The cars on the expressway continue to speed past, the building noise carries on, the water continues to flow down the river Meuse: nothing has actually changed here since the girl died, except the precise lump of concrete has been taken away. Jenny looks at the space where it was, and where the girl lost her life.

Jenny goes to see Julien and tells him about the girl. She shows him a still from the video footage, but he does not know her. Jenny says that when the bell went she felt like him – she wanted to answer. She says, 'I don't know what happened. I stopped you from going just because you wanted to: to get the upper hand.' He says nothing. She is clearly shaken, and asks for some water, so he lets her in to his room. Julien announces that he is moving out and giving up medicine. Jenny apologises for judging his emotions, but he tells her it is not because of what she said. She asks if she can call him, but he says he will not change his mind. She tells Julien she is sure he could make a very good doctor.

Jenny goes to see her predecessor, Dr Habran (Yves Larec) who is in hospital and tells him about the girl. Habran says, 'You couldn't have known but you should have let her in.' This is realistic but hard to hear. Habran is caring and sincere. He says with certainty that the girl never came to his practice, although there is a possibility she could have as a child. He says he has 'at least forty African families on my books'. Jenny asks if she can tell the police so they can check their names and he says of course. He asks Jenny to put up a notice on the board at the faculty of medicine to see if any young doctor would like to take over his practice, before he has to close it. Jenny has made the decision to move to the Kennedy Centre practice. A nurse comes in to give Dr Habran his injection, and he smiles welcomingly. He is shown to be a kindly man, who cares about his patients and remembers them, and has spent his life working in public healthcare, as opposed to the Kennedy Centre where Jenny has her new job.

Jenny calls Inspector Mahmoud to tell him of her conversation with Dr Habran and asks if the internal autopsy had been done on the girl's body. Although we do not hear his response, Jenny says 'so she struggled' and looks saddened by the news. She asks if the inspector will tell her when she will be buried. Jenny goes back to talk to Dr Habran. She tells him that the girl had haemorrhagic bruising on both wrists, from the attacker, as they either stopped her from escaping or threw her down the bank. There was no sign of intercourse. Jenny says she cannot accept that the girl will be buried with no name. She says, 'No one will know it is her in the ground.' She adds, 'If I had opened the door she would still be alive, like me.' Dr Habran sighs, and says that this is true, but then again, Jenny is not the one who killed her. Then he gets on with work, using one arm to type, as if he has had a stroke. Jenny looks at him and says, 'I'm going to take over your practice.' He looks like he is going to cry at the news, and says, 'That's good for my practice, but patients on medical insurance rates aren't what you wanted.'[5] Jenny says she has changed her mind. Clearly her conscience has been bruised by this experience with the girl. The suggestion is that she feels she should atone for her error by working for those who are needier and of lower social standing.

In the next scene, any naïvety about her patients is dispelled by an aggressive confrontation with a patient and her partner who want a fake medical certificate. She says Jenny signed one for her brother, but Jenny says he was sick. The woman calls her a bitch and the man picks up her stethoscope to steal. She tells him to leave it and he yells in her face, twice, forcing her back onto the couch, breathless. They leave, but this is an unpleasant encounter with patients, demonstrating that not all state insurance patients are genuine and grateful, or 'virtuous'. She treats a man's ulcerated foot in his home, and talks to him about his difficulties getting to the meter to pay for his gas, and his worries that he will be cut off. She says she will call social services, and he says he will show people the photo of the girl if she emails it to him. He seems to live in one scruffy room, with a rundown kitchen. Her duffle coat seems at home here, and on the grey expressway, the building site and the banks of the river: it is grey and blue and seems to be her only coat. He offers her a coffee and she agrees to make it, using instant coffee in a saucepan on the stove. Her next house call is the depressed woman who drinks too much. She is feeling better, and has baked waffles, which she offers to Jenny. Jenny examines her son, Bryan (Louka Minnella) and shows him the photo of the girl. He says he hasn't seen her. She calls Inspector Mahmoud, saying there is nothing to report from the photos, and he realises he forgot to tell her the girl was buried this afternoon. She asks which cemetery and he has to go and get the file. She goes back to get her thermometer from Bryan which she says she forgot: but it is actually because his pulse went much faster once she'd shown him the photo of the girl, making her think he knows something. He won't say anything. Jenny tries to make him think of how he would feel if it was his mother, but he just says no.

Jenny moves bedding and food into the accommodation at the practice. She has waffles and tea, and looks out over the cars zooming along the expressway and the Meuse, thinking about the girl's fate. She goes to the cemetery and buys a plot for the girl by a tree. It costs 420 euros, and lasts for ten years, but she hopes that her family will come forward and want her buried somewhere. She's brought a large plant with yellow flowers. Back at the surgery, Jenny sees an elderly lady, with a cough, who is scared of dying alone without 'her Snowy', a little dog. Bryan comes to the surgery with his school supervisor, saying he has indigestion. She gives him some antacid, and asks him again about the girl. He vomits in the bathroom, she holds him, and says it is because of stress. He should tell her what he knows and he'll feel better. She cares for him, and says she won't tell anyone, and he says, 'Not my mum or dad?' He then tells Jenny that he saw the girl, performing fellatio on an old man in a camper van, on the night she was found. He and his friend had hidden and watched. He tells her where the van is, so she goes to find it. The owner knows her from when she came out to see his mother, who died a week later. He thinks she is there to buy the van, and when she explains he gets angry, and says he's never seen the girl. She says she is not accusing him, but he is defensive. She says if anyone is guilty she herself is: she just wants the girl's name so she can let her family know what has happened. However, he throws her out, shouting at her, and saying he doesn't like her attitude.

Jenny then goes to the hospital to visit the van owner's father, Mr Lambert (Pierre Sumkay). His son has told him not to talk to her, and while she is speaking to him he has a seizure. She helps him sit down, and diagnoses a small coronary spasm. She gives him his medication, shuts the door and checks his pulse. He has pain in his arm and chest, but she says it should soon pass as his pulse is steady. He begins to speak. It was him in the van. He says that the girl said nothing about herself, but that she spoke French. His son brings him a prostitute, 'that's all', but that he is scared in case Jenny discovers his illegal garage. Lambert tells her that he goes to Liege, Rue St Marguerite, because it is handier, as they don't have to go in to the city. They wait 'in a place where there are phone calls'. Then the son comes into the room, and gets physically violent, threatening to hit the father and then Jenny.

Jenny leaves, clearly determined to follow the leads that she is collecting. She goes to the cybercafé, to make a phone call to Julien, and leaves a message saying she wants to visit him. She shows the girl's photo to the woman at the desk, and to the men in the café, but there is no response from anyone. The next morning, Bryan's father (Jérémie Renier) calls at the surgery very early, while Jenny is still asleep there. He tells her that Bryan was trying to excuse himself but it was actually just him watching the girl and the old man, and that he was embarrassed. He thanks her for her care, and she tries to show him the photograph, but he says he saw her picture in the paper and doesn't know her.

Jenny goes to visit Julien, taking a thermos of coffee from the lady at the house, who is Julien's grandmother. She hands over the coffee, and Julien pours her some. They talk about the girl, and about her possible murder. She asks Julien why he is giving up, if it isn't because of what she said. She tells him he can still change his mind, and reminds him that he had said he had always dreamt of being a doctor. Julien then explains what happened for him when the boy had a seizure. He tells Jenny that when he saw the kid fitting on the floor, he saw himself as a kid when his dad used to hit him:

> All I got from him was beatings. I wanted to be a doctor to treat him or treat myself I don't know. Or to be a better doctor than ours who thought I bruised myself playing. I'm glad you yelled. I can't be a doctor. I think of my dad all the time. I'm sick of him being in my head.

Jenny makes no reply.

We then see Jenny getting called back to below a patient's window to catch a panettone! It is a feature of Jenny's home visits that patients offer her food and drink, as if she is a guest in their home. As she is driving along, a car pulls alongside her, and one of the men from the cybercafé gestures to her to stop, and, when she doesn't, pulls the car over in front of her. He tries to force her to wind down her window, and another man smashes her car windscreen with a crow bar, then he says she is rude for not lowering her window. He threatens her, telling her to stop asking about the girl, unless she wants them 'to send her some sick guys'. They drive away, and Jenny stays in the car. Her eyelids flutter and she breathes heavily. This threatening encounter occurred very close to her face. She is about to get out of her car but then sees Bryan on his bicycle and she follows him, catches him up, and finds him hiding in some derelict buildings. She asks Bryan about the girl again, he pushes her into a pit and runs away. She shouts at him to help her out. After a while, he goes back and slides a fence panel down into the pit so she can climb out.

Back at the surgery, she is drying her hair, and making a simple dinner, chopping a tomato. Julien telephones to say he has decided to go back to medicine, and this makes her happy. Her doorbell rings, and it is Bryan's parents. They have come to say she must stop seeing Bryan about the girl. They say that they understand her feeling guilty but she can't make their son ill over it, and they are changing doctor. She says that she understands. She has a cigarette out of the window – looking over the river again where the girl died. Later she receives a telephone call from Bryan's father, who had wanted to change doctors. She visits him, in her duffle coat with the hood up. She goes in by entryphone. He's on the floor in a lot of pain. She places a pillow under his leg, and says it might be a slipped disc. He says he can tell it's like the last time this happened, and doesn't want an ambulance. She suggests that he knew the girl. He shouts at her and denies it.

The inspector calls her and tells her off for showing the photo to the men in the cybercafé, who, he says, have now become less cooperative. She apologises and asks about cause of death, and he says, 'None of your business doctor. We know our business.' But he does say he now knows more about the girl: 'Her name is Serena Ndong, dob July 3 1995. Libreville, Gabon.' When she arrives back at the surgery, cars zooming behind her on the expressway, Bryan's father is there, saying he'd like to talk to her. He's emotional. He says he was driving home, saw the girl on the expressway, saw she was a prostitute and did a U-turn. Bryan and his friend saw him. They decided to say he was alone so his friend wouldn't be questioned. She queries his saying, 'We decided?', but he aggressively says, 'Let me speak! Think this is easy?' He explains how Bryan had run after him, and when the girl refused him and began to run, he got back into his car and followed her. He continues,

> I wouldn't have done it if Bryan had called out or I'd seen him. When she rang your bell I'd lost her behind the parked cars. Then she ran across the road to catch a bus. She missed it. So I stopped. I offered her a deal. She accepted, provided she didn't get into my car. We were on the towpath. And I wanted more. Don't look at me! Turn around! Turn around! For pity's sake. She ran to get away from me, towards the Meuse. I followed her. She ran across the building site and tripped over something. She fell down the bank.

Jenny's calm attentive stare is too much for Bryan's father, who cannot bear her to look at him (Figure 7.3).

Figure 7.3 Dr Jenny Davin's (Adèle Haenel) steady attention yields results, in *The Unknown Girl/ La Fille Inconnue* (2016), directed by Jean-Pierre Dardenne and Luc Dardenne.

Jenny challenges the story and says that the autopsy says she had been grabbed by the wrists. He says, 'I did but before she ran off. When she turned me down, I tried to hold her back.' Jenny pushes him on his story, and why he did not go back to check on her when she fell. He says, unconvincingly, that he thought she had fainted and that she would wake up. Then Jenny tells him, and we hear for the first time, that the autopsy says she didn't die from the impact, but from blood loss while unconscious. The realisation of what this means becomes clear to him, as he says, 'You mean I let her die?' He then grabs Jenny and shouts at her, then apologises, sits down and says he cannot sleep because the girl is in his head all the time. He says to Jenny that if she had opened her door this would not have happened, and she says she knows it: she's in Jenny's head all the time too. Jenny tells him he must tell the truth to the police, but he fears losing his job, his wife, and going to prison.

The man says, 'Why would I ruin my life?' Jenny replies, 'Because she's asking us to. The girl.' He says, 'She doesn't care, she's dead.' But, Jenny replies, 'If she was dead she wouldn't be in our heads.' The man goes into the bathroom and tries to hang himself from a pipe, but it collapses. She gets him upright, and he says she can call the police: but she says he has to do that himself.

In the next scene, Jenny is treating a baby for a throat infection and happily can reassure the parents that it is nothing serious and can be treated with linctus. The woman from the reception at the cybercafé comes in to the surgery. She says to Jenny that before going to the police, she wanted to thank her for coming to the cybercafé and showing her the photo of the girl, who was her sister. The woman weeps as she tells Jenny that because she came to the café, she felt ashamed and made up her mind. She says, 'I was afraid my guy would put me back on the streets. He gave a fake passport so the police wouldn't know he made Félice work. She wasn't eighteen yet.' Her name was Félice Koumba. Her sister says she will claim her now and take care of everything. She thanks Jenny, as the surgery buzzer goes off again and Jenny admits another patient. The sister turns to Jenny and says, 'I didn't help my sister just because I was afraid of my guy. I was jealous of her too. She lived with us. My guy was attracted to her. When she vanished, I felt better.' Jenny can offer no words of comfort in response to this, but asks if she may hug her, and they hug each other.

Without time to process this visit, Jenny goes back into the waiting room, and helps an elderly lady to negotiate the stairs, offering to take her bag. She says, 'May I?' and takes her arm. They go around the corner of the stairs, and the film ends. Over the closing credits, there is no music, but the sounds of cars on the expressway zooming past the practice. The ending of the film confirms that all carries on, and we are left to ponder the meaning of Félice's life, and her death.

Murdoch writes how 'much, in some cases most, of our spiritual energy and understanding comes from non-reciprocal relationships with what is beyond and other' (MGM: 478). As with Susanne and her vision of Lotte, this idea is not just about comfort for us, in fact it can be far from that. As Jenny says, Félice is in their heads because she is demanding that they do the right thing. This is not to suggest that Félice is somewhere sending out commands, but rather that the circumstances that led to her death are calling to be faced as is the realisation that many people share responsibility. What is called for, here, is humility. And Jenny learns this starkly through the direct consequences of her arbitrarily imposing her authority on Julien on the night of Félice's death. As Murdoch writes,

> Freedom, we find out, is not an inconsequential chucking of one's weight about, it is the disciplined overcoming of self. Humility is not a peculiar habit of self-effacement, rather like having an inaudible voice, it is selfless respect for reality and one of the most difficult and central of all virtues. (SGC: 378)

What Jenny, Bryan's father and Félice's sister come to learn is that they have to face up to their own failings. For Jenny, this entails finding the family; for Bryan's father, confessing that he pushed her and left her to die, and for Félice's sister that she put 'her guy' ahead of her younger sister. In fact, meeting one's duty can be enough in such circumstances, as Murdoch proposes, 'Duty can appear when moral instinct and habit fail, when we lack any clarifying mode of reflection, and seek for a rule felt as external' (MGM: 302).

Jenny is a still, calm character, who makes a serious mistake by angrily misusing her authority. She uses calm attentiveness to listen to others and observe their reactions, in order to get to the bottom of what happened. The stillness of Jenny's personality, and her tenacity both with helping Julien's predicament and finding out the identity of the girl, display resilience and compassion, as well as recognition of the need for humility. The film affectively conveys the physical intimidation that she faces, and that this is gendered: the patient who shouts at her, the van owner, the pimp from the café and Bryan's father are all threatening towards Jenny, confronting her with masculine aggression and adding a layer of physicality to her daily life that might be absent, or certainly differently experienced, if she were a man. This is a realistic way of conveying Jenny's gender as part of her story, without mentioning it verbally. In this way, the specificity of Jenny's experience is depicted, within her professional context, by showing what the consequences are for her of being a woman.

CLEAR REALISTIC VISION WITH COMPASSION: *GIRLHOOD*

In *Girlhood*, we share the journey of Marieme (Karidja Touré), a young black girl living in the Parisian banlieue, with her mother and sisters, and an abusive domineering brother. Marieme's prospects are poor as she does not have good enough grades to stay on at school or go to college. Her mother does not seem to have much interest in her, or indeed to have any time in which to take an interest, and her brother Djibril (Cyril Mendy) is a bully, including physical, and possibly sexual, assault. Marieme and her younger sister Bébé (Simina Soumaré) care for the youngest girl Mini (Chance N'Guessan). She finds friendship, attention and inclusion, by joining a local girl gang. They bully, intimidate and steal from people, but she feels good by being included and finds a forum where she has some skills and knowledge which are valued. She straightens her hair to look more like the others, and becomes more physically confident and mature.

It is in relation to this film that perhaps we can most clearly see how Murdoch's thinking about personal, individual moral pilgrimage, and human stories, might be in tune with contemporary intersectional feminism. Murdoch is concerned with the rights of minority groups, including those so defined by race, class and gender, and the inclusion of those who are normally excluded from philosophical, intellectual and moral conversations. She is also, most of all, passionately committed to the vital importance of education, especially for girls. Marieme, therefore, is someone who Murdoch wants to include, and wants us to understand.

The film begins with a game of American football, with the players poised, padded, protected and battling. As Sue Harris describes, 'They roar as they play, deafening us with yelling that segues into jubilant laughter as the game ends and the helmets come off' (Harris 2015: 73). The footballers are revealed to be young women, who are thrilled and excited, 'revelling in the joy of their own strength' (ibid.). As they walk back to their homes in various directions on the estate, however, they come across groups of boys, and their voices quieten, their heads go down and their body shapes droop, as they go their own ways. As Harris describes, this is a sobering illustration of how joyous and freeing female solidarity is quashed and contained by the gendered social structures and relationships that restrict their lives. Emma Wilson describes the intersectional foundations of the film, and that it is concerned with 'different struggles against oppression' (Wilson 2017: 11). Marieme and her friends embody these different struggles, and the film conveys these in bodily, affective ways. For Wilson, the director Sciamma's feminist politics attend to pathos and hurt:

> Attention to singular bodies, their sensory loveliness, their strength, and their susceptibility to damage, to the full gamut of bodily feelings, risks, and violations, is a means of claiming visibility and value. It is a way of doing politics through sensuous cinema, through a relay of feelings. The hurt Sciamma shows, and the vulnerabilities she exposes, sharpen responses, deepening feelings. (2017: 12)

Wilson describes the blue, turquoise and green colours of the film's visual environments, as well as a 'nauseous yellow', seeing this careful crafting of sensory overload as 'a commitment to a filmic synaesthesia', which carries these intense feelings of hurt, rapture and sensation (ibid.: 12). The physicality of the film is a powerful means for conveying Marieme's experiences of herself and her world. The film captures the physical exhilaration of sport and the joy of dance, as well as the challenge and fierceness of fighting, the pain of assault, the vulnerability to attack and the sensual pleasure of sexual encounters. Through this array of bodily feelings, Marieme's multi-dimensional, intersectional life is conjured and conveyed.

In a scene that is strikingly static, Marieme is interviewed by her teacher regarding her options. The camera stays on Marieme's face for the whole take, as she realises that her choices are shrinking, and her emotions are becoming stronger and more desperate (Figure 7.4). She is told she can only take the vocational training, but she wants to go to college. Her teacher insists her grades are not good enough. When Marieme says, 'It's not my fault', the teacher asks whether there is something she should know: but Marieme does not reply. She is not able, or willing, to tell the teacher about her home circumstances, her responsibilities and the abuse she suffers.

Figure 7.4 Marieme (Karidja Touré) realises she cannot go to high school, in *Girlhood* (2014), directed by Céline Sciamma.

As she leaves the meeting, she meets three members of a girl gang, Lady (Assa Sylla), Adiatou (Lindsay Karamoh) and Fily (Mariétou Touré), and decides to join them when she realises they are friendly with Ismael (Idrissa Diabaté), the boy she likes. Marieme seems to grow more and more into liking what the girls do, whether it is looking at clothes, bullying and harassing other girls, dancing on the Metro, or getting into fights. The film does not endorse all the gang's activities. As So Mayer writes, 'Marieme both enjoys and questions the stakes in being one of the gang' (2016: 137). For Mayer, Marieme is 'one of Sciamma's watchful, thoughtful, powerful leads, defining herself through interaction with a magnetic group of peers' (ibid.). This watchfulness, conveyed by Touré's restrained, intelligent performance, and the film's patient, contemplative style, enables us to keep a balanced view of the gang as offering Marieme camaraderie, fun and strength, alongside its threatening, violent and criminal aspects. As Wilson observes, 'the gang is seen with a mix of adoration and painful skepticism' (2017: 15).

In a set-piece scene that conveys all that the girls stand for in Marieme's eyes, they dance together in a hotel room to Rihanna's 'Diamonds'. They have saved up, stolen for and looked forward to this night, where they do each other's hair and makeup, eat pizza, smoke dope and dance together, wearing stolen clothes, complete with security tags, and creating a fleeting fantasy of glamour and belonging. Lady gives Marieme a necklace saying, 'Vic – as in Victory.' Again this is an ambivalent scene. The girls have had to go to great lengths for this freedom, which so many more privileged teenage girls can do in their or their friends' bedrooms. Such is their desire for this time together, however, that they have made it happen, even if it means ignoring a phone call from her brother which she knows will lead to trouble later. The lyrics to 'Diamonds' add further poignancy, conveying how much they love and admire each other, and how, in this place, now, they can fulfil their potential to each other: 'You're a shooting star I see, a vision of ecstasy; Shine bright, tonight, you and I, we're beautiful, like diamonds in the sky.' The palette of the dance sequence is blue and silver, lighting the girls' skin as if in a nightclub, with the camera moving around them, joining in like a member of the group.[6] Vic's face shows her joy and her sorrow, 'her eyes full of pleasure and grief' (Wilson 2017: 16), as she appraises the others dancing, before she joins in, moving gracefully and sexily, loved by the others and loving them. This is a moving sequence of escapism and fantasy, which has to end, and the girls return to their normal lives.

Angry at her overnight absence, Djibril, whisperingly, takes his sister in a chokehold. It is a sinister, menacing assault, and the sadness of her home life is evident again in her traumatised, desperate eyes. There is an arranged fight between Lady and a member of another gang, and Lady comes off worse. The other girl stands over her and says, 'I wasted you, slut.' Marieme tries to care for her, but Lady just says, 'Get off me.' But then Ismael holds out his hand to Marieme, and they go off together and kiss. Marieme begins to change more rapidly now. She goes to where her mother is cleaning, because she has a 'try out' for work there. She dresses in the cleaning clothes and helps, but she physically intimidates the cleaning boss to tell Asma (Binta Diop), her mother, that she doesn't need her for the summer after all. Marieme rejects her mother's work, and, through the physicality of the girl gang, she has learnt to use violence and intimidation as a means of getting by.

As she stands alone, surveying the city at night, inspirational electronic music conveys the impression that Marieme is making plans. She thinks of the fight and of Lady's body on the ground. The girls meet in the park. Lady is low, and Fily has brought her sisters, saying her mother 'dumped' then on her. They want to do something different. They go to play in the park, with a golf club and a model Eiffel tower, and they argue about how to play the ball in an environment that looks too square and unadventurous for them. Lady looks young and vulnerable; her hair is not straightened, it is short and scraped back off her face. A group of boys taunt Lady and it turns out that her father cut off her hair to shame her because of the fight. Other girls mock them in the café, and they all tough talk each other. Then the previous 'fourth one' from the gang, the girl who Marieme/Vic replaced, arrives in the café, and it emerges that she left because she was pregnant.

They meet another gang for a fight, and this time it is not Lady fighting in their name, it is Vic. She fights fiercely, punching and kicking, wins, and cuts off her opponents' bra with a knife she secreted from her home kitchen earlier. The girls are full of joy and happiness and go splashing water over each other in the fountain in the park. As she waves the scarlet bra like a trophy, Wilson observes that she is 'more than Victory here: she is Liberty leading the people, brandishing red fabric' (2017: 16). Lady arrives, and Vic says she did it for her: Lady believes Vic did it for herself, but she still hugs her. Djibril is really happy with her and, for the first time, plays a computer football game with her. He offers her the team of Brazil, but Vic chooses France: perhaps indicating that she has ambition but also wants to belong and achieve.

She is now calling herself Vic, and has become far more assertive. She has become sexually empowered too. She orders Ismael to undress, and he does what she says. She undresses too, and we infer they make love. We next see her smiling face, as she is with a group of women dancing at La Défense: she and Lady are dressed the same and do a double act. Vic is confident, at one with the leader, and happy to share the spotlight. She sees her sister Bébé robbing a girl with a gang, scolds her, hits her and tells her to go home. Bébé says back to her, 'You're just like him.' They both realise the pain this comment causes, and what it means, and Vic says let's go home, and they go together. She is curt and non-committal with Lady as they leave, showing that Vic is no longer keen to please her. Back at the flat the sisters hold hands and Vic strokes Bébé's hair. Her brother calls her, her little sister tries to help; but he beats up Vic for 'doing it' with Ismael, and calls her a slut. She goes out to a diner on her own, where Abou (Djibril Gueye), a local drug dealer, approaches her because of the wounds on her face, and flatters her for her fighting win. He recruits her to work for him. Consequently, she moves out of the family flat. Her little sister hugs her from behind as she leaves, and Vic's face registers the pain she feels at leaving Bébé and Mini in Djibril's hands.

Vic is assertive and tough with the other girls who criticise her choice to work for Abou. She sees selling drugs as a move up. 'What else can I do?' She says she won't work as a cleaner, or 'get hassled as a slut'. They all cry and hug and it turns out Lady is actually called Sophie. Vic has moved beyond the leader of the gang and now sees her as she really is. We next see Vic in a short red dress, high heels and a platinum blonde wig, completing a drugs drop-off at a party. Aside from this glamorous costume, Vic appears to be dressing and moving in a far more masculine way. She moves into a flat with some men who know Abou, and who say to her, 'Playing the guy doesn't mean you're not a bitch.' She's with them all, laughing and joshing, as they lean on a wall and casually torment the girlfriend of one of them. Alone with Ismael, as she undresses, she reveals that she has been binding her breasts. Ismael is really angry and asks her why, and says he's had enough. She says, 'There's a hooker next door' if that is what he wants. She gets made up for another drugs job, looks very glamorous and older than her years. She goes to Abou's party, where she dances sensuously with another girl. Abou tries to bully her into kissing him. She hits him and he goes mad, and she leaves. In these scenes, Vic is exaggerating and disguising her gender as she sees fit, adopting both femininity and masculinity as masquerades to ease certain situations, but not looking comfortable as either.

She goes to see Ismael, and he apologises for what he said last time. He asks her to stay with him, to marry him, saying, 'You're a decent girl if we marry.'

But she doesn't want 'to be a "little" wife and have kids'. She asks if he really means it, and he says he'd marry her tomorrow. This does make her happy and she kisses him, but she says she can't do that, because she doesn't want that life.

She goes home to her old family flat and buzzes, but she cannot face going in. She knows she cannot go back. She stands and cries, and this feels like rock-bottom for Marieme: she has lost her name, her school identity, family identity, boyfriend and friends, and has moved through adolescence, to girl gang, to androgyny, to glamour girl, to this. Where does she go now? Her tears and her slow, heavy movements suggest how depressed and lost she might be. Wilson observes how 'as she slips out of the frame, the film shows blurred, tearful images of trees and towerblocks' (2017: 18). But the film defies this ending for Marieme, and she re-enters the frame, determined, crossing the frame from right to left, heading off towards something, as the inspirational electronic music replays, suggesting she is making a plan.

Marieme's demeanour and striding pace suggest determination and positivity: in relation to what, we do not know. For Wilson, the film 'is an ongoing riposte to the teacher who shut her out of education' (2007: 18), but that teacher alone is not to blame for Marieme/Vic's situation. The film does not hold any one individual responsible, but rather shows, through criss-crossing, matrix-filmmaking, how structures and conventions, realities and personalities, construct and imprison us. Marieme can be understood as a Murdochian individual through thinking about education and her family, as well as her race and her gender, but most particularly as somebody on her way to learning about herself, what matters to her and what she needs to do. She cannot seek solace in family or in work, and wants more than a conventional marriage has to offer. We leave her at the point where she breaks away, and we do not know what she will do next. We have seen her watchfulness, her experimentation with her gender and her physicality, and her arrival at decisions about others and herself. We have seen Marieme's conceptual framework change rapidly, as she has moved through the various stages of the film. Marieme may be socially and economically disadvantaged, but she could not be considered to fit a 'virtuous peasant' archetype, as Altorf describes it. And, Marieme's life is not unexamined. *Girlhood* shows the fallacy of conflating low socio-economic status with the unexamined life. Marieme is examining her life, her conscience, her friends and her family throughout the film, but has other factors that dictate her choices and her decisions as well as this reflection. This is why her face is so often a picture of the 'mixed emotions' that Murdoch knows a face can show: 'spirit and matter intensely fused' (OTC: 98). For Marieme, the spirit is expansive and ambitious, but the matter is circumscribed and oppressed.

Murdoch writes 'since reality is incomplete, art must not be too much afraid of incompleteness' (AD: 295). Marieme's story is incomplete, but this final scene is what Murdoch describes when she writes of how individual consciousness 'is a place where the moral and the aesthetic join' (MGM: 245). Marieme's consciousness is a site of moral challenge, not merely for her, but also for us, as we have to accept the inconclusiveness of the ending and the limited hope that it offers. We have been through the ambiguities of Marieme's experiences with joining and leaving the gang, and so have been led to a place where we view her with realism, compassion and respect, whilst being aware that her next move is limited. And with this, we have to be satisfied.

Looking at these films overall, and the women in them, we have a collection of characters who are seeking various things. Whether it is to understand their world, to escape from it, to find love within it, to atone for their wrongdoing, or to find a way to live, these are human stories, about searching:

> We can only move properly in a world that we can see, and what must be sought for is vision. (MGM: 303)

> We are all the time building up our own value world and exercising, or failing to exercise, our sense of truth in the daily hourly minutely business of apprehending, or failing to apprehend, what is real and distinguishing it from illusion. (Ibid.: 304)

The specificity of each vision sought by Laura, Gina, the rancher, Jenny and Marieme is an ongoing, ever present activity, revealed in the minutiae of their daily lives. Cinema can show us this activity, like no other art form, and in this way is truly a fresh vision of Murdochian moral philosophy.

NOTES

1. Gary Browning explains the significance of Murdoch's incorporation of homosexuality into her novels and how it performs a political role (2018: 127). Also, in her 1964 essay 'The Moral Decision about Homosexuality', she argues in favour of the liberalisation of the law on homosexuality, which was not made legal in Britain until 1967.
2. Judith Buchanan's edited collection, *The Writer on Film* (2013), explores various aspects of the ways in which gender stereotypes play out in the depiction of, amongst others, female writers and male poets.
3. See detailed discussion at p. 62.
4. The fact that Murdoch uses a capital 'L' for Liberalism suggests she is referring to the individual of classical Liberalism. For a discussion of the various types of individual, see MGM: 350–8.
5. This is a reference to the compulsory state-sponsored Belgian health insurance scheme.
6. I am grateful to Alice Pember for her insights into the camerawork in this scene and the film's politics as a whole, in her as yet unpublished PhD research.

CHAPTER 8

Metaphysics as a Guide to Movies

A philosophy cannot be a total system because the world is contingent and infinitely various, and systematic philosophy is often made more readable as well as more reasonable by the personal interests of the philosopher, by the way in which his analyses and examples stray toward particular matters which have amazed him or frightened him or pleased him; so that his book may have turned out to be more personal and accidental than he intended. (SRR: 38)

'Truth' is something we recognise in good art when we are led to a juster, clearer, more detailed, more refined understanding. Good art 'explains' truth itself, by *manifesting* deep conceptual connections. Truth is clarification, justice, compassion. This manifestation of internal relations is an image of metaphysics. (MGM: 321)

There are worse ends than the pursuit of an unexacting happiness; it is better to be cheered up by a silly magazine than by plans of revenge. (It is also of course true that we often ought to be out helping our neighbour rather than reading Proust or Tolstoy.) (MGM: 86)

Reading the first epigraph above is unnerving as I look back over the previous chapters and see how many of the films I have discussed are concerned with death and coping with grief and guilt. My inclusion of the personal and accidental is indeed unintended, and yet I have been amazed, frightened and pleased by the films I have written about. It is also the case that some of the films could have featured in more than one chapter. For example, *The Unknown Girl/La fille inconnue* could have been discussed in light of existentialism, goodness or morality, but I chose to focus on Dr Davin's experience in light of Murdoch's thinking about women. Similarly, Dr Cemal could have featured in the chapter on morality and goodness, as well as the existential hero. These films, like their protagonists and their moral world views, are multi-dimensional and overflowing with detail that make them almost inexhaustible resources for film philosophical enquiry. This is both an indication that, and a reason why, my investigation of Murdochian film philosophy cannot be a total system.

The first part of the same epigraph is important in relation to Murdoch, since her work is not a total system, and this is because she is committed to the reality of the contingent and infinitely various world in which we live. Her final work of philosophy, *Metaphysics as a Guide to Morals*, which I have drawn on throughout this book, has been described as a baggy monster, running hither and thither, heading off in all directions. Stephen Mulhall's analysis of the book accords with my understanding that this approach to philosophical writing is entirely Murdoch's intention. Mulhall considers that, to a reader, a first encounter with MGM is likely to give the impression that it is 'a bewilderingly dense and impenetrable confluence of several seemingly distinct ways of addressing its central concerns' (Mulhall 1997: 219). As Mulhall explains, 'To put it more bluntly: the trouble with *Metaphysics as a Guide to Morals* is that in general its sentences, its individual chapters and its overall structure appear to be extremely disorganized' (1997: 220). Mulhall argues, however, that this appearance is deceptive, and that the form of the text is 'a carefully calculated achievement or work of its writing', proposing:

> The form of this text is internally related to its content, that to present a discussion of these kinds of themes in any other kind of way would amount to a betrayal of the moral and philosophical vision the text aims to communicate, and that warnings to that effect are scattered liberally throughout its pages. (1997: 220–1)

Murdoch refers to the difficulties of the book when she warns: 'In the later part of the book we should recall the warning in the Preface that we shall have to travel over a wide field criss-cross in every direction' (MGM: 277). Mulhall sees that Murdoch is conveying to us, precisely through the style and form of the book, that traditional linear philosophical argumentation and reasoning are not suited to her conceptual thinking. Understanding this means letting go of the temptation to plot out and systematise Murdoch's philosophy, which does make it a challenging read but also compels us to draw on other, more figurative and contemplative elements of our imaginations. As Mulhall describes,

> She offers orientation to her reader by means of an image or figure, the idea of a field of force or tension; this not only suggests that the kind of unity she detects in moral experience is highly provisional or limited, but also indicates that images are part of the tissue of her thinking – not an ornament or optional extra but the thing itself. (1997: 221–2)

For Murdoch, philosophical thinking is creative thinking, and this involves more than language and words; images, pictures and metaphors are at the heart of our imaginations and our contemplations. Mulhall writes that, for Murdoch, 'Concepts depend upon the human faculty of imagination just as much as does imagery' (ibid.: 231). The role of the artwork is both to take us out of ourselves and then to challenge us to assess its limitations and its possibilities:

> When we are confronted by one particular ordering or patterning of our moral and metaphysical concepts, we must respect both its unity and the limitations of that unity. This means, on the one hand, attending to the internal relations that hold it together as a system; and on the other, attending to the phenomena and the concepts that this systematisation leaves out. (Mulhall 1997: 232)

We can think of a film in this way. It presents an ordering of the world, with physical and metaphysical concepts, images, of course, and a moral vision. We experience this, and are taken to a particular realisation or assessment, which we can then consider in light of the film world and in terms of our world, our lives, and the lives of others. In this way, film is using pictures and images in ways that penetrate our thinking and our own imaginaries, just as they did for Plato. Murdoch refers to 'Pictures, yes (such as Plato used, declaring them to *be* pictures), but explained, used, related to human life, surrounded by clear plain language' (MGM: 267). As Mulhall argues, 'any such pictures must always be regarded as limited or provisional wholes, as likely to impose a false unity on the reality they claim to represent. Any adequate analysis of them must question the neatness of the internal relations they crystallise, and unearth the concepts and the values they exclude' (1997: 234). This enables us to see how film can be both a limited whole, and 'a hall of reflection' (MGM: 296, 422), where 'ideas and intuitions can be unsystematically nurtured' (MGM: 422). This lack of a system, and lack of structure, throws emphasis on images, people and instants, and also invites fictional worlds to have as much relevance and value as our real world experiences to our moral progress as individuals. This viewpoint, aided by Mulhall's creative understanding of MGM and his acknowledgement of the importance of images, enables us to see clearly the relevance of Murdoch's thinking to film philosophy. There are some tensions and difficulties, such as when a certain film might be considered to be bad art, or poor philosophy (what Murdoch might call 'idea play' (L&P: 19)). In the rest of this chapter, I want to propose succinctly how Murdoch might become a significant voice in film philosophy, and make some overarching observations about what this book has shown, as well as suggest some ways to develop this relationship with other films and areas of thinking.

MURDOCHIAN FILM PHILOSOPHY

What does the philosophy of Iris Murdoch specifically bring to the field of film philosophy? I suggest there are at least three ways that Murdoch can make a significant contribution, as I have shown in this volume. Firstly, as a towering individual voice to rival those of 'the usual suspects': Carroll, Cavell, Deleuze, Derrida et al. Murdoch's body of work ranges from the 1950s to the 1990s, and as such can be positioned in relation to all of these thinkers, on both sides of the Atlantic. Murdoch is a unique voice for film philosophy: British, female, and working in the fields of philosophy most relevant to film, namely morality and aesthetics. Also, she was constantly grappling with philosophy in an interdisciplinary context; that is, how it is different from literature and how it relates to art. This has some parallels with the 'film as philosophy' debates, about how the disciplines connect, and enables Murdoch's voice to be more relevant than many. Secondly, and connected to this, she is a voice that encompasses both analytic and continental philosophical traditions, and indeed Eastern thought and Buddhist philosophy, and so is able to bridge some of those divides and take thinking in a fresh direction. Thirdly, her concept of attending to art as being practice, or training, for attending to reality, and as encouraging the same faculty of respectful, just discernment that is required to approach the Good, is consonant with cinematic ethics. Murdoch's proposals clarify the way in which films can affect us emotionally, cognitively and physically, as she explains how art, like nature, can pierce our self-centred veils and help us see beyond ourselves with compassionate vision. I have shown how some of the more traditional modes of moral philosophical thinking can be brought into dialogue with contemporary cinema with the twofold aim of showing the relevance of Murdoch's philosophical thinking, in tandem with showing how contemporary cinema is replete with ethical challenges, moral reflexivity, and means for us to 'grow by looking'.

Along with these aspects, there are many other ways in which Murdoch's thought can enrich our thinking about film. Her metaphysics, including talk of the Good, the soul and the spirit, provides a vocabulary and a framework for examining those aspects of cinema that can be hard to account for by formal analysis alone, and which we all know affect and move us to joy, tears and contemplation. The idea that Altorf develops from Le Dœuff, of Murdoch's philosophical imaginary, identifies the way in which philosophers have an array of images, myths, metaphors and stories that they use to explain their thoughts, and that we too have a similar range of visual examples and moments in our imaginations. As she says, 'Art work and value judgement are everywhere in self expression. Our evening story about the events of our day is a little evaluative work of art' (MGM: 94). These words encapsulate how art and imagination constantly infiltrate our minds, and are part of how we speak to others, tell stories, recount anything and create for ourselves. As Murdoch says, 'our perceptions, which so largely constitute our experienced-being, are intensely individual and polymorphous. Seeing, thinking and "interpreting" are mixed' (MGM: 278). We are in a constant state of adding to our inner visions, and our story-forming, and storytelling, imaginaries. This solves the problem that Murdoch poses here: 'The problem about philosophy, and about life, is how to relate large impressive illuminating general conceptions to the mundane ("messing about") details of ordinary personal private existence' (MGM: 146). According to Murdoch, 'This process of relating and fusing takes place largely instinctively when we attend to a work of art' (ibid.). Cinema is enfolded in the way that Murdoch links philosophy, life, art and the everyday. But where precisely is the philosophy going on?

Murdoch was resolute about her position that novels should not contain philosophy. In response to the question she was asked most frequently, about the difference between philosophy and literature, she expresses clearly that she has 'an absolute horror of putting theories or "philosophical ideas" as such into [her] novels' (L&P: 19). She says that she can only think of one good philosophical novel, which is Sartre's *La Nausée* (L&P: 20). However, she also states repeatedly how the novels of the nineteenth century, by Tolstoy in particular, are great works of art and how much we can learn from them; and she clearly believes that film can be a major art too, and that we can hone our moral thinking through our attention to art. So, the step to attending to film as being Murdochian moral training is a consistent one. This book argues that film can be more than part of that exercise, and that it can exist in a state of philosophical thinking, as do we when we watch it, and travel on a journey with it, and think about it afterwards. The filmic reality, as Rushton would name it, enhances our enduring connections with the films we watch, as they form part of our own moral imaginary, as images of dilemmas, decisions and processes (2011: 2). Dr Cemal's decision to lie about the autopsy, Dr Davin's decision to not let Julien answer the door, and Lisa's decision to lie about the red light, are more than isolated moments. They are the result of actions in the film world or lead to consequences that the film examines. These actions may be more extreme than some of us have encountered, or hopefully will ever encounter, but they resemble everyday matters and they engender everyday moral reflection. Importantly, through attending to these individuals, our thought processes investigate, assess and probably judge them, but the experience of the film as a whole hopefully enables us to do so with realism and compassion.

The question then is how this extends to our real lives, as we go about everyday as constantly occupied moral beings. The question itself suggests that there is a difference between how we relate to film lives and 'real-world' lives, and I suggest that Murdoch enables us to elide this difference. By showing how the change that happens when we experience the moral vision of cinema happens in us, then that change has occurred no matter that the prompt, or catalyst, is fictional and on-screen. We are doing the work: 'the (daily, hourly, minutely) attempted purification of consciousness [is] the central and fundamental "arena" of morality' (MGM: 293). Like M, as we perform the moral activity of travelling with the film, and assessing what we think of it, we are changed, no matter that there is possibly no outward evidence. Seeing the kestrel out of the window takes us out of ourselves and pierces the veil of our self-centred ego. Seeing the rancher's face as she rides the horse to and from the diner, with Elizabeth sitting closely behind her, compels us to consider her joy, and the depth of the meaning of this encounter to her. I have shown throughout the range of films and concepts in this book how Murdochian thought and filmic imagery can work together to explain and enhance the meaning of such moments.

> We are constantly puzzled by ambiguous 'perceptions' or 'seeings', we 'interpret' our surroundings all the time, enjoying as it were a multiple grasp of their texture and significance. We are doing it continuously and this includes intense imaginative introspection, evaluation, focusing upon an image, turning thoughts into things. Shall I do it? becomes a picture of it done. (MGM: 279)

This conveys the way in which we can envisage ourselves or a state of affairs as a way of thinking towards its completion, in the manner of creative visualisation techniques. Murdoch's notion of attending to art and images in our lives, coupled with the richness and complexity of film, enables us to understand how profoundly insightful and expansive cinema works to affect us at the time and beyond the end of the film. And Murdochian film philosophy is not limited to the films and concepts in this book, as I will now begin to demonstrate.

GOOD ART IN GENRE CINEMA

The selection of films in this book are from international cinemas, and vary from mainstream fare (*Jackie*, *Blue Jasmine*) to festival circuit favourites (*Stories We Tell*, *Compliance*) and independent or arthouse cinema (*Under the Skin, Graduation*). Murdoch's philosophical imaginary could certainly take in more conventional genre film, however, and productive encounters could be staged between Murdoch's thinking and romance, war, horror, comedy and science fiction. Keeping in mind the need Murdoch stressed for good art to not console, films that are reworking genres, or updating them to investigate or reflect contemporary concerns, could readily be in dialogue with Murdoch's thinking. For example, *Ex Machina* (Alex Garland, 2014), is a conventionally set-up film (based on a 'mad scientist in his castle' scenario), but challenges us to consider the possibility of artificial intelligence and the basis on which we form relationships. Through the intermingling of familiar relations with other humans, and ground-breaking confrontations with artificial beings, achieved through special effects as well as story and character, this film is able to lead us perplexingly through a philosophical minefield of ethical and psychological questions. Murdoch's thinking might lead us to consider what makes a life human and how the delusions of the protagonist, Caleb (Domhnall Gleeson), about the humanity of Ava (Alicia Vikander), ask questions about our perception of others and perhaps what makes us fall in love.

The Babadook (Jennifer Kent, 2014) is a visually stunning and atmospheric film, resembling German Expressionist films such as *The Cabinet of Dr Caligari* (Robert Wiene, 1920) but set in contemporary Adelaide, and centred around a child's sinister story book. Amelia (Essie Davis) wrestles with her grief for her husband and managing her challenging son, while the idiosyncratic little boy in turn has to manage his grief-stricken mother. Through the invocation of a terrifying creature arising out of the mysterious book, the film creates a vision of overwhelming and damaging grief, and invents a metaphor for coming to terms with powerful, dangerous, but ultimately controllable bereavement. The film ends with Amelia in charge of the Babadook, but it still lives in her cellar: they learn to live with him, rather than conquer him or make him go away. This figuration of learning to live with the omnipresence of grief, and the idea that it can be reduced but will persist, is a powerful way to imagine and picture grief in our own lives that perhaps resonates with our experience. 'These visual cases also have a metaphorical force. We instinctively dodge in and out of metaphor all the time, and in this sense too are fed or damaged spiritually by what we attend to' (MGM: 301).

In relation to love, Murdoch recognises that 'Eros may be wilful, but he is also said to be ingenious, and there are very many ways in which love between persons can exist and endure' (MGM: 346). This is something that is explored in less conventional depictions of marriage, such as *Certified Copy* (Abbas Kiarostami, 2010). This film explores the painful differences between husband and wife as they assess their relationship in terms of their different needs. Taking art and authenticity as a central concept about which they disagree, the film works around this concept to highlight the couple's differences in relation to companionship, romance and duty, and suggests that while she (Juliette Binoche) encounters and remembers life through images and the visual, he (William Shimell) is immersed in language and sound. Their differences, and their inability to really see each other, cause fundamental dysfunction between them as a couple.

Films about love, of course, need not be about romantic love, as I explored in Chapter 5. Love between parents and children, friends, and within families are all spheres where 'really looking' might improve relations. In *Still Alice* (Richard Glatzer and Wash Westmoreland, 2014), we are shown the devastating loss of cognitive ability for linguistics professor Alice (Julianne Moore) due to early onset dementia. The film explores the progress of Alice's illness within the context of her family. Her husband is initially supportive but struggles to cope; one daughter is prickly and selfish about it, but another daughter is interested and unafraid to be with her mother as her faculties lessen. Murdoch's examples of the love of the family, M for D, and the woman who has to juggle family needs, resonate with this type of supportive love between women in a family. The film depicts strong, loving devotion and explores the basis of the connection between mother and daughter, and the changes both women have to go through for the relationship to strengthen.

I have taken concepts and elements from Murdoch's work and discussed them in relation to film in order to open out the possibilities for connections. There are many more fruitful possibilities, not least in light of her non-theological metaphysics, and her political philosophy. In Gary Browning's book *Why Iris Murdoch Matters* (2018), he demonstrates her contemporary relevance and the breadth of her thinking, explaining how, 'Murdoch strikes a subtle balance between the styles and objects of thinking to which she attends. She does not dismantle the borders, but takes them to be open and mutually accessible' (ibid.: 2). Browning proposes that, in this post-metaphysical age, Murdoch's metaphysics 'does not shirk the dissonance and fragmentation of late modernity but maintains a continuing commitment to orient personal and moral development by attending to unifying notions of truth and goodness that are evidenced within lived experience' (ibid.: 7). So, religion can be valued 'for its orienting capacity to value experience as a whole rather than for its supernatural claims' (ibid.). Browning has examined the as yet unpublished Heidegger manuscript that is held in the Iris Murdoch archives at Kingston University.[1] In it, Murdoch uses the fabulous phrase, 'In philosophy, we go where the honey is' (Heidegger ms: 69; Browning 2018: 44). Browning discusses this briefly in light of Murdoch's use of Plato and Heidegger in

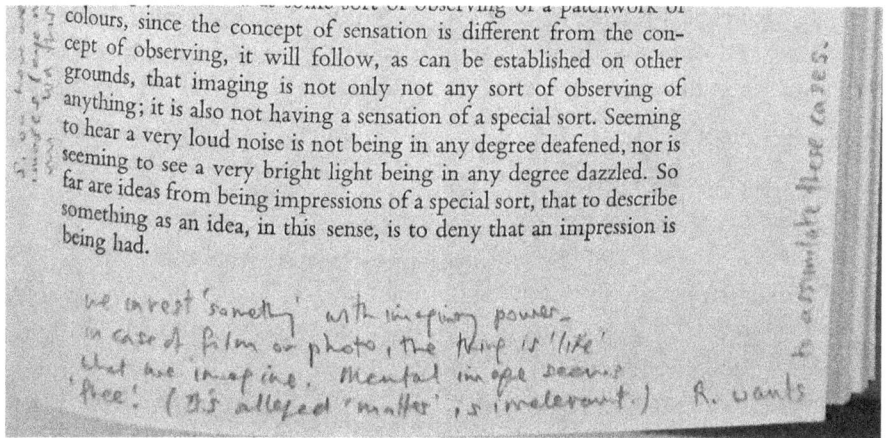

Figure 8.1 Iris Murdoch refers to film in an annotation on a page of her copy of Gilbert Ryle's *The Life of the Mind*. Photograph is author's own. From the Iris Murdoch Collections in Kingston University Archive. Copyright Kingston University.

the discussion of her own commitment to modernity and metaphysics, and this is also an apt description of what I have done with this book, in relation to Murdoch and cinema. I have looked for the ideas, passages and concepts that resonate with film, and used these to develop an approach that can be considered to be Murdochian film philosophy. I sensed honey in Murdoch's philosophy for enlarging our thinking about film, and I have discovered this to be the case. Other material that might supplement the published works I have looked at in this book include annotations to the books from Murdoch's Oxford libraries. These range from Murdoch's annotations or reactions in the margins, to detailed notes which can be found in the pages at the beginnings and ends of her books (Figure 8.1).

There are notebooks, including the notes taken at the Sartre lecture.[2] There is her extensive correspondence with a variety of individuals, including Philippa Foot, Brigid Brophy, Raymond Queneau and Elias Canetti. These letters have been collected into an anthology by Avril Horner and Anne Rowe, called *Living on Paper* (2015), which reveals insights into Murdoch's intellectual and personal relationships and perspectives on life. And, of course, there are her twenty-six novels, which are so frequently interpreted as putting her thinking about the world into action, through the individuals and particulars that she writes about. All of this material, as well as further study of the philosophical works that I have drawn upon in this book, offer a life's work which has potential for original and illuminating connections with film and the visual arts. There are two important areas where Murdoch's work can undoubtedly have a significant influence and which I do not have space to investigate fully in this book. The first is theology, and the second politics. I will consider both of these briefly in turn.

THEOLOGY

> We must stop thinking of 'God' as the name of a super-person, and indeed as a name at all. Can we then be saved by a mystical Christ who is the Buddha of the west? (MGM: 137)

For someone who did not believe in God, Murdoch wrote a lot about Christianity and religion. She was also very interested in Buddhism, and considered a combination of the two to be the ideal spiritual state. Murdoch considers herself to be 'a neo-Christian or Buddhist Christian or Christian fellow traveller' (MGM: 419). As discussed in Chapter 5, Murdoch considered religious contemplation and meditation to be akin to the type of Weilian attention that she was interested in. Also, she was tolerant of religious devotion, even envying those who believe in Christ, but was certain that she could not. She considers that addressing God is a means of consoling oneself, but does not criticise those who have faith and who pray: 'who can say, when a man prays, whether this is "mere superstition" or "something casual" or "the real thing"?' (MGM: 416). For Murdoch herself, however, her position on religion is clear and consistent. In 1977 she said:

> I am not myself a Christian believer, but I was brought up as a Christian and I feel close to Christianity. I believe in religion, in some sort of non-doctrinal sense – in a Buddhist sense. I think people miss this particular steadying influence, this spiritual home and spiritual centre. (Dooley 2003: 62)

This is a major difference between Murdoch and Weil, who was profoundly committed to religious thought. Murdoch approved of the moral characteristics of Jesus, and wanted to retain him, but denied the metaphysical assertion that he was both fully human and fully divine: 'Can the figure of Christ remain religiously significant without the old god-man mythology somehow understood? Can Christ, soon enough, become like Buddha, both real and mystical, but no longer the divine all-in-one man of traditional Christianity?' (MGM: 136). Murdoch describes God as a 'super-art-object' (MGM: 81), meaning that 'he' has been created by centuries of Christian art and this has formed our cultural imaginary. As she argues, 'There has always been a dangerous relationship between art and religion, and, where theology hesitates, art will eagerly try to explain' (F&S: 447).

Murdoch mentions the 'Motherhood of God' as discussed by Julian of Norwich (MGM: 84),[3] and the way in which 'the image-play of theology ... has always been an important part of religion but cannot be all of it' (ibid.). She opens up a path for feminist theology, calling on us to separate iconography and imagery from the spiritual contemplation that religious thinking can be, and this has significant potential for thinking about cinema. Firstly, when thinking about the terms that Murdoch uses such as 'virtue' and 'the Good', we are challenged to come up with new images and objects for these concepts. We might look for these notions in action rather than in abstract, or tied to stories from traditional religious texts. Also, cinema can rework these stories so as to provide fresh visions that can change how such concepts are conceived of in culture. For example, *Mary Magdalene* (Garth Davis, 2018) offers a fresh vision of the eponymous protagonist. There is none of the sexuality or nudity associated with the Mary Magdalene depicted by Christian art of the last two thousand years, which has directly fed into previous cinematic depictions, such as those by Barbara Hershey or Monica Bellucci.[4] This Mary (Rooney Mara) is an intelligent, unconventional and spiritual young woman who follows Jesus and has a unique understanding of him and his message. When Murdoch describes 'the woman who broke the alabaster box of very precious ointment' (VCM: 91), she is touching upon one of the New Testament stories that is often, wrongly, taken to refer to Mary Magdalene (Bourgeault 2010: 17–23). By not calling this woman Mary Magdalene, she is, knowingly or not, freeing Magdalene of the associations of crawling at Jesus's feet and anointing them with expensive nard, and is thereby opening up a space for Mary to be identified anew. Mary in the 2018 film understands Jesus to be preaching about a possible state of mind which is available to all, in this life, grounded in forgiveness. The disciples, however, are waiting for him to rise up and bring a new world, or a next world, that will answer their questions and win their battles. In this way, Mary Magdalene is a figure who preaches a spirituality that could be conceived of as Murdochian: it entails care, attention and forgiveness, and is spirituality understood as intellectual and practical (Figure 8.2).

For Murdoch, we picture concepts, because 'picturing is so natural' (MGM: 36): 'In thinking about abstract matters one instinctively produces images, such as duty being like a laser beam coming from above; an image which may itself elicit figurative rejoinders' (ibid.). Murdoch considers that philosophers are artists, 'and metaphysical ideas are aesthetic' (ibid.: 37). It is clear that cinematic images can be Murdochian metaphysical ideas, and that the duty is on us to explore them.

Figure 8.2 Mary Magdalene (Rooney Mara) as a spiritual leader, in *Mary Magdalene* (2018), directed by Garth Davis.

POLITICS

> We argue about how far religion and art should play political or 'social' roles. Should the church be enlivening personal spirituality or defending the poor? Should the artist create his own best work of art or advocate a better society? (MGM: 350)

The role of the church is relevant in contemporary Britain, in its involvement with food banks, the homeless and overseas charities in today's society. The question of 'personal spirituality' is less a part of public discourse in relation to the church, but concepts such as mindfulness and meditation are prevailing discourses in popular psychology. Perhaps Murdoch's call for compassionate vision is something that could be considered as a way of lifting us out of our self-centredness and towards considering others. In this way, Murdoch can be seen to be calling for imagination in politics: 'to imagine the consequences of policies, to picture what it is like for people to be in certain situations (unemployed, persecuted, very poor), to relate axiomatic moral ideas (for instance about rights) to pragmatic and utilitarian considerations' (MGM: 322). This is perhaps a way of thinking about the individual and the collective, the personal and the structural. Murdoch writes with vigour about the effects of television on our imaginations and consciences:

> We should also reflect upon the deep effects of television, for instance upon the fact that so many citizens go to bed at night with their heads full of overwhelmingly clear and powerful images of horror

and violence. Television can show us beautiful and fascinating things, distant landscapes and works of art, detailed pictures of animals and revealing close-ups of human faces, but it can also commit terrible crimes against the visible world. I am inclined to think that it blunts our general sense of colour and light and reduces rather than enhances our ability to see the detail of our surroundings. It is an instance, and indeed an image or parable, of how the packaged services of our increasingly perfected technology reduce our ability to think and imagine for ourselves. (MGM: 329–30)

Murdoch wrote this in the early 1990s: one can only imagine what she would make of the advances in technology since then, and our reliance upon smartphones and apps to tell us what to think and imagine. Her use of words such as 'colour', 'light' and 'detail' again calls attention to the need she perceives for us to really look; to study, and to attend. And she sees this as a moral matter, just as for her television 'commit[s] terrible crimes against the visible world'. This seems to be a matter of mediation and selection; the problem being that we are shown snippets, or 'structured glimpses', without the opportunity to make our own selection of both content and focus.

In language that is fitting for our time, especially in relation to certain individuals in international politics, Murdoch speaks about the fact that certain people rise to power, and that we elect them.

A dominating figure is that of the demonic individual. Perhaps the individual liberated or created by capitalism had a golden age of integral being and virtuous idealism, reflected in the great art forms of the nineteenth century, but now, it is said, has disintegrated and become unconfident and even corrupt. We see (it may be argued) his demonic descendants in ruthless tyrannical regimes and persons, and, in western democracies, in egoistic materialistic 'go-getters', in pursuit of money, fame, prestige and sex, who are now our most conspicuous citizens . . . Tyrants' subjects may even admire and value the egoistic anti-moralism of their leaders. That someone very grand exists who can satisfy every caprice may, while causing scandal, produce a warm feeling, and patriotism too can feed on such images. Neither public cruelty nor riotous private living need make a tyrant unpopular in his lifetime or later. Our best-known, best-loved, monarch is Henry the Eighth. (MGM: 352–3)

Murdoch describes the way in which swathes of a populace can be intoxicated by the excesses of a demonic individual and their 'anti-moralism'. This rings depressingly true for our current times, and Murdoch expands with great insight into the functioning of states.

> Of course the satisfaction felt at the overthrow of tyrants is a stronger, and better, emotion! That exceptional (for whatever reason) people are often valued and not hated for living lives of exemplary luxury and selfishness is perhaps a general feature of human societies, such people may be felt to live vicarious lives for the rest of us. In this way film stars, pop stars, television personalities, tycoons, and so on may be expected to live with obvious luxury and even disorder. To take a different though similar example, a majority of people in Britain value the Royal Family, and even like to see them dressed up and riding in their coaches. They are not envied. Here the advantages of a hereditary monarchy and head of state are evident. We (now) expect them to observe traditional moral standards but the odd one who is out of line does the institution no harm, rather the contrary. They play a popular symbolic role, and a beneficent political role in so far as by being 'mock tyrants' they are a protection against real tyrants. (MGM: 353)

At a time when the royal family in Britain is enjoying a resurgence in global popularity, it is pertinent to consider their contemporary appeal. The concept of a 'mock tyrant' is perhaps insightful. Unelected, the family's roles and functions are social, ceremonial and charitable, and, although non-political, their role in society is interesting to compare to that of politicians. Given the tradition of heritage films featuring British royalty (*Mrs Brown*, *Shakespeare in Love*, *The King's Speech*) and the international popularity of royal family sagas on television (*Wolf Hall*, *The Crown*), it is an area that merits attention in the way it has peaks and troughs of popularity, and also how certain members of the royal family are discussed and reported, given the increasing number of documentaries and biopics that are produced.[5]

The concept of the moral conduct of those in office, whether royal or political, is relevant here. Murdoch believes that,

> The machinery of the decent state is continually serviced by an atmosphere of moral good will and high ideals which is essential to its survival. This thoroughly mixed-up continually changing atmosphere is kept fresh by innumerable lively moralists, not least artists (especially writers) and their clients. (MGM: 358)

This language conveys Murdoch's conception of citizens as political beings, of which she considered herself to be one. As Browning argues, 'She does not disqualify herself entirely from politics, and as a citizen she takes politics seriously and it informs her philosophical and literary work' (2018: 117).

Murdoch's private political allegiances are well covered in other texts, notably Peter Conradi's authorised biography (2001), but, as with her feminism, it is important to remember the social and political times in which she lived. A member of the Communist Party at Oxford, she gave up membership after the war, when she worked for the Treasury. She changed in this post-war period, when, as Browning explains, 'morals and politics become mechanisms promoting and responding to burgeoning individualism' (2018: 122). In MGM, she reflects, 'We should recall how much popular existentialism meant to the post-1945 generation; and also ask why, as a popular philosophy, it has now waned' (MGM: 354). For Murdoch, real lived experience is inextricably linked with politics and morals. She is subversive in her support of civil disobedience, and philosophically questions the mechanics of the state:

> When is a bad law a law, is it always a law? The idea of 'natural law' belongs especially in this discussion. (MGM: 356)

> (Is it all right to cheat the Income Tax authorities? If one can cheat them is it not their fault?) (MGM: 357)

She also does write about social change and the realistic ways in which this can come about:

> A high moral as well as intellectual level of political debate is to be hoped for, and lip service at least is paid to its importance. Lip service is not to be despised. The triumph of good causes partly depends on people, at some point, becoming ashamed of saying certain things. (For instance of making anti-Semitic remarks or talking about women in certain ways.) (MGM: 358)

Murdoch is concerned with the relationship between axioms and private thought, such as when she notes that, 'Arguments about capital punishment involve a more evident appeal to axiom, when people argue (as I would) that the state should never (legally, in cold blood, etc.) take life' (MGM: 359). She is here expressing political and moral opinions, with an admittedly limited engagement to the actual workings of political systems or collective action. She is interested in the idea of 'natural law' and human rights, as a 'general ethical viewpoint which is separate both from politicised social theory and from traditional personal morals' (MGM: 361). She includes in this

> the promotion of women's rights, black rights, animal rights, the rights of the planet (ecology), one could even add liberation theology where the identification of Christ with the poor inspires a passion for justice which is *sui generis* and not a subsection of either Marxism or dogmatic Christianity. The flag of natural rights or natural law has often been that of revolutionary change. (MGM: 361)

Murdoch approaches political issues from the perspective of moral philosophy in MGM, and this opens up a range of creative, imaginative possibilities for exploring and envisioning political ideas. She wants to examine the welfare state, and does so with the question, 'When does a nanny become a tyrant?' (MGM: 363). She challenges the connection between freedom and happiness, always acutely aware of the threat of the totalitarian state who would deny human variety 'and the rights which *the fact* of variety carries' (MGM: 363). Murdoch calls for resistance to totalitarian reasoning, and its false reliance on scientific reasoning, and the despair and ignorance it leads to. She recounts,

> When I was in China I asked a question about 'homosexuality', a word with which our otherwise excellent interpreter was unfamiliar. When I explained its meaning in other terms, I was told that there was no such thing in China. So if homosexuals do not exist they clearly cannot have rights. (MGM: 364)

Murdoch's concern for the rights of minority groups, and the infinite variety of human beings, makes her philosophical analysis of political thinking a fertile ground for developing in relation to diverse identities and communities. As Browning observes, the political dimension to her philosophy and her novels has been overlooked. There is 'honey' in Murdoch's ideas about politics, however, perhaps particularly in the problems she poses, and these are reflected in her philosophical critique of the relationship between individual choice and the common good. Films that might be considered in light of these questions of rights and law might be *Selma* (Ava du Vernay, 2014) which recounted Martin Luther King's campaign to secure equal voting rights by way of the Selma march in 1965; or *Milk* (Gus Van Sant, 2008) which told the story of Harvey Milk's fight to secure political office as an openly gay man in San Francisco in the 1970s. These films tell stories about historical political campaigns within structures of oppression; but the way in which individuals in the films are shown to us, in the maelstroms of their decision making and prioritisation, enables us to attend to some of the philosophical questions that their stories raise, as well as engendering affective emotional engagement with the issues that concerned them. This might well be a Murdochian way in to analysing this type of political cinema, which is not documentary or straight biopic.

In the last filmic example in this book, I am turning to something perhaps unexpected in this context. *Only Lovers Left Alive* (Jim Jarmusch, 2013) is a vampire film that is not only beautiful to look at and listen to, with an exquisitely detailed *mise en scène* and an atmospheric soundtrack, but also has contemporary geo-political resonances. It sets the lead characters, the vampires, in philosophical, literary and aesthetic histories. It challenges the conception of vampirism and juxtaposes this with modern Detroit and Tangiers, calling into question how history will judge our modern age, what will endure and what will disappear. Adam (Tom Hiddleston) and Eve (Tilda Swinton), have spent the centuries of their lives rubbing shoulders with the great and the innovative in the worlds of literature, art, music and science. Adam's wall is adorned with photographs of Oscar Wilde, Christopher Marlowe, Buster Keaton and Joe Strummer. But, as Adam repeats, he has no heroes: it is the vampires who are the creators. Adam gave his adagio to Schubert to pass off as his own, just as vampire Christopher Marlowe's (John Hurt) work was willingly attributed to the 'illiterate zombie philistine' Shakespeare. Zombie is the term these vampires use to describe humans, and the neat conceit here is that the vampires would draw too much attention to themselves if they published under their own names. They allow inferior zombies to pass off the work as their own, so that the vampires might keep to their shadowy liminal lives and stay undetected by society, under the radar. Their motivation is to 'get the work out there'.

Adam is depressed because of the zombies and their – our – treatment of the world. Ruled by fear, dry of innovation and skill, Adam feels that 'all the sand's at the bottom of the hourglass'. For Eve, however, a self-professed survivor, this self-obsession is 'a waste of living', when Adam could be appreciating nature, nurturing kindness and friendships, 'and dancing'. These exchanges get to the heart of this peculiarly reassuring film. Adam and Eve are cultured aesthetes, with a sense of bafflement and isolation that makes it easy to identify with them whether as outsiders in a foreign city, or physically vulnerable bodies. Eve samples the riches that each era has to offer. Here is a vampire who relishes life and the living of it, from the relationships that endure with her to the contemporary updates on culture and the long view on how the world works. For example, the film shows Detroit to be like a wasteland, with closed factories and desolate streets. Detroit, she says, will rise again because 'it is a city that has water'. As Eve assembles her travelling library she scans the volumes with her eyes and fingers, devouring every image, character and letter, 'seemingly reading them with her hands' (Hastie 2014: 66). As she lowers the needle on the forty-five record of Charlie Feathers's 'Can't Hardly Stand It', the riffing chord changes sound like the pinnacle of musical achievement. As Adam executes scales on his violin, strums the strings on his 1905 Gibson or caresses the wooden bullet he has commissioned for the suicide he toys with, his exquisite sensory and intellectual acumen is enviably realised.

This playful fable aims to convey the need to embrace the cosmos in all its beauty in order to endure. Eve observes that red-spotted fungi are emerging at the wrong time of year and tells them that they are too early. The idea that the world and what matters in it has a very long history and an uncertain future is hardly original, but the notion that vampires have the cultural high ground as a result of their longevity invites us to indulge our pleasures and yet also to realise that they don't have to worry about the little matter of death.

What does this have to do with Iris Murdoch? Well, she believes in enjoying life, whether it is a silly magazine, Proust, Tolstoy or a Danny Kaye movie. In 1962 she said:

> The cinema upsets me terribly when it's sad. Life is sad enough without that too. Crying at music is a kind of pleasure, but in the cinema I just get filled with a dangerous sort of self-pity. The only films I go to now are Danny Kaye'. (Dooley 2003: 4)

As I noted in the introduction, Murdoch's own cinema-going decreased despite her admiration for its potential as a transformative art. She clearly did still get pleasure from the Danny Kaye films, however, and the impulse to indulge is not one that she would deny us. In *Only Lovers Left Alive*, the lovers do not just love each other, but they love beautiful words, notes, fabrics and textures. Their long view saddens Adam, but frees Eve, and the film invites us to contemplate our place in relation to what matters: what we can change, what we should worry about, and what beautiful things we can enjoy. As Hastie observes, the film 'offers a model for spending time, even if it is one seemingly outside the time of everyday life' (2014: 67). We can all achieve what Eve recommends to Adam, however, when she observes that his self-obsession is a waste of living, which, she says, could be spent on 'surviving things, appreciating nature, nurturing kindness and friendship. And dancing!' (Figure 8.3).

Figure 8.3 Eve (Tilda Swinton) encourages Adam (Tom Hiddleston) to dance, in *Only Lovers Left Alive* (2013), directed by Jim Jarmusch.

CONCLUDING WORDS

> There is . . . something in the serious attempt to look compassionately at human things which automatically suggests that 'there is more than this' . . . [which] must remain a very tiny spark of insight, something with . . . a metaphysical position but not metaphysical form. But it seems to me that the spark is real, and that great art is evidence of its reality. Art indeed, so far from being a playful diversion of the human race, is the place of its most fundamental insight, and the centre to which the more uncertain steps of metaphysics must constantly return. (OGG: 359–60)

Thinking about film as Murdochian art shows it to be a place of fundamental insight, but also one that can effect lasting change in us. This change happens as a result of the images we see, and the characters and stories on-screen, but also as a result of our sustained attention to the film and our contemplation afterwards. Film's renowned ability to 'take us out of ourselves' is given fresh significance if seen in this light, as unselfing and material for moral change. The concepts and language that Murdoch uses to discuss moral philosophy and our own moral journeys provide a rich vocabulary for understanding how we take films seriously. If we understand film as Murdochian moral thinking in action, this enables us to study, think and reflect anew, and to realise the role that film can play in our consciences, imaginations and relationships with others. Murdoch may say she has a man in mind, but we know she is speaking to all of us, about everyone else:

> The man I have in mind, faced by the manifold of humanity, may feel, as well as terror, delight, but not, if he really sees what is before him, superiority. He will suffer that undramatic, because un-self-centred, agnosticism which goes with tolerance. To understand other people is a task which does not come to an end. (SBR: 283)

NOTES

1. Murdoch prepared 'Manuscript on Heidegger' for possible publication in 1993, but, as Browning explains, she decided against publication and it has not yet been published (2018: 44).
2. See Chapter 1, note 1.
3. See *Revelations of Divine Love*, Julian of Norwich (1998: LIX, LXXXVI).
4. Barbara Hershey plays Mary Magdalene in Martin Scorsese's *The Last Temptation of Christ* (1988), and Monica Belluci plays her in Mel Gibson's *The Passion of the Christ* (2004).
5. *Mrs Brown* (John Madden, 1997); *Shakespeare in Love* (John Madden, 1998); *The King's Speech* (Tom Hooper, 2010), *Wolf Hall* (Peter Kosminsky, six episodes, 2015); *The Crown* (Philip Martin, Benjamin Caron, Stephen Daldry, Julian Jarrold and Philippa Lowthorpe, two seasons so far, 2016–). Topics such as costume, politics, melodrama and television are investigated in the anthology *The British Monarchy on Screen* (Merck 2016).

Bibliography

Altorf, M. (2007), 'Reassessing Iris Murdoch in the light of feminist philosophy: Michèle Le Dœuff and the philosophical imaginary', in A. Rowe (ed.), *Iris Murdoch: a Reassessment*. Basingstoke and New York: Palgrave Macmillan, pp. 175–86.
Altorf, M. (2008), *Iris Murdoch and the Art of Imagining*. London: Continuum.
Andersen, N. (2014), *Shadow Philosophy: Plato's Cave and Cinema*. London and New York: Routledge.
Antonaccio, M. (2000), *Picturing the Human: The Moral Thought of Iris Murdoch*. New York and Oxford: Oxford University Press.
Antonaccio, M. (2012), 'The virtues of metaphysics: A review of Iris Murdoch's philosophical writings', in J. Broackes (ed.), *Iris Murdoch, Philosopher*. Oxford: Oxford University Press, pp. 155–79.
Antonaccio, M. and W. Schweiker (1996), *Iris Murdoch and the Search for Human Goodness*. Chicago and London: University of Chicago Press.
Arendt, H. [1963] (2006), *Eichmann in Jerusalem*. New York: Penguin Books.
Arnheim, R. (1957), *Film as Art*. Berkeley and London: University of California Press.
Atwood, M. (1996), *Alias Grace*. London: Bloomsbury.
Balsom, E. and G. Vincendeau (2017), 'Crossing the line', *Sight and Sound*, 27:4, 33.
Barthes, R. [1957] (1993), 'The Face of Garbo' in *Mythologies*, trans. A. Lavers. London: Vintage.
Barton-Fumo, M. (2017), 'Elle', *Film Comment*, 53:1, 46.
Benjamin, W. [1935] (1968), *Illuminations*, ed. and with an introduction by Hannah Arendt, trans. Harry Zohn. New York: Harcourt Brace Jovanovich.
Benjamin, W. [1935] (2007), 'The Work of Art in the Age of Mechanical Reproduction', in Hannah Arendt (ed.), *Illuminations: Essays and Reflections*. New York: Schocken Books.
Bergson, H. [1900] (2008), *Laughter: An Essay on the Meaning of the Comic*, trans. Cloudesley Brereton. Rockville: Arc Manor.
Blum, L. (2014), 'Visual metaphors in Murdoch's moral philosophy', in Justin Broackes (ed.), *Iris Murdoch, Philosopher*. Oxford: Oxford University Press, pp. 307–23.
Bolton, L. (2009), 'Remembering flesh: Morvern Callar as an Irigarayan Alice', in Jenny Chamarette and Jennifer Higgins (eds), *Guilt and Shame: Essays in French Literature, Thought and Visual Culture*. Bern and Oxford: Peter Lang, pp. 189–200.
Bolton, L. (2014), 'Solving suicide: Facing the complexity of *The Hours*', in Warren Buckland (ed.), *Hollywood Puzzle Films*. London and New York: Routledge, pp. 265–78.

Bolton, L. (2015a), 'Mia in *Fish Tank*: Being a modern girl in modern Britain', in Fiona Handyside and Kate Taylor (eds), *Global Girlhood and International Cinema*. London: Palgrave Macmillan.
Bolton, L. (2015b), 'Winslet, Dench, Murdoch and Alzheimer's disease: Intertextual stardom in *Iris*', in Laura Mulvey and Anna Backman Rogers (eds), *Feminisms*. Amsterdam: University of Amsterdam Press.
Bolton, L. (2017a), 'Attention to the details of film and form: *Blue Jasmine* as Murdochian moral vision', special issue 'Iris Murdoch and Visual Culture', *Iris Murdoch Review*, 8, 54–62.
Bolton, L. (2017b), 'Murdoch and *Margaret*: Learning a moral life', *Film-Philosophy*, 21:3, 265–80.
Bolton, L. (2017c), 'Introduction', special issue 'Iris Murdoch and Visual Culture', *Iris Murdoch Review*, 8, 4–8.
Bolton, L. (2017d), Anne Rowe, author of *The Visual Arts and the Novels of Iris Murdoch* (2002) in interview with Lucy Bolton, *Iris Murdoch Review*, 8, 21–8
Bordwell, D. (1989), 'A case for cognitivism', *Iris*, 9, 11–40.
Bourgeault, C. (2010), *The Meaning of Mary Magdalene*. Boulder: Shambhala.
Bradshaw, P. (2011), '*Margaret*', *The Guardian*, 1 December, <https://www.theguardian.com/film/2011/dec/01/margaret-film-review> (last accessed 31 October 2018).
Brans, J. (1985), 'Virtuous dogs and a unicorn: An interview with Iris Murdoch', *Southwest Review*, 70:1, 43–54.
Breger, C. (2014), 'Configuring affect: Complex world making in Fatih Akin's *Auf der anderen Seite* (*The Edge of Heaven*)', *Cinema Journal*, 54:1, 65–87.
Broackes, J. (2012), *Iris Murdoch, Philosopher*. Oxford: Oxford University Press.
Broackes, J. (2017), 'Iris Murdoch's first encounters with Simone Weil', *Iris Murdoch Review*, 8, 17–20.
Broucek, F. J. (1991), *Shame and the Self*. New York: The Guilford Press.
Browning, G. K. (2018), *Why Iris Murdoch Matters: Making Sense of Experience in Modern Times*. London and New York: Bloomsbury.
Buchanan, J. (ed.) (2013), *The Writer on Film: Screening Literary Authorship*. Basingstoke and New York: Palgrave Macmillan.
Carroll, N. (2008), *The Philosophy of Motion Pictures*. Malden, MA and Oxford: Blackwell.
Carroll, N. (2014), *Humour: A Very Short Introduction*. Oxford: Oxford University Press.
Cavell, S. [1971] (1979), *The World Viewed: Reflections on the Ontology of Film*. Cambridge, MA, and London: Harvard University Press.
Chagollan, S. (2014), 'Cate Blanchett infuses *Blue Jasmine* with literary complexity', *Variety*, 30 January, <https://variety.com/2014/film/features/cate-blanchett-blue-jasmine-santa-barbara-film-festival-1201073028/> (last accessed 17 December 2018).
Conradi, P. [1986] (2001b), *Iris Murdoch: The Saint and the Artist*. London: HarperCollins.
Conradi, P. (1994), 'Platonism in Iris Murdoch', in Anna Baldwin and Sarah Hutton (eds), *Platonism and the English Imagination*. Cambridge: Cambridge University Press, pp. 330–42.
Conradi, P. (ed.) (1997), *Existentialists and Mystics*. New York and London: Penguin.
Conradi, P. (2001), *Iris Murdoch: A Life*. London: HarperCollins.
Cooper, S. (2013), *The Soul of Film Theory*. Basingstoke and New York: Palgrave Macmillan.
Cox, L. (2015), 'Standing up against the rape joke: Irony and its vicissitudes', *Signs: Journal of Women in Culture and Society*, 40:4, 1–22.
Critchley, S. (2002), *On Humour*. New York and Oxford: Routledge.
Cunningham, M. (1998), *The Hours*. London: Fourth Estate.
Diamond, C. (2010), 'Murdoch the explorer', *Philosophical Topics*, 38:1, 51–85.
Dipple, E. (1982), *Iris Murdoch: Work for the Spirit*. London: Methuen.
Doane, M. A. (2003), 'The close-up: Scale and detail in the cinema', *differences: A Journal of Feminist Cultural Studies*, 14:3, 89–111.

Dooley, G. (ed.) (2003), *From a Tiny Corner in the House of Fiction: Conversations with Iris Murdoch*. Columbia: University of South Carolina Press.
Downing, L. (2013), *The Subject of Murder: Gender, Exceptionality, and the Modern Killer*. Chicago: University of Chicago Press.
Downing, L. and L. Saxton (2010), *Film and Ethics: Foreclosed Encounters*. London: Routledge.
Eaton, O. (2017), 'The past is present: Jacqueline Kennedy Onassis in American chaos, pre/post 9/11', *Celebrity Studies*, 9:3, 291–306.
Ebert, R. (2012), '*Compliance*', RogerEbert.com, 29 August, <https://www.rogerebert.com/reviews/compliance-2012> (last accessed 31 October 2018).
Edwards, N. (2015), 'Obliged to sympathise: Infanticide in *Il y a longtemps que je t'aime* and *A perdre la raison*', *Australian Journal of French Studies*, 55:2, 174–87.
Epstein, J. [1921] (1977), *Magnifications and Other Writings*, trans. Stuart Liebman, *October*, 3, 9–25.
Faber, M. (2000), *Under the Skin*. Edinburgh and New York: Canongate Books.
Feinberg, S. (2013), 'Cate Blanchett interview', *The Hollywood Reporter*, 26 July, <https://www.hollywoodreporter.com/race/cate-blanchett-blue-jasmine-woody-594161> (last accessed 31 October 2018).
Fiddes, P. S. (2012), 'Murdoch, Derrida and *The Black Prince*', in Anne Rowe and Avril Horner (eds), *Iris Murdoch: Texts and Contexts*. Basingstoke and New York: Palgrave Macmillan.
Forsberg, N. (2013), *Language Lost and Found: On Iris Murdoch and the Limits of Philosophical Discourse*. New York and London: Bloomsbury.
Freeland, C. A. (2001), *But is it Art?: An Introduction to Art Theory*. Oxford: Oxford University Press.
Friedan, B. [1963] (1997), *The Feminine Mystique*. New York and London: W. W. Norton.
Gardner, E. (2014), 'Six year battle over Kenneth Lonergan's *Margaret* finally ends', *The Hollywood Reporter*, 2 April <https://www.hollywoodreporter.com/thr-esq/six-year-legal-battle-kenneth-692235> (last accessed 31 October 2018).
Hämäläinen, N. (2015), 'Reduce ourselves to zero? Sabina Lovibond, Iris Murdoch, and Feminism', *Hypatia*, 30:4, 743–59.
Handy, B. (2013), 'Woody Allen's *Blue Jasmine* is perhaps his cruelest ever film', *Vanity Fair*, 26 July, <https://www.vanityfair.com/news/2013/07/movie-review-blue-jasmine-woody-allen> (last accessed 31 October 2018).
Harris, S. (2015), *Girlhood*, *Sight & Sound*, 25:5, 73–4.
Harris Williams, M. (2017), 'The Oedipal wound in two stories by Kafka: *The Metamorphosis* and *A Country Doctor*', *Psychodynamic Practice*, 23:2, 120–32.
Haskell, M. (2016), 'Agents provocateurs', *Film Comment*, 52:6, 38–41.
Hastie, A. (2014), 'Blood and photons: The fundamental particles of *Only Lovers Left Alive*', *Film Quarterly*, 68:1, 63–8.
Horner, A. and A. Rowe (eds) (2015), *Living on Paper: Letters from Iris Murdoch 1934–1995*. London: Chatto & Windus.
Ide, Wendy (2017), '*Certain Women* review: Kelly Reichardt fashions a minor miracle', *The Observer*, 5 March, <https://www.theguardian.com/film/2017/mar/05/certain-women-observer-film-review> (last accessed 26 August 2018).
Jacobowitz, F. (2012), '*Once upon a Time in Anatolia*', *Cineaction*, 59–61.
James, N. (2017), 'Darkness visible', *Sight and Sound*, 27:4, 28–32.
Julian of Norwich (1998), *Revelations of Divine Love*, trans. Elizabeth Spearing. London: Penguin.
Kern, L. (2012), 'Shock value', *Film Comment*, 48:2, 64–5.

Klevan, A. (2011), 'Notes on Stanley Cavell and philosophical film criticism', in Havi Carel and Greg Tuck (eds), *New Takes in Film-Philosophy*. Basingstoke and New York: Palgrave Macmillan.

Koehler, R. (2012), '*Compliance*', *Cineaste*, 37:4, 55–7.

Laverty, M. (2007), *Iris Murdoch's Ethics: A Consideration of her Romantic Vision*. London: Continuum.

Leeson, M. (2010), *Iris Murdoch: Philosophical Novelist*. London: Continuum.

Leigh, D. (2014), '*Under the skin*: Why did this chilling masterpiece take a decade? *The Guardian*, 6 March, <https://www.theguardian.com/film/2014/mar/06/under-the-skin-director-jonathan-glazer-scarlett-johansson> (last accessed 17 December 2018).

Lim, D. (2016), 'The well-told tale', *Film Comment*, 52:4, 66.

Lita, A. (2004), The moral regard for others', *The Philosopher*, 92:1.

Locke, J. (1690), *An Essay Concerning Human Understanding*, first edition. London: Thomas Bassett, Book 2, Chapter XI, p. 147.

Lonergan, K. (2012), '*Margaret*: Inside the 'fall' of a teenager', National Public Radio Interview, 11 July, <http://www.npr.org/2012/07/11/156565706/margaret-inside-the-fall-of-a-teenager> (last accessed 30 July 2018).

Lovell, J. (2012), 'Kenneth Lonergan's thwarted masterpiece', *The New York Times*, 19 June, <https://www.nytimes.com/2012/06/24/magazine/kenneth-lonergans-thwarted-masterpiece.html> (last accessed 17 December 2018).

Lovibond, S. (2011), *Iris Murdoch, Gender and Philosophy*. London: Routledge.

Lovibond, S. (2015), 'Iris Murdoch and the ambiguity of freedom', in *Essays on Ethics and Feminism*. Oxford: Oxford University Press, pp. 242–58.

Lowell MacDonald, R. (2016), *The Appreciation of Film: The Postwar Film Society Movement and Film Culture in Britain*. Exeter: University of Exeter Press.

McGill, H. (2013), '*Compliance*', *Sight & Sound*, March, 82.

MacIntyre, A. [1966] (1998), *A Short History of Ethics: A History of Moral Philosophy from the Homeric Age to the Twentieth Century*. London: Routledge.

Marks, L. U. (2000), *The Skin of the Film: Intercultural Cinema, Embodiment, and the Senses*. Durham, NC: Duke University Press.

Marks, L. U. (2002), *Touch: Sensuous Theory and Multisensory Media*. Minneapolis: University of Minnesota Press.

Mayer, S. (2016), *Political Animals: The New Feminist Cinema*. London: I. B. Tauris

Meszaros, J. (2016), *Selfless Love and Human Flourishing in Paul Tillich and Iris Murdoch*. Oxford: Oxford University Press.

Mennel, B. (2009), 'Criss-crossing in global space and time: Fatih Akin's *The Edge of Heaven* (2007)', *Transit*, 5:1.

Merck, M. (ed.) (2016), *The British Monarchy on Screen*. Manchester: Manchester University Press.

Moi, T. (2014), '"Something that might resemble a kind of love": fantasy and realism in Henrik Ibsen's *Little Eyolf*', in Susan Wolf and Christopher Grau (eds), *Understanding Love: Philosophy, Film and Fiction*. Oxford: Oxford University Press, pp. 185–207.

Moore, S. H. (2010), 'Murdoch's fictional philosophers: What they *say* and what they *show*', in Anne Rowe and Avril Horner (eds), *Iris Murdoch and Morality*. Basingstoke and New York: Palgrave Macmillan, pp. 101–12.

Morgan, D. (2010), *With Love and Rage: A Friendship with Iris Murdoch*. Kingston: Kingston University Press.

Morin, E. [1956] (2005), *The Cinema, or The Imaginary Man: An Essay in Sociological Anthropology*, trans. Lorraine Mortimer. Minneapolis: University of Minnesota Press.

Mulhall, S. (1997), 'Constructing a hall of reflection: Perfectionist edification in Iris Murdoch's "Metaphysics as a Guide to Morals"', *Philosophy*, 72:280, 219–39.

Murdoch, I. [1951] (2017), '"Waiting on God": A radio talk on Simone Weil', *Iris Murdoch Review*, 8, 10–16.
Murdoch, I. [1953] (1987), *Sartre: Romantic Rationalist*. London: Chatto & Windus.
Murdoch, I. (1954), *Under the Net*. London: Chatto & Windus.
Murdoch, I. (1961), *A Severed Head*. London: Chatto & Windus.
Murdoch, I. (1962), *An Unofficial Rose*. London: Chatto & Windus.
Murdoch, I. (1964), 'The Moral Decision about Homosexuality', *Man and Society*, 7, Summer, 3.
Murdoch, I. (1970), *The Sovereignty of Good*. London: Routledge.
Murdoch, I. (1978), *The Sea, the Sea*. New York: Viking Press.
Murdoch, I. (1986), *Acastos: Two Platonic Dialogues*. London: Chatto & Windus.
Murdoch, I. [1992] (2003), *Metaphysics as a Guide to Morals*. London: Penguin.
Murdoch, I. (1993), 'Taking the plunge', *The New York Review of Books*, 4 March, <https://www.nybooks.com/articles/1993/03/04/taking-the-plunge/> (last accessed 17 December 2018).
Onstad. K. (2017), '*Alias Grace*: 20 years in the making but on TV at the right time', *The New York Times*, 25 October, <https://www.nytimes.com/2017/10/25/arts/television/alias-grace-margaret-atwood-sarah-polley.html> (last accessed 1 January 2019).
Orange, M. (2017), 'Professional lives: Career women on film', *Virginia Quarterly Review*, 93:2, 178–81.
Osterweil, A. (2014), '*Under the Skin*: The perils of becoming female', *Film Quarterly*, 67:4, 44–51.
Perkins, V. F. (1972), *Film as Film: Understanding and Judging Movies*. London: Penguin.
Pinkerton, N. (2014), *Blue Jasmine*, *Sight & Sound*, 23:10, 62–3.
Puchner, M. (2010), *The Drama of Ideas: Platonic Provocations in Theatre and Philosophy*. New York and Oxford: Oxford University Press.
Righelato, R. (2015), 'Men with no name: The return of the existential hero', *The Guardian*, 16 March, <https://www.theguardian.com/film/filmblog/2015/mar/16/return-existential-hero-sean-penn-the-gunman> (last accessed 28 October 2018).
Renzi, B. G. and Rainey, S. (eds) (2006), *From Plato's Cave to the Multiplex*. Newcastle: Cambridge Scholars Press.
Rowe, A. (2002), *The Visual Arts and the Novels of Iris Murdoch*. Lewiston, NY and Lampeter: E. Mellen Press.
Rushton, R. (2011), *The Reality of Film: Theories of Filmic Reality*. Manchester: Manchester University Press.
Ryle, G. (1960), *The Concept of Mind*. London: Hutchinson.
Schwartz, M. (2009), 'Moral vision: Iris Murdoch and Alasdair MacIntyre', *Journal of Business Ethics*, 90, 315–27.
Shaw, D. (2012), *Morality and the Movies: Reading Ethics through Film*. London and New York: Continuum.
Shoard, C. (2013), 'Woody Allen on *Blue Jasmine*', *The Guardian*, 26 September, <https://www.theguardian.com/film/2013/sep/26/woody-allen-blue-jasmine-tantrums> (last accessed 31 October 2018).
Singer, P. (1979), *Practical Ethics*. Cambridge: Cambridge University Press.
Sinnerbrink, R. (2016), *Cinematic Ethics: Exploring Ethical Experience through Film*. London: Routledge.
Smith, William G. (2004), *Plato and Popcorn: A Philosopher's Guide to 75 Thought Provoking Movies*. Jefferson, NC and London: McFarland & Co.
Snow, N. E. (2013), 'Learning to look: Lessons from Iris Murdoch', *Teaching Ethics*, 13:2, 1–22.

Sobchack, V. C. (1992), *The Address of the Eye: A Phenomenology of Film Experience*. Princeton and Oxford: Princeton University Press.
Sobchack, V. C. (2004), *Carnal Thoughts: Embodiment and Moving Image Culture*. Berkeley and London: University of California Press.
Steinbauer, A. (2015), 'Lawyers, blondes and Irishmen', *Philosophy Now*, 111, <https://philosophynow.org/issues/111/Lawyers_Blondes_and_Irishmen> (last accessed 31 October 2018).
Stopes, M. C. (1919), *Married Love*. London: Fifield and Co.
Taubin, A. (2012), 'In search of wild things', *Film Comment*, 48:2, 60–2.
Teays, W. (2012), *Seeing the Light: Exploring Ethics through Movies*. Malden, MA: Wiley-Blackwell.
Thomson-Jones, K. (2008), *Aesthetics and Film*. London and New York: Continuum.
Vincendeau, G. (2017), 'Crossing the line', *Sight and Sound*, 27:4, 33.
Von Der Ruhr, Mario (2006), *Simone Weil*. New York and London: Continuum
Warnock, M. (ed.) (1996), *Women Philosophers*. London: J. M. Dent.
Weil, Simone [1949] (2002a), *The Need for Roots*. London and New York: Routledge.
Weil, Simone (2002b), *Gravity and Grace*. London: Routledge.
Wheatley, C. (2009), *Michael Haneke's Cinema: The Ethic of Image*. New York and Oxford: Berghahn.
Widdows, H. [2005] (2016), *The Moral Vision of Iris Murdoch*. London and New York: Routledge.
Wilson, E. (2017), 'Scenes of hurt and rapture: Céline Sciamma's *Girlhood*', *Film Quarterly*, 70:3, 10–22.
Wolf, S. (2014), 'Loving attention: Lessons in love from *The Philadelphia Story*', in Susan Wolf and Christopher Grau (eds), *Understanding Love: Philosophy, Film and Fiction*. Oxford: Oxford University Press, pp. 369–86.
Woolf, V. (1925), *Mrs. Dalloway*. London: L. & V. Woolf.
Woolf, V. [1926] (2009), 'The cinema', *Virginia Woolf Selected Essays*, Oxford: Oxford University Press, pp. 172–6.
Young, I. M. (2005), *On Female Body Experience: 'Throwing Like a Girl' and Other Essays*. Oxford: Oxford University Press.

Filmography

Atomic Blonde, directed by Davie Leitch. Germany, Sweden: 87Eleven, 2017.
Babadook, The, directed by Jennifer Kent. Australia: Screen Australia, 2014.
Birth, directed by Jonathan Glazer. UK, France: New Line Cinema, 2004.
Black Swan, directed by Darren Aronofsky. USA: Fox Searchlight Pictures, 2010.
Blue Jasmine, directed by Woody Allen. USA: Gravier Productions, 2013.
Box, The, directed by Richard Kelly. USA: Warner Bros, 2009.
Brief Encounter, directed by David Lean. UK: Cineguild, 1945.
Cabinet of Dr Caligari, The (*Das Cabinet des Dr. Caligari*), directed by Robert Wiene. Germany: Decla Bioscop AG, 1920.
Certain Women, directed by Kelly Reichardt. USA: Film Science, 2016.
Certified Copy, directed by Abbas Kiarostami. France, Italy: MK2 Productions, 2010.
Clockwork Orange, A, directed by Stanley Kubrick. UK, USA: Warner Brothers, 1971.
Clouds of Sils Maria, directed by Olivier Assayas. France, Germany: CG Cinéma, 2014.
Compliance, directed by Craig Zobel. USA: Bad Cop Bad Cop Film Productions, 2012.
Days of Heaven, directed by Terrence Malick. USA: Paramount Pictures, 1978.
Death of Stalin, The, directed by Armando Iannucci. France, UK: Quad Productions, 2017.
Edge of Heaven, The (*Auf der anderen Seite*), directed by Fatih Akin. Germany, Turkey: Anka Film, 2007.
Elle, directed by Paul Verhoeven. France, Germany: SBS Productions, 2016.
Les Enfants du Paradis (*Children of Paradise*), directed by Marcel Carné. France: Société Nouvelle Pathé Cinema, 1945.
Ex Machina, directed Alex Garland. UK: Universal Pictures International, 2014.
Girlhood (*Bande de Filles*), directed by Céline Sciamma. France: Hold Up Films, 2014.
Gladiator, directed by Ridley Scott. USA, UK: Dreamworks, 2000.
Good People, directed by Henrik Ruben Genz. USA, UK: Millennium Films, 2014.
Graduation (*Bacalaureat*), directed by Cristian Mungiu. Romania, France: Canal+, 2016.
Hours, The, directed by Stephen Daldry. USA, UK: Paramount Pictures, 2003.
Indecent Proposal, directed by Adrian Lyne. USA: Paramount Pictures, 1993.
Innocence, directed by Lucile Hadzihalilovic. Belgium, France: Ex Nihilo, 2004.
Italian Straw Hat, The (*The Horse Ate the Hat*), directed by René Clair. France, Germany: Films albatross, 1928.
Iris, directed by Richard Eyre. UK, USA: BBC Films, 2001.

I've Loved You So Long (*Il y a longtemps que je t'aime*), directed by Philippe Claudel. France, Germany: UGC YM, 2008.
Jackie, directed by Pablo Larraín. Chile, France: Fox Searchlight Pictures, 2016.
King's Speech, The, directed by Tom Hooper. UK, USA: See-Saw Films, 2010.
Last Temptation of Christ, The, directed by Martin Scorsese. Canada, USA: Universal Pictures, 1988.
Magnificent Ambersons, The, directed by Orson Welles. USA: Mercury Productions, 1942.
Manchester by the Sea, directed by Kenneth Lonergan. USA: Amazon Studios, 2016.
Manifesto, directed by Julian Rosefeldt. Germany: Bayerischer Rundfunk, 2015.
Margaret, directed by Kenneth Lonergan. USA: Fox Searchlight Pictures, 2011.
Mary Magdalene, directed by Garth Davis. UK, USA: See-Saw Films, 2018.
Milk, directed by Gus Van Sant. USA: Focus Features, 2008.
Miserables, Les, directed by Tom Hooper. UK, USA: Universal Pictures, 2012.
Mrs Brown, directed by John Madden. UK, Ireland: BBC Scotland, 1997.
Murderers Among Us (*Die Mörder sind unter uns*), directed by Wolfgang Staudte. Germany: Deutsche Film, 1946.
Nocturnal Animals, directed by Tom Ford. USA: Focus Features, 2016.
Once Upon a Time in Anatolia (*Bir Zamanlar Anadolu'da*), directed by Nuri Bilge Ceylan. Turkey: Zeynofilm, 2011.
Only Lovers Left Alive, directed by Jim Jarmusch. Germany, UK: Recorded Picture Company, 2013.
Passion of the Christ, The, directed by Mel Gibson. USA: Icon Productions, 2004.
Ratcatcher, directed by Lynne Ramsay. UK, France: Pathé Pictures International, 1999.
Sang d'un poète, Le (*The Blood of a Poet*), directed by Jean Cocteau. France: Vicomte de Noailles, 1932.
Selma, directed by Ava du Vernay. UK, USA: Pathé, 2014.
Seven Samurai, directed by Akira Kurosawa. Japan: Toho Company, 1954.
Shakespeare in Love, directed by John Madden. USA, UK: Universal Pictures, 1998.
Still Alice, directed by Richard Glatzer and Wash Westmoreland. USA, UK: Lutzus-Brown, 2014.
Stories We Tell, directed by Sarah Polley. Canada: National Film Board of Canada, 2012.
Streetcar Named Desire, A, directed by Elia Kazan. USA: Charles K. Feldman Group, Warner Bros., 1951.
Under the Skin, directed by Jonathan Glazer. Switzerland, Poland: Film 4, 2013.
Unfaithful, directed by Adrian Lyne. USA, Germany: Fox 2000 Pictures, 2002.
Unknown Girl, The (*La fille inconnue*), directed by Jean-Pierre Dardenne and Luc Dardenne, Belgium, France: Les Films du Fleuve, 2016.
We Need to Talk about Kevin, directed by Lynne Ramsay. UK, USA: BBC Films, 2011.

Index

Note: illustrations are indicated by page numbers in **bold**

abortion, 52, 102
Acastos: Two Platonic Dialogues (Murdoch), 6
Adams, Amy, 33
Affleck, Casey, 155, **160**, 165
'Against Dryness' (Murdoch), 51, 176–7, 201
Alias Grace (Attwood), 38
Allen, Woody, 61
Altorf, Marije, 26, 167–8, 170, 173–5, 201, 206
Andrici, Rares, 99
animals, 52, 109, 144–6, 148, 173, 178, 180–6, 218
Anscombe, Elizabeth, 3, 5
Antonaccio, Maria, 77, 107
archetypes, 10–11, 13, 184
Arendt, Hannah, 136
Aristotelian Society, 3, 4, 8
Arletty, 14
Arnheim, Rudolf, 24, 31, 49
art
    attention to, 18, 12, 21, 128, 132, 143, 154, 206, 207, 221
    cinema as art, 8, 9–19, 22–5, 33–50, 207, 221
    and comedy and tragedy, 132, 135, 142–3, 161–6
    distinction between high art and mass art, 23
    function of, 29
    good and bad art, 26, 28–33, 143, 162, 186, 203, 205, 208–12
    and goodness, 25, 108, 109, 128, 176, 206
    and morality, 58, 73, 143
    in Murdoch's novels, 26, 28
    Murdoch on, 3, 7, 9–19, 21–2, 25–33, 58, 128, 132, 135, 161–6, 169, 176, 203, 206–7, 221
    and philosophy, 25–8, 206
    and politics, 214
    and religion, 213–14
    and truth, 203
'Art and Eros' (Murdoch), 27–8
asylum, 114
Athenaeum Club, 168–9
Atlas, James, 169
Atomic Blonde (2017), 30
attention
    to art, 12, 18, 21, 128, 132, 143–4, 154, 206–7, 221
    in *Blue Jasmine*, 60–7
    and the close-up, 31–2
    Murdoch on, 8, 12, 18, 62–3, 66–7, 77–9, 95, 106, 108, 116, 128, 132, 143–4, 154, 206–7, 221
    Weil's concept of, 4, 7, 8, 63, 66, 77–9, 171, 212
Attwood, Margaret, 38
Auberjonois, Rene, 180
Auclair, Zoé, 31–2
Auf der anderen Seite see *Edge of Heaven*
authority, 68–74
Ayer, A. J., 3

Babadook, The (2014), 209
bad art, 28–33, 162, 205
Balázs, Béla, 49
Balsom, Erika, 152
banality, 12, 91, 134, 135, 136
Barthes, Roland, 33
Barton-Fumo, Margaret, 153
Baryshnikov, Anna, 158
Bayley, John, 5

Bazin, André, 2
BBC Radio, 3–4, 5
Beale, Simon Russell, 137
Beatles, The, 17
Bellamy, Michael O., 168
Bellucci, Monica, 213
Benjamin, Walter, 22–3, 33
Bergman, Ingmar, 2
Bergson, Henri, 130, 141, 154
Berkel, Christian, 146
Berling, Charles, 146
better person, becoming, 6–7, 18, 107, 132, 171, 175
Bible, 123, 173, 175, 186, 213
Biles, Jack I., 168
Binoche, Juliette, 76, 81, **88**, 210
Birsal, Taner, 91
Birth (2004), 31–2, **32**, 33
Black Swan (2010), 34
Blanchett, Cate, 32–3, 60–1, **65**
Blood of a Poet (1932), **15**, 15–16, 31
Bloquet, Jonas, 148
Blue Jasmine (2013), 51, 53, 60–7, **65**
bodies *see* human body
Bonnaud, Olivier, 187
Bordwell, David, 24
Bowes, Geoff, 39, 43
Box, The (2009), 73
Breger, Claudia, 115, 117–18
Brief Encounter (1945), 8, 14
Broackes, Justin, 3, 4, 5, 6, 7
Broadbent, Jim, 5
Broderick, Matthew, 159
Brophy, Brigid, 16–17, 211
Browning, Gary, 210–11, 216–17, 218
Buddhism, 52, 77–8, 133, 206, 212
Bugnar, Liz, 96
Burns, Heather, 158
Burton, Richard, 35–6
Buscemi, Steve, 137, **139**

Cabinet of Dr Caligari, The (1920), 47, 209
Cambridge University, 3
'Camelot' (Burton), 35–6
Camp, Bill, 70
Campion, Jane, 2
Canetti, Elias, 211
Cannavale, Bobby, 60
Carroll, Noël, 24, 206
Cavell, Stanley, 2, 11, 12, 206
Centre for Iris Murdoch Studies, 5
Certain Women (2016), 167, 177–87, **182**
Certified Copy (2010), 209–10
Chandler, Kyle, 155
Chaplin, Charlie, 14, 16, 31
Chichester University, 5

Christianity, 52, 77–8, 108, 120, 133, 212–13, 218
CinemaScope, 12
Clair, René, 49
Clockwork Orange, A (1971), 23
close-ups, 13, 31–7, 69, 71, 92–3, 117, 182, 215
Clouds of Sils Maria (2014), 76, 81–90, **88**
Cocteau, Jean, 13, 15–16, 31
comedy, 13, 14, 130–1, 136–44, 153–4, 161–2, 165–6; *see also* humour
communism, 136, 217
compassion, 60, 62, 94–5, 118–21, 125, 132, 176, 196, 206, 214, 221
Compliance (2012), 51, 53, 68–74, **70**
Concept of Mind (Ryle), 3
Conradi, Peter, 4–5, 6, 77–8, 217
consciousness, 9–10, 28, 53, 76, 131, 171, 201–2
Considine, Paddy, 137
Consigny, Anna, 145
consolation, 28–30, 44, 76, 80, 95, 109, 112, 117, 161, 209
convention, 95, 173
Cooper, Sarah, 49
corruption, 60, 98–102, 215
Cosar, Emre, 114
Cox, Lara, 153
Critchley, Simon, 130, 142
Crowley, Dermot, 138
Crown, The (Netflix), 216
Crudup, Billy, 34
Cunningham, Michael, 11

Davis, Essie, 209
Davrak, Baki, 110, **119**
Days of Heaven (1978), 12
de Beauvoir, Simone, 167–8
death
  in *Blue Jasmine*, 62, 64
  in *Clouds of Sils Maria*, 82, 84, 86
  in *The Death of Stalin*, 137–40
  in *The Edge of Heaven*, 105, 111–12, 115–18, 120
  in *Elle*, 149–50, 151, 154–5
  and grief, 34, 116–17, 128, 157, 158, 160, 163–4, 203, 209
  in *I've Loved You So Long*, 121–2
  in *Jackie*, 33–7
  in *Manchester by the Sea*, 155–65
  in *Margaret*, 54–6
  by murder, 90–5, 111–12, 115, 121–2, 124–7, 137, 149, 151, 154–5
  in *Once Upon a Time in Anatolia*, 90–5
  by suicide, 62, 64, 82, 84, 86, 88, 93–4, 150, 194
  and tragedy, 131
  in *The Unknown Girl*, 188–95
  in *We Need to Talk about Kevin*, 124–7

Death of Stalin (2017), 130, 136–44, **139**
Deleuze, Gilles, 206
Dench, Judi, 5
Deren, Maya, 2
Dern, Laura, 177
Derrida, Jacques, 173, 175, 206
despair, 13–14, 76, 89, 116, 161
Diabaté, Idrissa, 198
Diamond, Cora, 66–7
Dickens, Charles, 25, 143
Dijan, Philippe, 152
Diop, Binta, 199
Dipple, Elizabeth, 73
disaster movies, 162
distance, 10, 22, 30, 33, 49
Doane, Mary Ann, 31
Dowd, Ann, 68
Dragus, Maria, 96, **100**
dreams, 9, 11, 30, 89, 108–9
Durham University, 5
duty, 79, 115, 124–5, 195, 210, 213

Ebert, Roger, 72
Edge of Heaven (2007), 13, 105, 109–20, **119**, 128, 133
editing, 22, 24, 41
education, 96–102, 111–12, 120, 168, 185, 196, 201
Edwards, Natalie, 122
Efira, Virgine, 146
ego, 21, 30, 66, 76, 77, 80–2, 86, 89, 90, 108, 122, 143, 171, 208, 215
Ehrenreich, Alden, 61
Eichmann, Adolf, 136
Eidinger, Lars, 83
Eisenstein, Sergei, 2
Elle (2016), 130, 144–55, **150**
emotional affect, 25, 47–8, 206
empathy, 25, 30, 95, 105, 121
Enfants du Paradis, Les (1945), 18–19
entertainment, 9, 14
Epstein, Jean, 2, 31, 33, 49
Erdogan, Yilmaz, 91
escape, 9, 199
ethics, 51–2, 77, 106
euthanasia, 52
everyday life, 6–7, 57, 63, 106–8, 116, 123, 128, 134–6, 161–2, 184–6, 207–8
evil, 28, 95, 108, 117, 127, 135–6, 143
Ex Machina (2014), 209
existentialism, 4, 7, 75–102, 175, 203–4, 217
'Existentialist Bite' (Murdoch), 75
'Existentialist Hero, The' (Murdoch), 6
existentialist heroes, 80–1, 89, 94
'Existential Political Myth, The' (Murdoch), 75
Existentialists and Mystics (Conradi), 6; *see also* individual essays

Faber, Michel, 44
'Face of Garbo' (Barthes), 33
faces *see* human face
family, 37–44, 56, 96–102, 110–18, 121–7, 146–50, 155–65, 179–80, 186, 210; *see also* fatherhood; marriage; motherhood
fantasy, 8, 26, 29–30, 44, 77, 95, 109, 117, 164, 176, 199
fatherhood, 39–44, 92–4, 96–102, 110–12, 118–20, 148, 150
female beauty, 15–16, 45
Feminine Mystique, The (Friedan), 167
feminism, 45, 167–77, 196–7, 213, 217
Fiddes, Paul S., 105
Fille inconnue see *Unknown Girl*
film noir, 81
film phenomenology, 25
film philosophy, 2–3, 7, 18–19, 51, 174–5, 205–8
film studies, 2–3, 24
'Fire and the Sun' (Murdoch), 6, 21, 130, 142–3, 164, 213
flashbacks, 34, 60–1, 155–8, 162
Foot, Philippa, 3, 5, 17, 211
Forsberg, Niklas, 2
Freeland, Cynthia, 22–3
French cinema, 17
Freud, Sigmund, 142, 175
Friedan, Betty, 167
Friend, Rupert, 138

Gabin, Jean, 14
gender, 122–3, 167–202
gender equality, 167–9
genre cinema, 208
German cinema, 17, 209
Gerwig, Greta, 36
Girlhood (2014), 167, 196–202, **198**
Gladiator (2000), 12
Gladstone, Lily, 180, **182**
Glazer, Jonathan, 44–5
Gleeson, Domhnall, 209
God, 80, 104, 107, 108, 120, 165, 212–13
good art, 26, 28–33, 143, 162, 186, 203, 208–12
Good People (2014), 73
goodness, 4–5, 7, 18–19, 25, 66, 67, 79–80, 102, 104–28, 136, 175–6, 184–5, 203–4, 206
Goulehi, Ange-Déborah, **189**
Graduation (2016), 76, 96–102, **100**
Grévill, Laurent, 121
grief, 34, 116–17, 128, 157, 158, 160, 163–4, 203, 209
Guardian, 54
Gueye, Djibril, 200
Gulkin, Harry, 39–41, 43, 44
Gyllenhaal, Jake, 33

Haenel, Adèle, 30, 187, **194**
Haffenden, John, 29
Hale, Sheila, 169
Hämäläinen, Nora, 167, 170–3
Hampshire, Stuart, 3, 175
happiness, pursuit of, 79, 203
Hare, R. M., 3, 4, 5, 106
Harris, Jared, 178
Harris, Sue, 197
Haskell, Molly, 152–3, 154
Hastie, Amelie, 220
Hathaway, Anne, 13
Haubruge, Bérangère, 31–2
Haunts of the Black Masseur (Sprawson), 18
Hawkins, Sally, 60
Hayward, Kara, 156
Hazanavicius, Serge, 120
Hegel, G. W. F., 25, 79
Heidegger, Martin, 210–11
Hershey, Barbara, 213
Hiddleston, Tom, 219, **221**
Hobbes, Thomas, 142
Hobson, Harold, 168–9
homosexuality, 52, 169, 218
Hopkins, Gerard Manley, 56
Horgan, Cara, 138
Horner, Avril, 211
horror, 47, 135, 141, 148, 155, 214–15
Hours, The (2003), 11
Hours, The (Cunningham), 11
'House of Theory' (Murdoch), 136
Howard, Trevor, 14
human body, 13, 30–1, 44–9, 197
human face, 13, 15–16, 30–7, 48, 49, 92–3, 117, 120, 215
human rights *see* rights
humility, 58, 90, 119, 195
humour, 14, 61, 91, 130–1, 135, 136–44, 153–4, 161, 165–6; *see also* comedy
Huppert, Isabelle, 145, **150**, 152–3
Hurt, John, 219

Ide, Wendy, 184
'Idea of Perfection' (Murdoch), 1, 7–8, 62–3, 67, 73, 78, 80, 81, 106–7, 116, 175–6
images, 133–6, 143, 173–4, 204–5, 206, 210, 213
imagination, 9, 23, 58, 109, 132, 134, 204–5, 206–7, 214–15
incongruity theory, 142
Indecent Proposal (1993), 73
individuality, 4, 7–8, 28, 53, 76–81, 89, 106–7, 132–3, 144, 154, 168–9, 171–3, 176, 184–7, 201–2
inner life, 3, 13, 28, 57–9, 95, 102, 105, 107–8, 171, 173

Innocence (2004), 31–2
intersectionality, 167, 196–7
Iris (2001), 1, 5
Iris Murdoch: A Life (Conradi), 5, 217
Iris Murdoch Archive, Kingston University, 3, 5, 16, 210–11
Iris Murdoch Research Centre, 5
Iris Murdoch Review, 5
Isaacs, Jason, 139
Isaaz, Alice, 148
isolation, 76, 78, 80–1, 121, 164, 180, 184
Italian Straw Hat, The (1928), 14
Ivanov, Vlad, 96
I've Loved You So Long (2008), 105, 120–4, **123**, 128, 161

Jackie (2016), 33–7, **36**
Jacobowitz, Florence, 92, 94–5
James, Nick, 152
Japanese cinema, 15
Johansson, Scarlett, 45–6, **48**
Johnson, Celia, 14
Jour se lève, Le (1939), 14
Julian of Norwich, 213

Kafka, Franz, 135
Kant, Immanuel, 135, 142
Karamoh, Lindsay, 198
Kaye, Danny, 220
Kennedy, Jackie, 33–7
Kermode, Frank, 169
Kern, Laura, 72
Kidman, Nicole, 31–2, **32**, 33
Kierkegaard, Søren, 78, 142
King, Martin Luther, 218
King Lear (Shakespeare), 130, 131–2
King's Speech, The (2010), 216
Kingston University, 3, 5, 16, 210–11
'Knowing the Void' (Murdoch), 78–9
Koehler, Robert, 72
Köse, Nursel, 110
Krishnamurti, Jiddu, 169
Kubrick, Stanley, 23
Kurtiz, Tuncel, 110
Kurylenko, Olga, 137

Lafitte, Laurent, 146
Lane, Diane, 13
language, 8, 27, 58, 67, 175–6, 210
Larec, Yves, 190
Laverty, Megan, 172
Le Dœuff, Michele, 173–4, 206
Leeson, Miles, 5
LeGros, James, 177
Leigh, Vivien, 61

Lepkowski, Gerald, 140
Levi, Mica, 33–4, 45
Lim, Dennis, 153
Lita, Ana, 78
'Literature and Philosophy' (Murdoch), 21, 25–7, 205, 207
Living on Paper (Horner & Rowe), 211
Locke, John, 9–10
loneliness, 76, 78, 80–1, 165
Lonergan, Kenneth, 53, 55, 56, 157
love, 14–15, 79, 95, 104–9, 115, 118–27, 171, 175, 176, 187, 209–10
Lovell, Joel, 54
Lovibond, Sabina, 79, 80, 170–1, 174, 185
loving gaze, 8, 63, 95, 106, 108, 125–6, 171
Lumière brothers, 49

McDowell, John, 5
McGill, Hannah, 72
McLoughlin, Adrian, 137
Magee, Bryan, 25, 26, 169
Magnificent Ambersons, The (1942), 8, 10, 13–14
Manchester by the Sea (2016), 130, 155–66, **160**
Manifesto (2017), 33
Mann, Michael, 81
Manovici, Malina, 96
Mara, Rooney, 213, **214**
Margaret (2011), 51, 52–3, 54–9, **55**, 133
Marks, Laura, 25, 45
marriage, 38–9, 52, 60, 62, 96–7, 100–1, 126, 167, 179–80, 209–10
Married Love (Stopes), 167
Marxism, 75, 79, 218
Mary Magdalene (2018), 213, **214**
Mayer, So, 198
Mazet, Arthur, 145
meditation, 7, 58, 105, 107, 108, 212, 214
memory, 41–4, 45, 76, 134, 157, 162
Mendy, Cyril, 196
Meszaros, Julia, 78–9
Metamorphosis (Kafka), 135
'Metaphysics and Ethics' (Murdoch), 3–4, 66–7, 75, 106
Metaphysics as a Guide to Morals (Murdoch)
  on art, 28, 30, 73, 131, 143, 162, 187, 203, 205, 206–7
  on attention, 66, 79, 207
  on comedy and tragedy, 130, 131, 133–6, 141, 143, 144, 161–6
  critique of Derrida, 173
  on death, 117, 131, 163–4, 209
  on despair, 161
  on duty, 195, 213
  on everyday life, 207–8
  on goodness, 104, 122, 125, 128
  on images, 133–6, 143, 205, 213
  on individuality, 78, 144
  on love, 104, 109, 115, 209
  on moral vision, 201–2
  Mulhall's analysis of, 204–5
  on natural law, 217–18
  on politics, 214–18
  on religion, 78, 104, 107–8, 212–14
  on rights, 217–18
  on spirituality, 128, 133, 144, 165, 195, 212–13
  structure of, 6, 204
  on television, 134, 162, 214–15
  on transcendence, 165
  on truth, 202, 203
  on tyranny, 215–16, 218
  on Weil, 78–9
  and women's stories, 173
Meyers, Jeffrey, 169
Midgley, Mary, 3, 5
migration, 109–16
Milk (2008), 218
Milk, Harvey, 218
Miller, Lee, **15**, 15–16
Minnella, Louka, 191
minority groups, 52, 196, 218
Miserables, Les (2012), 13
Mrs Brown (1997), 216
Mrs Dalloway (Woolf), 11
Moi, Toril, 106
Moll, Gretchen, 155
moments, 9–10, 11–12
Moore, G. E., 66, 106
Moore, Julianne, 210
Moore, Scott H., 27
moral experience, 53, 107, 135–6, 204
moral fables, 51–74
moral realism, 6, 95
moral relevance, 51, 52–3, 58
moral responsibility, 73
moral training, 6, 19, 207
moral vision, 7–8, 18, 28, 49–50, 52–3, 57, 62–3, 67, 73, 95, 128, 175–6, 202, 205
moralism, 51–2
Moretz, Chloë Grace, 83
Morgan, David, 16
Morin, Edgar, 49
motherhood, 62, 97, 110–18, 121–7, 146, 148, 149–50, 210
Mulhall, Stephen, 204–5
Münsterberg, Hugo, 31
murder, 90–5, 111–12, 115, 121–2, 124–7, 137, 149, 151, 154–5; *see also* death

Murdoch, Iris
  academic background, 3
  academic interest in, 5
  Alzheimer's disease, 5
  annotations and marginalia, **211**, 211
  on art, 3, 7, 9–19, 21–2, 25–33, 58, 128, 132, 135, 161–6, 169, 176, 203, 206–7, 221
  on attention, 8, 12, 18, 62–3, 66–7, 77–9, 95, 106, 108, 116, 128, 132, 143–4, 154, 206–7, 221
  on cinema, 8–18, 207, 220
  biographies, 1, 5, 217
  civil service career, 3
  on comedy and tragedy, 13, 130–6, 141–4, 154–5, 161–6
  correspondence, **16**, 16–18, 211
  and existentialism, 4, 7, 75–81, 89–90, 175, 217
  and feminism, 167–77, 196, 217
  on goodness, 4–5, 7, 18–19, 25, 66–7, 79–80, 102, 104–9, 112, 118–28, 136, 175–6, 184–5, 206
  Heidegger manuscript (unpublished), 210–11
  influence of Weil, 4–5, 7, 63, 66, 77–9, 171–2, 175
  interviews, 17–18, 19, 25–6, 130, 167, 168–9, 173
  key philosophical concerns, 6–8
  on love, 115–17, 123–7, 171, 175, 176, 209–10
  and moral fable, 51–3, 56–9, 62–3, 66–7, 73
  notebooks, 3, 211
  novels, 3, 5, 19, 26, 27–8, 169, 207, 211, 218; *see also individual titles*
  philosophical works *see individual titles*
  and politics, 136, 214–20
  and religion, 6, 52, 58, 77–8, 108, 127, 133, 210, 212–14
  review of *Haunts of the Black Masseur*, 18
  review of *Notebooks of Simone Weil*, 4
  and women's stories, 122–3, 167–77, 185–7
music, 12, 33–4, 37–8, 45, 54, 59, 70, 85–7, 110, 157, 159, 198–9, 201, 220
mystical heroes, 80–1, 94

narrative, 10–11, 37–44, 58–9, 133, 206–7
natural law, 217–18
nature, 21, 30, 86, 108, 109, 180, 185, 186, 206
Nausée, La (Sartre), 207
New York Times, 54
N'Guessan, Chance, 196
Nocturnal Animals (2016), 33
Notebooks of Simone Weil, 4, 117

O'Brien, Ben, 156
Olympic Games, 18

'On "God" and "Good"' (Murdoch), 51, 73, 104, 108–9, 123–4, 125, 176, 221
'On the Cinema' (Murdoch), 8–16, 21–2, 30–1, 201
Once Upon a Time in Anatolia (2011), 76, 90–5, **93**, 102, 133
Only Lovers Left Alive (2013), 219–20, **221**
Orange, Michelle, 184
Oxford University, 3, 5, 7, 106, 217

Palin, Michael, 137
Paquin, Anna, 54–5, **55**
Payne, Stephen, 69
Pears, David, 169
Pearson, Adam, 48
Penn, Sean, 81
Perkins, Victor, 24
Philadelphia Story, The (1940), 27
Philosopher's Pupil, The (Murdoch), 18
philosophical imaginary, 173–5, 206
Plato, 4–5, 6, 9, 25, 27–9, 73, 77, 107, 109, 130, 142–4, 175, 205, 210–11
politics, 136, 214–20
Polley, Diane, 38–44, **42**
Polley, Johnny, 38, 39, 40, 41
Polley, Michael, 38–44
Polley, Sarah, 37–44
Portman, Natalie, 33–7, **36**
poverty, 52, 165
power, 64, 69, 122, 141–2, 171, 215–16
prayer, 105, 108
prison, 60, 85, 111, 114, 119, 120–1, 124–5, 146, 150, 184
Prisor, Lucas, 145
private realm, 170
prostitution, 110, 191–2, 193–4
psychoanalysis, 2, 175
public realm, 170
Puchner, Martin, 25
Pudovkin, Vsevolod, 49

Qian, Ruibo, 155
Queneau, Raymond, 16, 17, 211
Quick, Diana, 138

Ramsay, Lynne, 124
rape, 23, 96–7, 130, 140, 144–55
Ratcatcher (1999), 12
Reichardt, Kelly, 2, 177, 184
relief theory, 142
religion, 6, 52, 58, 77–8, 105, 108, 127, 133, 149, 151–2, 159, 210, 212–14
Renier, Jérémie, 192
Republic (Plato), 9
Riefenstahl, Leni, 18

Righelato, Rowan, 81
rights, 79, 196, 214, 217–19
Rin Tin Tin, 16
Riseborough, Andrea, 138
Rodier, Sara, 179
romanticism, 4, 7, 76, 77, 161
Rowe, Anne, 5, 26, 28, 211
royalty, 216
Rushton, Richard, 176, 207
Ryle, Gilbert, 3, 106, 175, 211

Saint and the Artist (Conradi), 5
saintliness, 122
Sang d'un Poète see *Blood of a Poet*
Sarsgaard, Peter, 35, 64
Sartre, Jean-Paul, 3, 4, 7, 23, 25, 30, 75, 76, 78, 79, 89, 175, 207, 211
Sartre: Romantic Rationalist (Murdoch), 1, 6, 7, 23, 75–9, 89, 203
satire, 141–2
Schopenhauer, Arthur, 142
Schrader, Paul, 81
Schwartz, Michael, 73
Schweiker, William, 107
Schygulla, Hanna, 113, **119**
Sciamma, Céline, 197
science, 67, 78, 92, 94–5, 175, 218
Scott Thomas, Kristin, 105, 120, **123**
Scruton, Roger, 24
Sea, the Sea (Murdoch), 5
Second Sex, The (de Beauvoir), 167–8
self-delusion, 44, 63–4, 78, 94, 95, 108, 112
self-forgetting, 8, 23, 25, 30, 172
self-reflection, 4, 57–9, 172
Selma (2014), 218
sentimentality, 28, 143, 164, 165, 174, 183, 185
Sesonske, Alexander, 24
Seven Samurai (1954), 8, 10–11, 13, 15, 24
Severed Head, A (Murdoch), 5
sexuality, 48, 52, 96–7, 110, 121, 144–53, 156, 158–9, 167, 169, 177, 197, 200, 213
Shakespeare, William, 25, 130, 131–2
Shakespeare in Love (1998), 216
Shaw, Dan, 51
Shimell, William, 210
Shoard, Catherine, 61
silent film, 14, 24
Singer, Peter, 51–2
Sinnerbrink, Robert, 53
slapstick, 14, 61, 137, 138
Slaymaker, William, 29
Snow, Nancy E., 95
Sobchack, Vivien, 25
solipsism, 4, 75, 76, 81, 89, 90
soul, 49, 125, 132–3, 206

Soumaré, Simina, 196
sound, 14, 33–4, 37–8, 45, 47, 94, 162, 183, 210, 219; *see also* music
Sovereignty of Good, The (Murdoch), 6
'Sovereignty of Good over Other Concepts' (Murdoch), 6–7, 30, 66, 81, 118–19, 122, 126–7, 130, 132, 143–4, 176, 195
Spectator, 4
spirituality, 4, 13, 28, 107, 117, 128, 133, 143–4, 165, 195, 212–14
Sprawson, Charles, 18
'Spring and Fall' (Hopkins), 56
Stalin, Joseph, 136–44
star bodies, 45
star faces, 32–3, 34, 120
Steinbauer, Anja, 142
Stevens Heusel, Barbara, 173
Stevenson, Charles, 106
Stewart, Kristen, 81, 180
Still Alice (2014), 210
Stopes, Marie, 167
stories *see* narrative
Stories We Tell (2012), 33, 37–44, **42**
Streetcar Named Desire (1951), 61
'Sublime and the Beautiful Revisited' (Murdoch), 81, 222
'Sublime and the Good' (Murdoch), 132, 133, 154
suicide, 62, 64, 82, 84, 86, 88, 93–4, 150, 194; *see also* death
Sundance Film Festival, 72
surrealism, 11, 12, 22, 91, 135
Swinton, Tilda, 124, **126**, 219, **221**
Sylla, Assa, 198

Tambor, Jeffrey, 137, **139**
Tanis, Firat, 90
Taubin, Amy, 72
technology, 22, 24, 215
television, 134, 162, 214–15, 216
theology, 212–13; *see also* religion
Theron, Charlize, 30
'Thinking and Language' (Murdoch), 3
Thomson-Jones, Katharine, 24, 30
time, 9–10, 91, 220
Titieni, Adrian, 96, **100**
Tolstoy, Leo, 26, 207
totalitarianism, 29, 136–44, 218
Touré, Karijda, 196, **198**, 198
Touré, Mariétou, 198
tragedy, 13, 130–6, 155–66
tragic fragments, 131, 162
transcendence, 7, 18, 78, 105–8, 119, 124, 129
travel films, 11
truth, 41–4, 67, 95, 121, 144, 203
tyranny, 136–44, 215–16, 218

Under the Net (Murdoch), 3
Under the Skin (2013), 33, 44–50, 48, 133
Under the Skin (Faber), 44
Unfaithful (2002), 13
universality, 52, 57–9
Unknown Girl, The (2016), 30, 167, 187–96, 189, 194, 203
Unofficial Rose, An (Murdoch), 169
unselfing, 8, 23, 25, 30, 77, 95, 170–2, 221
Uzuner, Muhammet, 90, 93

vampirism, 219–20
Verhoeven, Paul, 152–3
Vikander, Alicia, 209
Vincendeau, Ginette, 152
virtuous peasant, 174, 185
'Vision and Choice in Morality' (Murdoch), 4, 6, 7, 8, 52–3, 56–9, 73, 176, 186–7, 213
visual metaphors, 7–8, 18, 206
Vogue magazine, 8–16, 30–1
voiceover, 39, 40, 41–2

Walker, Dreama, 69, 70
Warnock, Mary, 3
water, 17–18
We Need to Talk about Kevin (2011), 105, 124–7, 126, 128

Weil, Simone, 4–5, 7, 51, 63, 66, 77–9, 117, 171–2, 175, 212
welfare state, 218
Welles, Orson, 10, 13–14
Wendy and Lucy (2008), 184
Why Iris Murdoch Matters (Browning), 210–11
Widdows, Heather, 106, 107
Williams, Esther, 18
Williams, Michelle, 157, 179, 184
Wilson, C. J., 155
Wilson, Emma, 197, 198, 201
Winslet, Kate, 5
Wittgenstein, Ludwig, 3, 6
Wolf, Susan, 125–6
Wolf Hall (BBC), 216
women's stories, 122–3, 167–202
Woolf, Virginia, 2, 10, 47, 49
work, 184–5
'Work of Art in the Age of Mechanical Reproduction' (Benjamin), 22
World Viewed, The (Cavell), 11

Yesilçay, Nurgül, 112
Young, Iris Marion, 172

Ziolkowska, Patrycia, 13, 113
Zobel, Craig, 72
Zylberstein, Elsa, 120, 123

EU representative:
Easy Access System Europe
Mustamäe tee 50, 10621 Tallinn, Estonia
Gpsr.requests@easproject.com

www.ingramcontent.com/pod-product-compliance
Lightning Source LLC
Chambersburg PA
CBHW071836230426
43671CB00012B/1980